# Annual Report of Lands Under Control of the U.S. Fish & Wildlife Service

*as of September 30, 2003*

## On the cover:
## Baca National Wildlife Refuge

On April 10, 2003, the Service acquired 3,302 acres via transfer from the Bureau of Reclamation to establish the Baca National Wildlife Refuge in the San Luis Valley of Colorado. The establishment of the refuge is authorized by the Great Sand Dunes National Park and Preserve Act of 2000, Public Law 106-530.

The establishment of this refuge will protect water resources; protect and maintain irrigation water rights necessary for the protection of monument, park, preserve, and refuge resources; and minimize to the extent consistent with protection of national wildlife refuge resources, adverse impacts on other water users. The approved refuge boundary will consist of approximately 92,500 acres of wetlands, sagebrush, and riparian lands, of which a total of 53,500 acres will be acquired and managed by the Service, with the remaining 35,700 acres in private and State ownership. Other land features within the refuge include sand dunes, forested areas, and several thousand acres of ditch-serviced and irrigated lands.

The refuge boundary abuts lands owned or managed by other conservation entities such as The Nature Conservancy, the National Park Service, the U.S. Forest Service, and the Colorado Land Board of Commissioners. The Service along with these neighboring landowners will manage the largest and most diverse assemblage of wetlands in the State of Colorado. Most of these wetlands are identified as Conservation Sites by the Colorado Natural Heritage Program. These wetlands provide habitat for a myriad of water birds, including the largest nesting colonies of snowy egrets, white-faced ibis, and black-crowned night herons. This area also provides critical migration habitat for the entire Rocky Mountain population of greater Sandhill cranes. Under the preservation of the Service, the wetlands can be managed in a coordinated fashion for the benefit of nationally significant water bird populations and rare plant communities of global significance. The refuge lands offer unique hydrological, educational, wildlife, recreational, and other diverse resources which will be preserved for future generations.

*Cover Photo Courtesy of:*
*Karen R. Hollingsworth,*
*Three Black Ducks*

# Annual Report of Lands Under Control of the U.S. Fish and Wildlife Service as of September 30, 2003

*Compiled By: Division of Realty*

# Message from the Director

For more than a century, the National Wildlife Refuge System has succeeded in conserving irreplaceable ecosystems, even as our nation's population has skyrocketed and urbanization has spread. This extraordinary and vast expanse of lands, now encompassing 542 wildlife refuges across 95 million acres of some of the world's best wildlife habitat, is our gift to the "unborn generations" for whom President Theodore Roosevelt created the refuge system on Pelican Island, Florida, March 14, 1903.

This year's report includes the addition of two new refuges—Baca National Wildlife Refuge in Colorado and Mountain Longleaf National Wildlife Refuge in Alabama. Baca NWR was established April 10 when the Fish and Wildlife Service accepted the transfer of 3,302 acres of developed wetlands on the White Ranch from the Bureau of Reclamation. Mountain Longleaf NWR, the first mountain refuge in the Southeast, was established May 29 and will protect the best remaining forests of mountain longleaf pine, habitat for the endangered gray bat and many neo-tropical migratory birds.

Today, the refuge system protects a rich diversity of fish and wildlife, including more than 700 species of birds, 220 species of mammals, 250 reptile and amphibian species and more than 200 species of fish.

Wildlife refuges are tools that have been used to rescue and recover species from extinction, providing habitat for more than 250 threatened or endangered plants and animals. Each year, millions of migrating birds use wildlife refuges as steppingstones on which to rest as they migrate thousands of miles south for the winter and return north for the summer.

Perhaps most importantly, wildlife refuges are a consistent and visible promise by the United States to its citizens that species, wild and free, will forever have a place on the land and in the national consciousness.

Refuge landscapes are enormously diverse, ranging from tiny islands of less than three acres to vast expanses in Alaska. Habitats are equally diverse—from arctic tundra and towering mountain peaks in Alaska to tallgrass and wet prairies in the Dakotas, and tropical tree islands in the Florida Keys.

In addition to managing refuges, the refuge system also administers 37 wetland management districts that encompass thousands of waterfowl protection areas in 203 counties across the United States.

Wildlife refuges have been called America's best-kept secret. The yearlong Refuge System Centennial is changing that perception. Nearly 40 million people have visited wildlife refuges in the past year, coming in droves to festivals, dedications, fishing derbies, hunting expos, and family days where they learned the extraordinary story of the refuge system and the wonders of unspoiled nature.

The future of wildlife is best assured by giving people the chance to experience it firsthand. A new generation will develop a love for the natural world only if youngsters have a chance to cast their fishing lines into the waters of a nearby creek, listen to the whistling wings of mallards, or search for songbirds among a canopy of 100-year-old trees. With a wildlife refuge just an hour's drive from most metropolitan areas, the refuge system offers the best chance for today's

youth—too often trapped in front of a television screen—to see firsthand our nation's outdoor heritage.

The refuge system is also the embodiment of Interior Secretary Gale Norton's "Four C's"—consultation, cooperation, communication, all in the service of conservation. Some 38,000 volunteers form a cooperative workforce 10 times larger than the refuge system staff. Volunteers accomplish 20 percent of the work done on refuges. More than 240 community Friends groups are key partners in achieving refuge goals, often raising funds for projects.

In 2003 alone, more than 1,400 partners—especially our Friends groups—donated more than $10 million in money, services, and labor to the refuge system, adding $5 of value to every $3 budgeted.

The seed of an idea that began in 1903 on a tiny Pelican Island—that each generation has a responsibility to pass on some untouched, unmarred places of natural wonder—has blossomed into the National Wildlife Refuge System, the world's most expansive network of protected lands dedicated to wildlife conservation.

Now, we begin to celebrate the second century of the refuge system. There is no better was to salute the refuge system's achievements than by visiting a wildlife refuge with binoculars, fishing rod, shotgun or camera in hand, surrounded by the next generation of conservationists and outdoor enthusiasts in tow. So come out and enjoy your National Wildlife Refuge System.

*Steve Williams*

Director

# KEY TO REAL PROPERTY NUMBERS

## SEPTEMBER 30, 2003

| No. | Name |
|-----|------|
| 3 | Hecala NFH, MO |
| 5 | Leadville NFH, CO |
| 6 | Craig Brook NFH, ME |
| 11 | Bozeman Fish Technology Cen., MT |
| 14 | Erwin NFH, TN |
| 15 | Nashua NFH, NH |
| 17 | D.C. Booth NFH, SD |
| 18 | Warm Springs NFH, GA |
| 19 | Edenton NFH, NC |
| 22 | White Sulphur Springs NFH, WV |
| 23 | Private John Allen NFH, MS |
| 25 | Pelican Island NWR, FL |
| 26 | Mammoth Spring NFH, AR |
| 27 | Bratton NWR, LA |
| 28 | Stump Lake NWR, ND |
| 29 | Mountain Wildlife Ref., OK |
| 30 | Huron NWR, MI |
| 31 | Passage Key NWR, FL |
| 32 | Shell Keys NWR, LA |
| 33 | Three Arch Rocks NWR, OR |
| 34 | Copalis NWR, WA |
| 47 | Flattery Rocks NWR, WA |
| 52 | Quillayute Needles NWR, WA |
| 53 | Key West NWR, FL |
| 58 | Lower Klamath NWR, CA & OR |
| 40 | Malheur NWR, OR |
| 41 | Chase Lake NWR, ND |
| 41-1 | Island Bay NWR, FL |
| 42 | Hawaiian Islands NWR, HI |
| 44 | Cold Spring NWR, OR |
| 46 | Deer Flat NWR, ID & OR |
| 47 | Minidoka NWR, ID |
| 52 | Culebra NWR, PR |
| 53 | Farallon NWR, CA |
| 58 | Fairport NFH, IA |
| 59-1 | National Bison Range, MT |
| 61 | Pittsford NFH, VT |
| 61 | Clear Lake NWR, CA |
| 63 | Fort Niobrara NWR, NE |
| 65 | Green Bay NWR, WI |
| 67 | Orangeburg NFH, SC |
| 68 | Gravel Island NWR, WI |
| 73 | Anaho Island NWR, NV |
| 74 | National Elk Refuge, WY |
| 75 | Upper Mississippi River Wildlife & Fish Refuge, IL, IA, MN, WI |
| 77 | Dungeness NFH, WA |
| 78 | White Lace NWR, MN |
| 79 | Wolf Lake NWR, AR |
| 81 | North Platte NWR, NE |
| 82 | Berkshire Trout Hatchery, MA |
| 85 | Nine-Pipe NWR, MT |
| 88 | Pablo NWR, MT |
| 89 | Sully Hill Natl. Game Preserve, ND |
| 91 | Blackbeard Island NWR, GA |
| 93 | Upper Mississippi River Wildlife & Fish Refuge, IL, IA, MN, WI |
| 96 | Johnston Island NWR, (Pacific Area Inset) |
| 98 | Savannah NWR, GA & SC |
| 100 | McKay Creek NWR, OR |
| 103 | Upper Klamath NWR, OR |
| 105 | Pathfinder NWR, WY |
| 108 | Tishomingo NWR, OK |
| 109 | Tule Lake NWR, CA |
| 113 | Bear River Migratory Bird Ref., UT |
| 114 | Cedar Keys NWR, FL |
| 115 | Benton Lake NWR, MT |
| 117 | Salt Plains NWR, OK |
| 118 | Cape Romain NWR, SC |
| 119 | Wolf Island NWR, GA |
| 121 | Salton Sea NWR, CA |
| 122 | Sheldon NWR, NV & OR |
| 124 | St. Marks NWR, FL |
| 125 | Crescent Lake NWR, NE |
| 126 | Genoa NFH, WI |
| 127 | Natchitoches NFH, LA |
| 128 | Back Bay NWR, VA |
| 129 | Hagerman NWR, ID |
| 131 | Ennis NFH, MT |
| 133 | Dexter NFH, NM |
| 135 | Lamar NFH, PA |
| 140 | Hutton Lake NWR, WY |
| 141 | Bamforth NWR, WY |
| 142 | Long Lake NWR, NC |
| 146 | Swanquarter NWR, NC |
| 149 | Blackwater NWR, MD |
| 159 | Hatchery Lake NWR, VA |
| 160 | Nantucket NWR, MA |
| 162 | Tranquilacu NWR, MI |
| 164 | Des Lacs NWR, ND |
| 165 | J. Clark Salyer NWR, ND |
| 167 | Arrowwood NWR, ND |
| 168 | Sand Lake NWR, SD |
| 169 | Lacreek NWR, SD |
| 170 | Lostwood NWR, ND |
| 172 | Medicine Lake NWR, MT |
| 173 | Lake Andes NWR, SD |
| 174 | Square Creek NWR, MO |
| 175 | Chautauqua NWR, IL |
| 176 | Waubay NWR, SD |
| 177 | Red Rock Lakes NWR, MT |
| 178 | Oregon Islands NWR, OR |
| 179 | Lake Isom NWR, TN |
| 180 | Seney NWR, MI |
| 183 | Valentine NWR, NE |
| 184 | Uvalde NFH, TX |
| 185 | Upper Souris NWR, ND |
| 187 | White River NWR, AR |
| 188 | Hart Mtn. Natl. Antelope Refuge, OR |
| 191 | Muleshoe NWR, TX |
| 192 | Rice Lake NWR, MN |
| 193 | Delta NWR, LA |
| 194 | Tamarac NWR, MN |
| 195 | Bowdoin NWR, MT |
| 196 | Kellys Slough NWR, ND |
| 199 | Bitter Lake NWR, NM |
| 200 | Desert NWR, NV |
| 201 | Swan Lake NWR, MO |
| 202 | Storm Lake NWR, ND |
| 203 | Tewaukon NWR, ND |
| 206 | Ardoch NWR, ND |
| 207 | Turnbull NWR, WA |
| 210 | Willapa NWR, WA |
| 211 | Camas NWR, ID |
| 213 | Okefenokee NWR, FL & GA |
| 214 | Yazoo NWR, MS |
| 215 | Charles M. Russell NWR, MT |
| 217 | Patuxent Research Refuge, MD |
| 218 | Bosque del Apache NWR, NM |
| 220 | Moosehorn NWR, ME |
| 221 | Sacramento NWR, CA |
| 223 | Union Slough NWR, IA |
| 224 | Bombay Hook NWR, DE |
| 225 | Agassiz NWR, MN |
| 231 | Chincoteague NWR, VA |
| 232 | Pea Island NWR, NC |
| 233 | Bear Butte NWR, SD |
| 235 | Santa Ana NWR, TX |
| 237 | Colusa NWR, CA |
| 234 | Montezuma NWR, NY |
| 238 | Lake Thibodeau NWR, MT |
| 240 | Lacassine NWR, LA |
| 241 | Ruby Lake NWR, NV |
| 242 | Aransas NWR, TX |
| 245 | Sabine NWR, LA |
| 248-1 | McKinney Lake NFH, NC |
| 247 | Black Coulee NWR, MT |
| 248 | Bock Bay NWR, LA |
| 249 | Hewitt Lake NWR, MT |
| 252 | Inks Dam NWR, TN |
| 253 | Hagerman NWR, TX |
| 254 | Corning NFH, AR |
| 255 | Tybee NWR, SC |
| 257 | Leavenworth NFH, WA |
| 259 | Wheeler NWR, AL |
| 260 | Valley City NFH, ND |
| 262 | West Sister Island NWR, OH |
| 263 | Cape Meares NWR, OR |
| 267 | Great White Heron NWR, FL |
| 268 | Mattole NFH, FL |
| 289 | Piedmont NWR, GA |
| 270 | Cabeza Prieta NWR, AZ |
| 271 | Kofa NWR, AZ |
| 272 | Meredith NFH, WI |
| 274 | Carolina Sandhills NWR, SC |
| 275 | Meridian NWR, MS |
| 278 | Mn London NFH, AZ |
| 281 | Little Pend Oreille NWR, WA |
| 286 | Buffalo Lake NWR, ND |
| 288 | Canfield Lake NWR, ND |
| 292 | Florence Lake NWR, ND |
| 295 | Johnson Lake NWR, ND |
| 306 | Lake George NWR, ND |
| 307 | Lake Ilo NWR, ND |
| 308 | Lake Nettie NWR, ND |
| 310 | Lake Zahl NWR, ND |
| 314 | McLean NWR, ND |
| 318 | Shell Lake NWR, ND |
| 320 | Hobart Lake NWR, ND |
| 322 | Stewart Lake NWR, ND |
| 323 | Edwin B. Forsythe NWR, NJ |
| 324 | Stewart Lake NWR, ND |
| 325 | Lake Alice NWR, ND |
| 329 | Maxbass NWR, ND |
| 330 | Little White Salmon NFH, WA |
| 334 | Entiat NFH, WA |
| 335 | Winthrop NFH, WA |
| 340 | Havasu NWR, AZ & CA |
| 341 | San Andres NWR, NM |
| 342 | Horicon NWR, WI |
| 349 | White Lake NWR, ND |
| 350 | Willow Lake NWR, ND |
| 352 | Imperial NWR, AZ & CA |
| 356 | Lake Mason NWR, MT |
| 359 | Reelfoot Lake NWR, KY & TN |
| 361 | Creston Coulee NWR, WA |
| 363 | Chassahowitzka NWR, FL |
| 364 | Parker River NWR, MA |
| 365 | Santee NWR, SC |
| 369 | Halfbreed Lake NWR, MT |
| 370 | Lamesteer NWR, MT |
| 380-1 | Coleman NFH, CA |
| 381 | Holstone NWR, MT |
| 382 | Missisquoi NWR, VT |
| 386 | Chincoteague NWR, MD & VA |
| 387 | Colusa NWR, CA |
| 388 | Cheran NWR, SC |
| 389 | Great Meadows NWR, MA |
| 390 | Orangeburg County NFH, SC |
| 391 | Nononay NWR, WA |
| 392 | Mingo NWR, MO |
| 393 | Columbia NWR, WA |
| 394 | Slade NWR, ND |
| 395 | Creston NWR, MT |
| 396 | Sutter NWR, CA |
| 400 | J.H. "Ding" Darling NWR, FL |
| 401 | Tennessee NWR, TN |
| 403 | Tishomingo NWR, OK |
| 404 | Hagerman NWR, TX |
| 406 | Laguna Atascosa NWR, TX |
| 412 | Michigan Islands NWR, MI |
| 413 | Wertheim NWR, NY |
| 415 | Crab Orchard NWR, IL |
| 419 | Stillwater NWR, NV |
| 423 | North Attleboro NFH, MA |
| 424 | Spring Creek NFH, WA |
| 426 | Bo Gine NFH, GA |
| 428 | Hiawatha Forest NFH, MI |
| 429 | Pendills Creek NFH, MI |
| 430 | Garrison Dam NFH, ND |
| 433 | Pinellas NWR, FL |
| 434 | Willard NFH, WA |
| 435 | Arthur R. Marshall Loxahatchee NWR, FL |
| 436 | Norwood NWR, CO |
| 450 | Norfix NWR, WA |
| 451 | Presquile NWR, VA |
| 452 | Eagle Creek NWR, OR |
| 456 | Shiawassee NWR, MI |
| 458 | National Key Deer Refuge, FL |
| 451 | Kirwin NWR, KS |
| 467 | Martin NWR, MD & VA |
| 468 | Elizabeth A. Morton NWR, NY |
| 477 | Quivira NWR, KS |
| 482 | McKay NWR, WA |
| 483 | Norfolk NWR, AR |
| 487 | Audubon NWR, ND |
| 492 | Gavins Point NFH, SD |
| 498 | Holla Bend NWR, AR |
| 501 | Abernathy Fish Technology Cen., WA |
| 501-1 | Jackson NFH, WY |
| 505 | Iroquois NWR, NY |
| 505-2 | Klamath Forest NWR, OR |
| 507 | Paint Bank NFH, WV |
| 509 | Bowden NFH, WV |
| 513 | Catahoula NWR, LA |
| 516 | Pidey NWR, NV |
| 517 | War Horse NWR, MT |
| 518 | Buffalo Lake NWR, TX |
| 519 | Delcan NWR, IA & NE |
| 522 | Fish Springs NWR, UT |
| 523 | Erie NWR, PA |
| 524 | Fish Farming Exp. Station, AR |
| 529 | Willow Beach NFH, AZ |
| 531 | Alchesay NFH, AZ |
| 538 | Kern NWR, CA |
| 541 | Great Swamp NWR, NJ |
| 542 | Modoc NWR, CA |
| 543 | Ouray NWR, UT |
| 547 | Jordan River NFH, MI |
| 549 | San Juan Islands NWR, WA |
| 550 | Nockay Islands NWR, NC & VA |
| 551 | Wassaw NWR, GA |
| 555 | Washita NWR, OK |
| 565 | Garrison Dam NFH, ND |
| 569 | Ottawa NWR, OH |
| 571 | Detroit River NWR, MI |
| 581 | Wytheville NFH, VA |
| 582 | Harris Neck NWR, GA |
| 586 | Sequoyah NWR, OK |
| 601 | Jones Hole NFH, UT |
| 603 | Delevan NWR, CA |
| 605 | Cross Creeks NWR, TN |
| 606 | Eastern Neck NWR, MD |
| 608 | Dale Hollow NWR, TN |
| 612 | Anahuac NWR, TX |
| 615 | John Heinz NWR at Tinicum, PA |
| 619 | Greers Ferry NFH, AR |
| 623 | Beulah Fish Technology Center, WY |
| 626 | Alamosa NWR, CO |
| 629 | Patuxent NWR, NV |
| 630 | Prime Hook NWR, DE |
| 632 | Merritt Island NWR, FL |
| 643 | Lake Woodruff NWR, FL |
| 651 | Choctaw NWR, AL |
| 654 | Mescalero NFH, NM |
| 655 | Lee Metcalf NWR, MT |
| 664 | Toppenish NWR, WA |
| 666 | Pee Dee NWR, NC |
| 674 | Clarence Cannon NWR, MO |
| 675 | Cedar Island NWR, NE |
| 676 | Cibola NWR, AZ & CA |
| 679 | Kootenai NWR, ID |
| 680 | Eufaula NWR, AL & GA |
| 683 | Hatchie NWR, TN |
| 684 | Cedar Point NWR, OH |
| 687 | Conboy Lake NWR, WA |
| 690 | Lahontan NFH, NV |
| 690-1 | Quinault NFH, WA |
| 691 | Ridgefield NWR, WA |
| 732 | Browns Park NWR, CO |
| 733 | Kooskia NFH, ID |
| 734 | Sherburne NWR, MN |
| 736 | Seedskadee NWR, WY |
| 745 | Hotchkiss NFH, CO |
| 746 | William L. Finley NWR, OR |
| 747 | Ankeny NWR, OR |
| 748 | Baskett Slough NWR, OR |
| 749 | Ridgefield NWR, WA |
| 751 | Las Vegas NWR, NM |
| 753 | Pine Island NWR, FL |
| 754 | Mattamuskeet NWR, FL |
| 755 | Colcoahatchee NWR, NM |
| 781 | Maxwell NWR, NM |
| 763 | Flint Hills NWR, KS |
| 788 | Muscatobuck NWR, TX |
| 770 | Brazoria NWR, TX |
| 771 | Rachel Carson NWR, ME |
| 772 | San Luis NWR, CA |
| 788 | Warm Springs NFH, GA |
| 789 | UL Bend NWR, MT |
| 781 | Target Rock NWR, NY |
| 782 | Bell Creek NFH, KY |
| 794 | St. Vincent NWR, FL |
| 795 | Green Lake NWR, ME |
| 796 | Bear Lake NWR, ID |
| 800 | Buck Island NWR, VI |
| 801 | Fisherman Island NWR, VA |
| 803 | Mason Neck NWR, VA |
| 804 | San Bernard NWR, TX |
| 805 | Amagansett NWR, NY |
| 806 | Oyster Bay NWR, NY |
| 807 | Hobe Sound NWR, FL |
| 809 | Umatilla NWR, OR & WA |
| 810 | Seatuck NWR, NY |
| 811 | Wapanocca NWR, AR |
| 814 | Supawna Meadows NWR, NJ & TX |
| 826 | Sequoyah NWR, OK |
| 827 | Ninigret NWR, RI |

# KEY TO REAL PROPERTY NUMBERS

## SEPTEMBER 30, 2005

| No. | Name |
|---|---|
| 831 | San Marcos NFH, TX |
| 834 | St. Johns NWR, FL |
| 835 | Conscience Point NWR, NY |
| 836 | Julia Butler Hansen NWR, OR & WA |
| 838 | Allegheny NFH, PA |
| 839 | Minnesota Valley NWR, MN |
| 840 | Seatauket Point NWR, RI |
| 842 | Plum Tree Island NWR, VA |
| 843 | Saddle Mountain NWR, WA |
| 845 | Lewis and Clark NWR, OR |
| 846 | Nomans Land Island NWR, MA |
| 847 | Wapack NWR, NH |
| 848 | Seal Island NWR, ME |
| 849 | Thacher Island NWR, MA |
| 851 | Attwater Prairie Chicken NWR, TX |
| 852 | Meredosia NWR, IL |
| 853 | Pond Island NWR, ME |
| 855 | Nantucket NWR, MA |
| 856 | Hanalei NWR, HI |
| 857 | Humboldt Bay NWR, CA |
| 858 | Swan River NWR, MT |
| 859 | Great Dismal Swamp NWR, NC & VA |
| 860 | Hulela NWR, HI |
| 861 | Ocoquan Bay NWR, VA |
| 862 | Wallops Island NWR, VA |
| 863 | White River NFH, VT |
| 864 | Rose Atoll NWR (Pacific Area Inset) |
| 865 | Franklin Island NWR, ME |
| 866 | Block Island NWR, RI |
| 867 | Anaganan Pupfish Station, NV |
| 868 | Kansomand NWR, WA |
| 870 | San Pablo Bay NWR, CA |
| 871 | Nisqually NWR, WA |
| 872 | Sevilleta NWR, NM |
| 875 | Oxbow NWR, MA |
| 876 | Cabo Rojo NWR, PR |
| 877 | Baker Island NWR (Pacific Area Inset) |
| 878 | Howland Island NWR (Pacific Area Inset) |
| 879 | Jarvis Island NWR (Pacific Area Inset) |
| 881 | Petit Manan NWR, ME |
| 882 | Mokah NFH, WA |
| 883 | Supawna Meadows NWR, NJ |
| 884 | Egmont Key NWR, FL |
| 888 | Trustom Pond NWR, RI |
| 889 | Hopper Mountain NWR, CA |
| 898 | San Francisco Bay NWR, CA |
| 900 | Optima NWR, OK |
| 901 | Hillside NWR, MS |
| 903 | Big Stone NWR, MN |
| 904 | Moody NWR, TX |
| 906 | Seal Beach NWR, CA |
| 907 | Felsenthal NWR, AR |
| 908 | D'Arbonne NWR, LA |
| 909 | Mississippi Sandhill Crane NWR, MS |
| 910 | Karl E. Mundt NWR, NB & SD |
| 912 | Pearl Harbor NWR, HI |
| 913 | Pinckney Island NWR, SC |
| 914 | Ellicott Slough NWR, CA |
| 915 | Kakahaia NWR, HI |
| 920 | Deschee NWR, TX |
| 921 | James Campbell NWR, HI |
| 923 | Iron River NFH, WI |
| 924 | Salinas River NWR, CA |
| 926 | Wilson Creek-Lurline WMA, CA |
| 928 | Morgan Brake NWR, MS |
| 928 | Panther Swamp NWR, MS |
| 929 | Bear Cay NWR, VI |
| 935 | Blowing Wind Cave NWR, AL |
| 937 | Upper Ouachita NWR, LA |
| 937 | Featherstone NWR, VA |
| 939 | Fox River NWR, WI |
| 940 | Lower Suwannee NWR, FL |
| 942 | Grasslands WMA, CA |
| 943 | Napa Valley WMA, NV |
| 944 | Crocodile Lake NWR, FL |
| 948 | San Joaquin River NWR, CA |
| 949 | Bon Secour NWR, AL |
| 950 | Texas Point NWR, TX |
| 965 | Antioch Dunes NWR, CA |
| 966 | Butte Sink WMA, CA |
| 967 | Lower Hatchie NWR, TN |
| 970 | Kirtland Warbler WMA, MI |
| 971 | Cross Island NWR, ME |
| 973 | Mathews Brake NWR, MS |
| 974 | Banks Lake NWR, GA |
| 977 | Overflow NWR, AR |
| 981 | Castle Rock NWR, CA |
| 982 | Tijuana Slough NWR, CA |
| 984 | Lower Rio Grande Valley NWR, TX |
| 985 | Watercress Darner NWR, AL |
| 988 | Bogue Chitto NWR, LA & MS |
| 991 | Alaska Maritime NWR, AK |
| 992 | Alaska Peninsula NWR, AK |
| 993 | Arctic NWR, AK |
| 994 | Bechanof NWR, AK |
| 995 | Innoko NWR, AK |
| 996 | Izembek NWR, AK |
| 997 | Kanuti NWR, AK |
| 998 | Kenai NWR, AK |
| 999 | Kodiak NWR, AK |
| 1000 | Koyukuk NWR, AK |
| 1001 | Nowitna NWR, AK |
| 1002 | Selawik NWR, AK |
| 1003 | Tetlin NWR, AK |
| 1004 | Togiak NWR, AK |
| 1005 | Yukon Delta NWR, AK |
| 1006 | Yukon Flats NWR, AK |
| 1008 | Bears Bluff NFH, SC |
| 1009 | Bon Cave NWR, AL |
| 1012 | Richard Cronin NFH, MA |
| 1015 | San Bernardino NWR, AZ |
| 1016 | Blue Ridge NWR, CA |
| 1018 | Tensas River NWR, LA |
| 1019 | Protection Island NWR, WA |
| 1021 | Bandon Marsh NWR, OR |
| 1024 | Big Boggy NWR, TX |
| 1025 | Moosehorn NWR, MA |
| 1026 | Crystal River NWR, FL |
| 1027 | Tehama–Colusa Fish Facility, CA |
| 1028 | Pierce NWR, WA |
| 1029 | Harbor Island NWR, WI |
| 1030 | Ash Meadows NWR, NV |
| 1031 | Alligator River NWR, NC |
| 1032 | Eastern Shore of Virginia NWR, VA |
| 1034 | San Simeon Field Station, CA |
| 1035 | Sandy Point NWR, VI |
| 1036 | Currituck NWR, NC |
| 1037 | Kilauea Point NWR, HI |
| 1038 | Buenos Aires NWR, AZ |
| 1039 | Stewart B. McKinney NWR, CT |
| 1040 | Chassaa NWR, TN |
| 1042 | Bitter Creek NWR, CA |
| 1043 | Wilson Creek-Lurline WMA, CA |
| 1044 | Coachella Valley NWR, CA |
| 1046 | Hakalau Forest NWR, HI |
| 1051 | Cache River NWR, AR |
| 1052 | Stagecoach Lake NWR, WA |
| 1053 | Ozark Plateau NWR, OK |
| 1054 | Atchafalaya NWR, LA |
| 1055 | Little River NWR, OK |
| 1057 | John Hay NWR, NH |
| 1060 | Little Sandy NWR, TX |
| 1062 | Pilot Knob NWR, MO |
| 1063 | San Joaquin River NWR, CA |
| 1065 | Midway Atoll NWR (Island Inset) |
| 1066 | Lake Ophelia NWR, LA |
| 1075 | McColl NFH, ID |
| 1076 | Sweetwater Marsh NWR, CA |
| 1078 | Sunkhaze Meadows NWR, ME |
| 1084 | Cameron Prairie NWR, LA |
| 1091 | Logan Cave NWR, AR |
| 1092 | Florida Panther NWR, FL |
| 1093 | Cape May NWR, NJ |
| 1094 | Pettaquamscutt Cove NWR, RI |
| 1113 | Laguna Cartagena NWR, PR |
| 1118 | Sacramento River NWR, CA |
| 1119 | Bond Swamp NWR, GA |
| 1122 | St. Catherine Creek NWR, MS |
| 1124 | Bayou Savage NWR, LA |
| 1125 | Pocosin Lakes NWR, NC |
| 1126 | Lyons Ferry NFH, WA |
| 1127 | Sawtooth NFH, ID |
| 1129 | Driftless Area NWR, IA |
| 1132 | Cypress Creek NWR, IL |
| 1137 | Grand Bay NWR, AL & MS |
| 1138 | Hamden Slough NWR, MN |
| 1139 | Roanoke River NWR, NC |
| 1140 | Ace Basin NWR, SC |
| 1142 | Franz Lake NWR, WA |
| 1143 | Grays Harbor NWR, WA |
| 1149 | Ohio River Islands NWR, KY, PA & WV |
| 1153 | James River NWR, VA |
| 1154 | Dahomey NWR, MS |
| 1155 | Tallahatchie NWR, MS |
| 1156 | Tucannon NFH, WA |
| 1158 | Nestucca Bay NWR, OR |
| 1159 | Neal Smith NWR, IA |
| 1161 | Archie Carr NWR, FL |
| 1166 | Nisqually NFH, WA |
| 1171 | Ozark Cavefish NWR, MO |
| 1174 | Middkill River NWR, NJ & NY |
| 1175 | North Central Valley WMA, CA |
| 1176 | Blue Ridge NWR, CA |
| 1178 | Balcones Canyonlands NWR, TX |
| 1179 | Bayou Cocodrie NWR, LA |
| 1180 | Marin Islands NWR, CA |
| 1181 | Morbanon Lake NWR, WY |
| 1182 | Grand Cote NWR, LA |
| 1183 | Moro NFH, NM |
| 1184 | Siletz Bay NWR, OR |
| 1205 | Two Ponds NWR, CO |
| 1206 | Marais Des Cygnes NWR, KS |
| 1207 | Great Bay NWR, NH |
| 1209 | Lake Umbagog NWR, ME & NH |
| 1210 | Tualatin River NWR, OR |
| 1213 | Harvey Broke NWR, LA |
| 1216 | Keolia Pond NWR, HI |
| 1218 | Bill Williams NWR, AZ |
| 1224 | Lake Wales Ridge NWR, FL |
| 1225 | Canaan Valley NWR, WV |
| 1225 | Pond Creek NWR, AR |
| 1226 | Pahero River NWR, FL |
| 1208 | Guam NWR (Pacific Area Inset) |
| 1209 | Bald Knob NWR, AR |
| 1210 | Deep Fork NWR, OK |
| 1212 | Emiquon NWR, IL |
| 1229 | Rocky Mountain Arsenal NWR, CO |
| 1231 | Big Branch Marsh NWR, LA |
| 1232 | Stone Lakes NWR, CA |
| 1235 | Big Muddy Nat. Fish & Wildlife Refuge, MO |
| 1241 | Mathews NWR, MA |
| 1244 | Rappahannock R. NWR, VA |
| 1245 | San Diego NWR, CA |
| 1247 | Mandaray NWR, LA |
| 1250 | Ouray NFH, UT |
| 1258 | Ten Thousand Islands NWR, FL |
| 1259 | Key Cave NWR, AL |
| 1261 | Black Bayou Lake NWR, LA |
| 1262 | Bogue Chute NWR, NE |
| 1267 | Silvio O. Conte Nat. Fish & wildl. Ref., MA, NH & VT |
| 1268 | Waccamaw NWR, SC |
| 1269 | Magic Valley Hatchery, ID |
| 1270 | Eagle (Fish) Lab, ID |
| 1271 | Blackfoot Valley WMA, MT |
| 1272 | Whittaway Creek, NWR, MT |
| 1273 | Clarks River NWR, KY |
| 1274 | Decorah NFH, ID |
| 1275 | Livingston Stone NFH, CA |
| 1276 | Inriga Fish Hatchery & Satellites, OR |
| 1277 | Lee-Inglass Fish Hatchery, WA |
| 1278 | Arrowbok NWR, NE |
| 1279 | Colorado River NWR, UT |
| 1280 | Lost Trail NWR, MT |
| 1281 | Novato Island NWR, SD |
| 1282 | Snowanguma Snowamom NWR, NY |
| 1283 | Whittaway Creek, NWR, MT |
| 1284 | Port Louisa NWR, IA & IL |
| 1285 | Great River NWR, IL & MO |
| 1286 | Two Rivers NWR, IL & MO |
| 1287 | Middle Mississippi River NWR, IL & MO |
| 1288 | Big Oak NWR, IN |
| 1289 | Cat Island NWR, LA |
| 1290 | John W. & Louise Seier NWR, NE |
| 1291 | Guadalupe–Nipomo Dunes NWR, CA |
| 1292 | North Dakota NWR, ND |
| 1293 | Clearwater NFH, ID |
| 1295 | Northern Tallgrass Prairie NWR, MN |
| 1296 | Caldwell River NWR, MS |
| 1297 | Oahu Forest NWR, HI |
| 1298 | Caddo Lake NWR, TX |
| 1299 | Palmyra Atoll NWR (Pacific Area Inset) |
| 1300 | Kingman Reef NWR (Pacific Area Inset) |
| 1301 | Assabet NWR, MA |
| 1302 | Vieques NWR, PR |
| 1305 | Dakota Tallgrass Prairie, NE & SD |
| 1309 | Bayou Teche NWR, LA |
| 1311 | Red River NWR, LA |
| 1312 | Cahaba River NWR, AL |
| 1313 | Baca NWR, CO |
| 1314 | Mountain Longleaf NWR, AL |

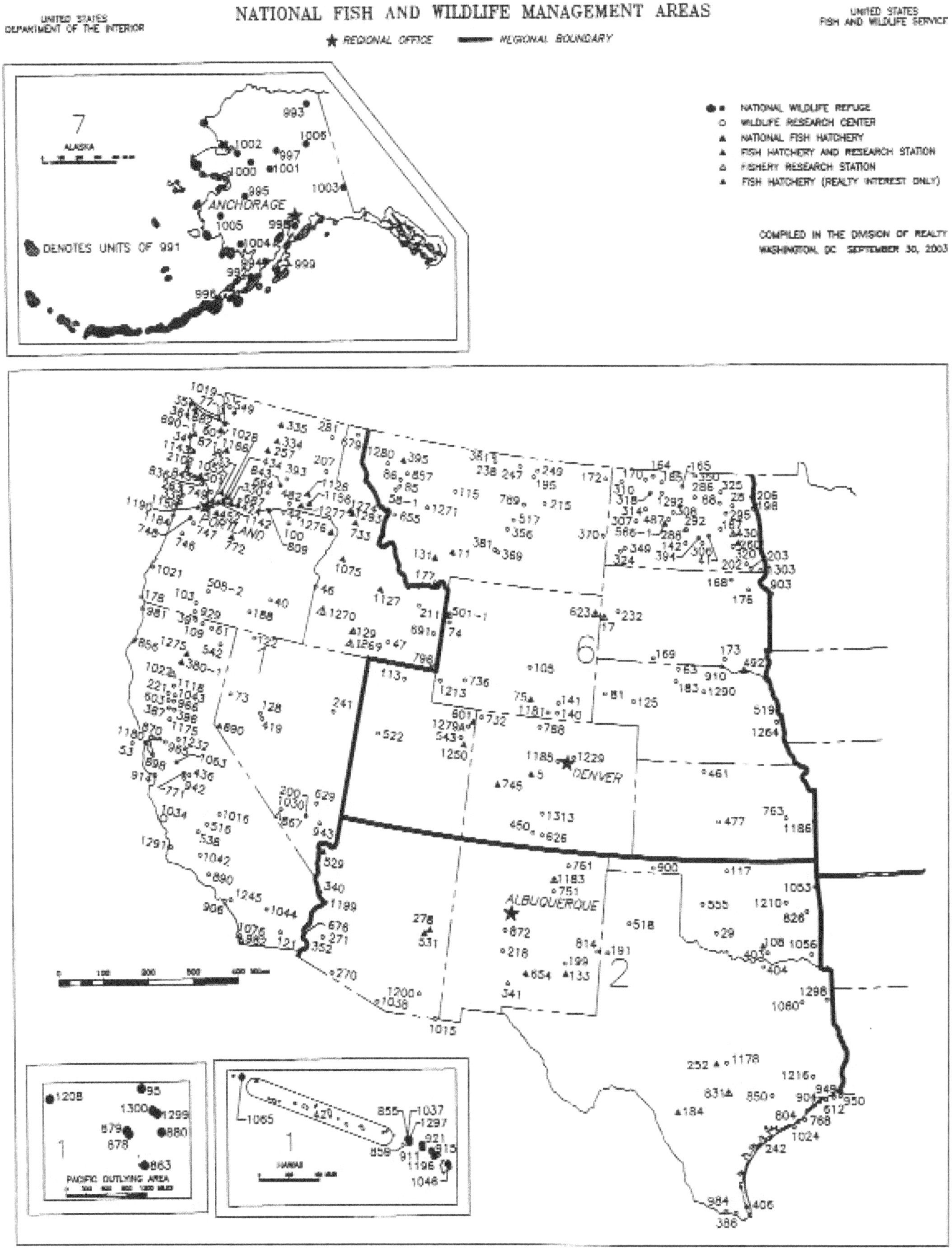

UNITED STATES DEPARTMENT OF THE INTERIOR
NATIONAL FISH AND WILDLIFE MANAGEMENT AREAS
UNITED STATES FISH AND WILDLIFE SERVICE
REGIONAL OFFICE
REGIONAL BOUNDARY
NATIONAL WILDLIFE REFUGE
WILDLIFE RESEARCH CENTER
NATIONAL FISH HATCHERY
FISH HATCHERY AND RESEARCH STATION
FISHERY RESEARCH STATION
FISH HATCHERY (REALTY INTEREST ONLY)
COMPILED IN THE DIVISION OF REALTY
WASHINGTON, DC SEPTEMBER 30, 2003
ALASKA
ANCHORAGE
DENOTES UNITS OF 991
PORTLAND
DENVER
ALBUQUERQUE
PACIFIC OUTLYING AREA
HAWAII

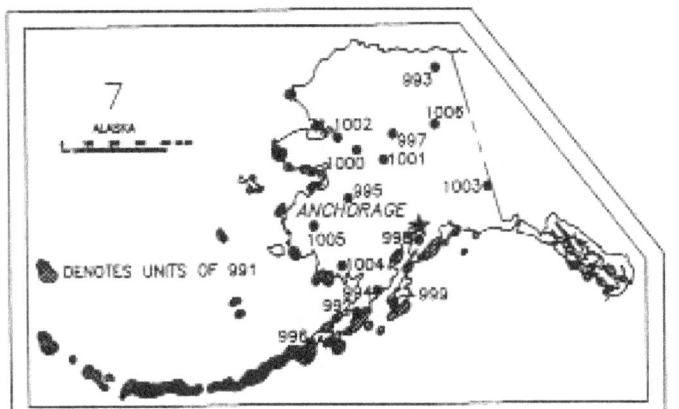

# NATIONAL FISH AND WILDLIFE MANAGEMENT AREAS

REGIONAL OFFICE ▬▬▬ REGIONAL BOUNDARY

UNITED STATES
DEPARTMENT OF THE INTERIOR

UNITED STATES
FISH AND WILDLIFE SERVICE

- ● National Wildlife Refuge
- ○ Wildlife Research Center
- ▲ National Fish Hatchery
- ▲ Fish Hatchery and Research Station
- △ Fishery Research Station
- ▲ Fish Hatchery (Realty Interest Only)

COMPILED IN THE DIVISION OF REALTY
WASHINGTON, DC   SEPTEMBER 30, 2003

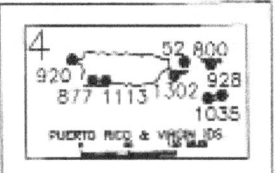

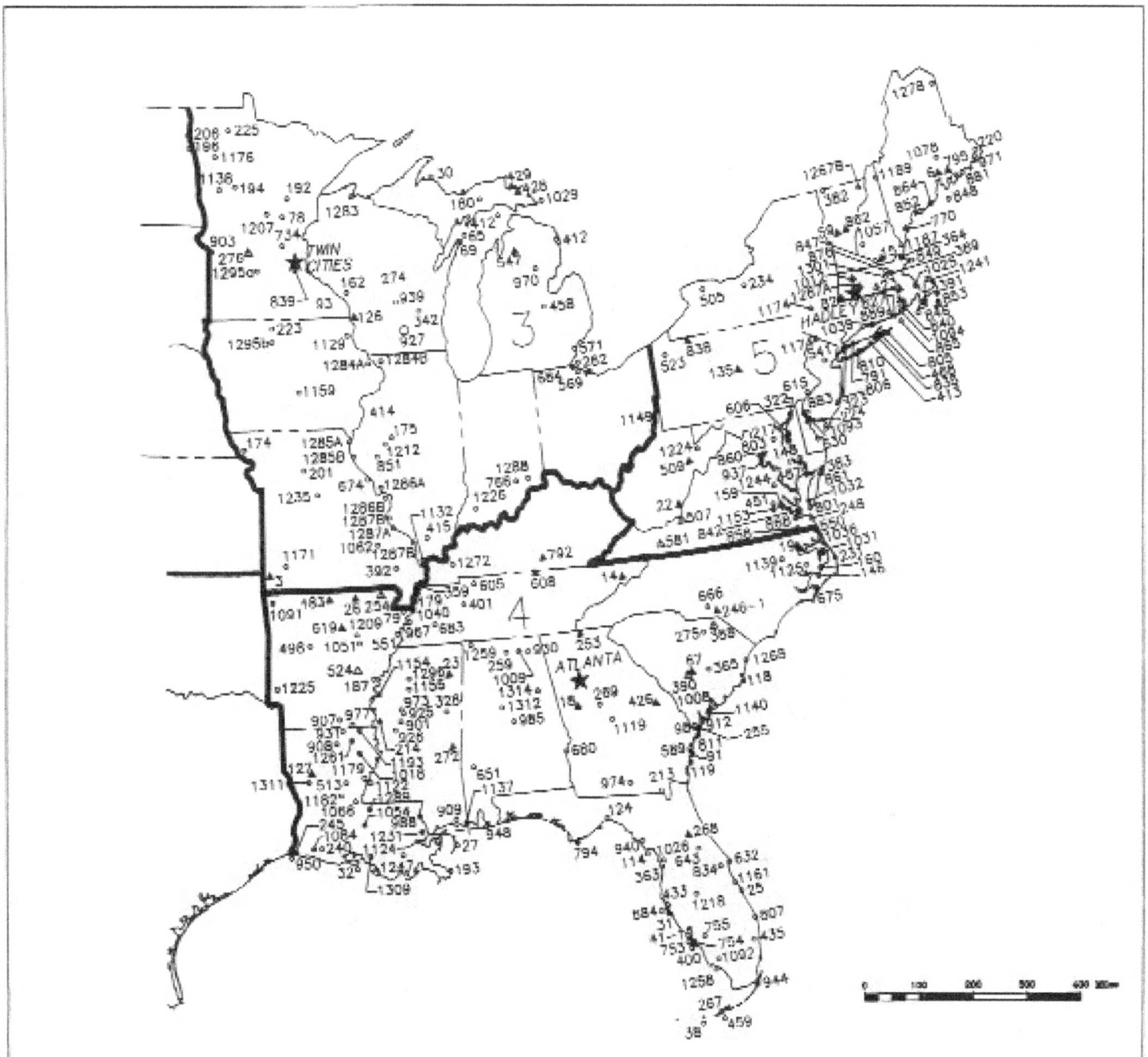

PUERTO RICO & VIRGIN IDS

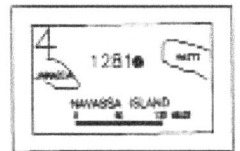

NAVASSA ISLAND

5

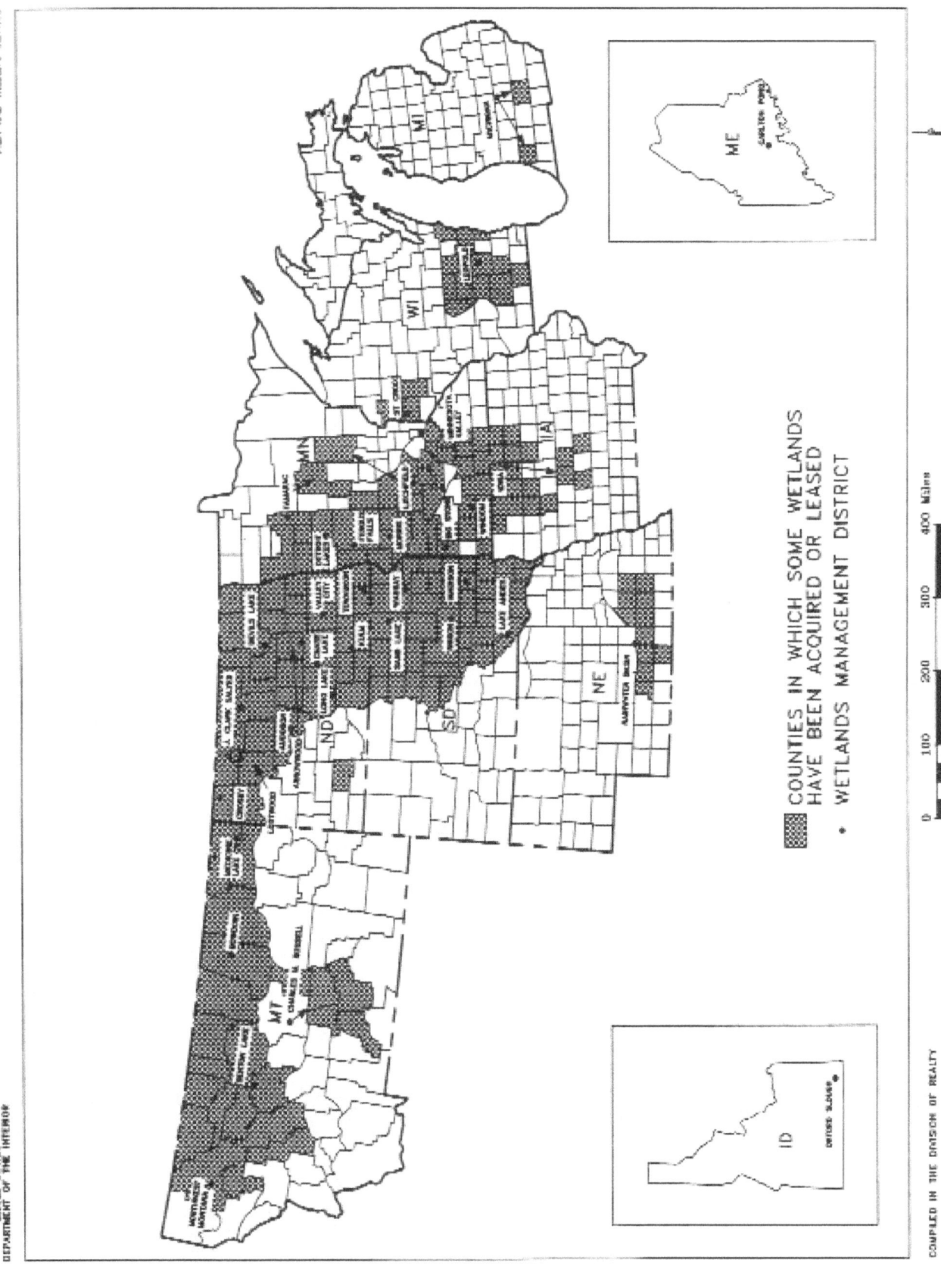

WATERFOWL PRODUCTION AREAS

COUNTIES IN WHICH SOME WETLANDS
HAVE BEEN ACQUIRED OR LEASED

• WETLANDS MANAGEMENT DISTRICT

0    100    200    300    400 Miles
0    161    322    482    644 Kilometers

COMPILED IN THE DIVISION OF REALTY

WASHINGTON, DC   SEPTEMBER 30, 2003

6

# Significant Land Acquisition Accomplishments in Fiscal Year 2003

The U.S. Fish and Wildlife Service acquired fee title or other interest in nearly 511,000 acres of land in Fiscal Year 2003, and the number of national wildlife refuges increased from 540 in FY 2002 to 542 in FY 2003. New units established as part of the National Wildlife Refuge System in Fiscal Year 2003 were the Baca National Wildlife Refuge (NWR) in Colorado and Mountain Longleaf NWR in Alabama, as authorized by law.

**Baca NWR**: Public Law 106-530 authorized the establishment of the Baca National Wildlife Refuge in San Luis Valley, Colorado. The San Luis Valley contains the largest and most important concentration of wetlands in Colorado. This refuge is established to protect water resources, maintain water rights, and minimize to the extent consistent with the protection of national wildlife resources, adverse impacts on other water users. The wetland areas are important habitat to a variety of water-dependent birds such as shorebirds and waterfowl (also see cover).

**Mountain Longleaf NWR**: Public Law 107-314 authorized the transfer of approximately 7,759 acres of the former Fort McClellan in Anniston, Alabama for the establishment of the Mountain Longleaf NWR. The refuge is established to enhance, manage and protect the unique mountain longleaf pine community. This forest type is being rapidly lost in the southeastern United States and this population may represent the largest and most pristine example of the mountain longleaf pine forest. The area also provides habitat for the endangered gray bat and has historically provided habitat for the endangered red-cockaded woodpecker.

Also, numerous partnership opportunities resulted in several additions to existing national wildlife refuges. The **Cahaba River NWR** experienced significant growth in Fiscal Year 2003. In partnership with The Nature Conservancy (TNC), the Service acquired an additional 1,857 acres. The refuge was established in 2000 and is now over eighty percent complete. The Cahaba River is one of the nation's most biologically diverse and threatened rivers. The river provides habitat for a number of rare and imperiled fish, mollusks, and plant species.

The **Red River NWR** is comprised of five units distributed along a 280 mile stretch in northwest Louisiana. Land acquisition efforts began in 2002, and an additional 2,960 acres have been acquired (Spanish Lake Bottoms Unit, Headquarters Unit and Bayou Pierre Unit) doubling the size of the refuge. These land acquisition efforts have been accomplished with the assistance of The Conservation Fund (TCF) and TNC. Eventually, the refuge will provide habitat and sanctuary for over 350 species of birds.

The Service acquired 6,924 acres at **Cat Island NWR** in Louisiana by partnering with TNC. This refuge contains one of the highest densities of old-growth bald cypress in the nation and the largest bald cypress known in the United States. The refuge provides habitat for a natural diversity of fish and wildlife, including non-game neotropical migratory birds, breeding and wintering waterfowl, woodcock, wading birds, and the threatened Louisiana black bear.

The Service acquired a 153-acre tract at **Detroit River International Wildlife Refuge**. This tract was formerly a diked farm on the estuary shore of the Detroit River and represents the first acquisition at the new international refuge. This vital acquisition will provide feeding and nesting habitat for thousands of ducks, including canvasbacks.

The Service, in cooperation with the State of California completed acquisition of the Cargill tract totaling 16,500 acres at **Don Edwards San Francisco Bay NWR**. The Service acquired approximately 9,600 acres, and the remaining acreage was acquired by the State. This property represents a unique environmental opportunity to restore wetlands at the edge of the San Francisco Bay where wetland loss has been significant.

The **Siletz Bay NWR** was established in 1991 to protect and restore important coastal wetland habitats and upland buffers for a variety of estuarine-dependent fish and wildlife resources. Land acquisition efforts are focused on acquiring former diked tidelands that can be restored. After six years of negotiations, the Service acquired two tracts of land totaling four acres. The acquisition of these tracts were essential for a major tidal marsh restoration project to proceed. The Millport Slough Tidal Marsh Restoration Project will restore 100 acres of tidal salt marsh. Our partners on this project include Pacificorp, Ducks Unlimited, Confederate Tribes of the Siletz Indians, Forest Service, Mid-Coast Watershed Council, Oregon Coastal Program, Oregon Habitat Joint Venture, and the American Land Conservancy.

The Service acquired three tracts of land that are essential to the tidal marsh restoration project within the Ni-les'tun Unit of the **Bandon Marsh NWR**. The Service purchased one tract, and TNC purchased another tract for eventual acquisition by the Service when appropriated funds are received. The third tract was donated and will preclude the need to construct expensive dikes and water control structures as part of the restoration project, thus resulting in considerable cost savings to the refuge. When completed, this restoration project will be the largest ever constructed in the state of Oregon. Partnerships with the Bandon Dunes Golf Resort, Ducks Unlimited, Coquille Indian Tribe, Confederate Tribes of the Siletz Indians, TNC, The Archaeological Conservancy, Shoreline Education for Awareness, South Slough National Estuarine Research Reserve, Port of Bandon, Oregon Coastal Program, and Oregon Habitat Joint Venture have allowed us to acquire 857 of the 1,000 acres in the approved acquisition boundary.

The **Nestucca Bay NWR** was expanded in 2000 to protect key habitats for threatened and endangered species such as Coho Salmon. This rare and unique coastal bog ecosystem provides a diversity of habitats for migratory birds, mammals, amphibians, as well as compatible wildlife-dependent recreational activities. The Service now preserves all tidal salt marsh within the refuge boundary. The Service also accepted a donation on the Marsh Unit that serves as a buffer between a housing development and the marsh.

**Palmyra Atoll NWR** provides nesting habitat for migratory seabirds. The Service purchased approximately 416 acres of this beautiful and resource rich atoll from TNC and established the land base of the refuge. This important acquisition also included a donation from TNC for access and rights to use the infrastructure and a site on Cooper and Menge Islands for refuge management purposes. The Service is working cooperatively with TNC to implement refuge management programs and permit compatible public use for: wildlife observation and photography, environmental education and interpretation, recreational fishing, and access by recreational sailboats and motorboats.

The Clark County Conservation of Public Land and Natural Resources Act of 2002 added 26,433 acres of land to the **Desert National Wildlife Range**. This land was previously under the jurisdiction of the Bureau of Land Management and will provide additional habitat for the bighorn sheep, desert tortoise, and a wide variety of flora and fauna found where the Mojave Desert and the Great Basin meet.

Public Law 106-398, as amended by Public Law 107-107 authorized the transfer of 14,573 acres from the Department of the Navy to the Secretary of the Interior for the **Vieques NWR** in Puerto Rico. On April 29, 2003, the General Services Administration transferred an additional 96 acres for a total of 14,699 acres. Vieques National Wildlife Refuge is the largest refuge in the Caribbean. The refuge contains several ecologically distinct habitats including: beaches, coastal lagoons, mangrove wetlands, and upland forested areas. The marine environment surrounding the refuge contains coral reefs and sea grass beds.

The U.S. Army and Department of the Interior signed a Memorandum of Agreement on September 26, 2003 to transition 9,404 acres of the Savanna Army Depot Activity in Savanna, Illinois, into the National Wildlife Refuge System.

On the same day, the Department accepted transfer of primary jurisdiction over two parcels totaling 3,022 acres. The area is now known as the Lost Mound Unit of the **Upper Mississippi River National Wildlife and Fish Refuge** and provides increased protection and conservation of the unique natural resources found there. Habitat at Lost Mound includes sand prairie and sand savanna—atypical sand formations at the southern zone of what is referred to as the "driftless" area—and contains one of the largest natural grasslands in the Midwest. Most of Lost Mound is riverine/flood plain forest that provides habitat for marsh and water birds, raptors, waterfowl, neotropical migrants, otter, beaver, muskrats and fish. Both the uplands and bottomlands of the Unit have excellent wildlife and biodiversity values. Lost Mound Unit will also provide future opportunities for public recreation and ecotourism in this area. The Service will manage the area while Army continues to clean up the hazardous substances and other environmental contaminants found there. Lost Mound is jointly managed by the Service and the Illinois Department of Natural Resources (ILDNR).

---

A complete list of new additions to the National Wildlife Refuge System is as follows:

| State | Unit Name | Acres | Date Est. |
|---|---|---|---|
| Colorado | Baca NWR | 3,302 | 4/10/2003 |
| Alabama | Mountain Longleaf NWR | 7,759 | 5/29/2003 |

TABLE 1 - SUMMARY BY CATEGORIES

| CATEGORY | | RESERVED FROM PUBLIC DOMAIN | | ACQUIRED BY OTHER FEDERAL AGENCY | | DEVISE OR GIFT | PURCHASED | | AGREEMENT EASEMENT OR LEASE | TOTAL ACRES |
|---|---|---|---|---|---|---|---|---|---|---|
| | | SOLE OR PRIMARY | SECONDARY | SOLE OR PRIMARY | SECONDARY | | ACRES | COST ($) | | |
| NATIONAL WILDLIFE REFUGES | 542 | 81,327,397.71 | 690,838.04 | 3,144,156.02 | 1,229,726.33 | 705,688.91 | 4,140,129.03 | 1,770,263,734.98 | 1,303,425.64 | 92,541,398.18 |
| WATERFOWL PRODUCTION AREAS | 203 | 15,897.64 | 0.00 | 26,758.41 | 0.00 | 13,240.96 | 685,530.71 | 192,197,575.74 | 7,253,670.50 | 7,991,096.77 |
| COORDINATION AREAS | 30 | 56,586.61 | 0.00 | 139,273.47 | 55,739.14 | 0.00 | 681.13 | 13,480.00 | 63,544.00 | 315,824.35 |
| TOTAL | 775 | 81,399,881.46 | 690,838.04 | 3,310,187.90 | 1,285,465.47 | 718,929.87 | 4,846,340.87 | 1,962,474,810.77 | 7,620,640.14 | 95,852,250.75 |
| ADMINISTRATIVE SITES | 47 | 50.95 | 36.00 | 7.40 | 0.00 | .75 | 1,025.15 | 10,570,469.05 | 37.04 | 1,157.29 |
| NATIONAL FISH HATCHERIES | 69 | 3,607.09 | 987.09 | 2,596.85 | 3,682.01 | 1,438.52 | 5,273.90 | 5,196,960.59 | 4,360.85 | 21,866.31 |
| TOTAL | 116 | 3,658.04 | 1,023.09 | 2,604.25 | 3,682.01 | 1,439.27 | 6,299.05 | 15,767,429.64 | 4,397.89 | 23,024.80 |
| GRAND TOTAL | 891 | 81,403,539.50 | 691,861.13 | 3,312,792.15 | 1,289,147.48 | 720,369.14 | 4,852,636.92 | 1,976,242,040.36 | 7,625,038.03 | 95,875,284.55 |

REPORT DEFINITIONS

THE FOLLOWING DEFINITIONS ARE USED SOLELY FOR ADMINISTRATIVE PURPOSES IN GROUPING LAND USE CATEGORIES FOR THIS REPORT AND DO NOT NECESSARILY REFLECT THE DEFINITIONS FOUND IN 50 CFR 25.12

ADMINISTRATIVE SITE: LAND USED TO SUPPORT ADMINISTRATIVE PROGRAMS, SUCH AS MAINTENANCE FACILITIES OR OFFICES, AND OFF-SITE VISITOR CENTERS (TABLE 6)

COORDINATION AREA: ANY AREA ADMINISTERED AS PART OF THE NATIONAL WILDLIFE REFUGE SYSTEM AND MANAGED BY THE STATE UNDER COOPERATIVE AGREEMENTS BETWEEN THE SERVICE AND A STATE FISH AND WILDLIFE AGENCY (TABLE 5).

MIGRATORY WATERFOWL REFUGE ON A FEDERAL WATER RESOURCE PROJECT: FEDERAL LAND MANAGED BY THE SERVICE AS PART OF THE NATIONAL WILDLIFE REFUGE SYSTEM TO MITIGATE A FEDERAL WATER RESOURCE PROJECT FOR THE BENEFIT OF MIGRATING WATERFOWL (AND OTHER WILDLIFE) UNDER THE FISH AND WILDLIFE COORDINATION ACT (TABLE 9).

NATIONAL FISH HATCHERY: FACILITY WHERE FISH ARE RAISED. HATCHERY OBJECTIVES ARE TO REPLENISH DEPLETED STOCKS, TO MITIGATE FEDERAL WATER PROJECTS, TO ASSIST WITH THE MANAGEMENT OF FISHERY RESOURCES ON FEDERAL (PRIMARILY SERVICE) AND INDIAN LANDS, AND TO ENHANCE RECREATIONAL FISHERIES (TABLE 7.)

NATIONAL WILDLIFE REFUGE: ANY AREA OF THE NATIONAL WILDLIFE REFUGE SYSTEM, EXCEPT COORDINATION AREAS AND WATERFOWL PRODUCTION AREAS (TABLE 4).

WATERFOWL PRODUCTION AREA: ANY WETLAND OR POTHOLE AREA ACQUIRED PURSUANT TO THE MIGRATORY BIRD HUNTING AND CONSERVATION STAMP ACT OR OTHER STATUTORY AUTHORITY AND ADMINISTERED AS PART OF THE NATIONAL WILDLIFE REFUGE SYSTEMS AND IDENTIFIED BY COUNTY DESIGNATION (TABLE 4).

WILDERNESS AREA: SERVICE LAND DESIGNATED BY CONGRESS TO BE MANAGED AS A UNIT OF THE NATIONAL WILDERNESS PRESERVATION SYSTEM, IN ACCORDANCE WITH THE TERMS OF THE WILDERNESS ACT OF 1964. ALL SERVICE WILDERNESS AREAS OCCUR WITHIN NATIONAL WILDLIFE REFUGES, WITH THE EXCEPTION OF MOUNT MASSIVE WILDERNESS AREA WHICH IS LOCATED AT THE LEADVILLE NATIONAL FISH HATCHERY (TABLE 8).

NOTE: FOR CONVERSION TO METRIC UNITS

1 ACRE = .405 HECTARES

TABLE 2 - SUMMARY BY STATES, ASSOCIATED GOVERNMENTS AND POSSESSIONS

| STATE | | RESERVED FROM PUBLIC DOMAIN | | ACQUIRED BY OTHER FEDERAL AGENCY | | DEVISE OR GIFT | PURCHASED | | AGREEMENT EASEMENT OR LEASE | TOTAL ACRES |
|---|---|---|---|---|---|---|---|---|---|---|
| | | SOLE OR PRIMARY | SECONDARY | SOLE OR PRIMARY | SECONDARY | | ACRES | COST ($) | | |
| ALABAMA | 11 | 0.00 | 0.00 | 16,114.00 | 37,821.62 | 1,214.59 | 12,713.34 | 38,432,070.00 | 1,317.69 | 69,181.24 |
| ALASKA | 48 | 76,243,206.75 | 66,687.00 | 1.87 | 0.00 | 45,185.98 | 380,850.81 | 127,925,511.65 | 145,462.54 | 76,779,394.77 |
| ARIZONA | 15 | 1,548,669.60 | 27,270.45 | 4,212.95 | 12,501.25 | 1,200.00 | 125,868.58 | 17,567,215.00 | 7,447.80 | 1,725,148.59 |
| ARKANSAS | 13 | 8,881.60 | 0.00 | 166,974.56 | 825.77 | 1,861.20 | 164,106.16 | 66,303,460.98 | 711.40 | 347,338.49 |
| CALIFORNIA | 42 | 81,073.58 | 45,118.29 | 35,580.77 | 6,467.04 | 10,623.79 | 154,178.16 | 198,564,875.06 | 127,111.85 | 479,954.86 |
| COLORADO | 12 | 16,402.00 | 0.00 | 4,285.05 | 17,000.00 | 509.53 | 48,866.06 | 14,192,978.36 | 1,770.07 | 88,829.53 |
| CONNECTICUT | 1 | 0.00 | 0.00 | 0.00 | 4.90 | 243.79 | 654.73 | 21,724,590.00 | 1.72 | 905.14 |
| DELAWARE | 2 | 0.00 | 0.00 | 541.50 | 0.00 | 29.60 | 24,622.16 | 7,896,752.76 | 954.19 | 26,126.45 |
| FLORIDA | 30 | 4,858.76 | 154.00 | 32,463.44 | 138,222.70 | 4,388.60 | 747,290.58 | 124,937,105.45 | 548,869.95 | 976,282.81 |
| GEORGIA | 10 | 0.00 | 0.00 | 39,575.46 | 3,273.80 | 25,579.36 | 408,369.57 | 8,896,077.04 | 4,089.33 | 480,633.54 |
| HAWAII | 15 | 254,418.10 | 0.00 | 72.80 | 61.15 | 91.59 | 43,791.46 | 38,574,518.60 | 945.95 | 299,380.44 |
| IDAHO | 15 | 25,907.10 | 26,758.15 | 1,175.46 | 1,070.52 | 581.26 | 21,349.66 | 4,270,852.86 | 15,617.48 | 92,009.42 |
| ILLINOIS | 11 | 65.15 | 0.00 | 46,187.61 | 67,101.81 | 3,917.79 | 32,241.61 | 17,801,885.73 | 444.81 | 149,953.28 |
| INDIANA | 3 | 0.00 | 0.00 | 719.05 | 51,000.00 | 412.58 | 13,061.86 | 7,950,397.60 | 0.00 | 64,699.49 |
| IOWA | 27 | 333.66 | 0.00 | 0.00 | 47,237.94 | 81.22 | 64,786.88 | 37,440,185.71 | 712.01 | 113,151.71 |
| KANSAS | 5 | 0.00 | 0.00 | 116.50 | 29,241.71 | 199.20 | 29,131.77 | 5,573,019.40 | 6.57 | 58,695.05 |
| KENTUCKY | 3 | 0.00 | 0.00 | 0.00 | 20.47 | 0.00 | 7,525.88 | 7,111,499.15 | 0.00 | 7,546.35 |
| LOUISIANA | 24 | 10,462.85 | 2,802.30 | 251,417.20 | 0.00 | 16,977.79 | 257,424.59 | 119,092,675.16 | 25,557.77 | 564,332.25 |
| MAINE | 12 | 0.00 | 0.00 | 11,536.27 | 0.00 | 4,252.99 | 45,464.96 | 34,810,766.02 | 754.82 | 61,789.04 |
| MARYLAND | 5 | 0.00 | 0.00 | 11,866.89 | 0.00 | 1,940.99 | 29,651.62 | 15,810,081.28 | 68.21 | 43,514.31 |
| MASSACHUSETTS | 12 | 0.00 | 0.00 | 4,454.58 | 0.00 | 780.69 | 11,718.21 | 71,018,748.74 | 81.58 | 16,975.01 |
| MICHIGAN | 13 | 2,999.51 | 121.72 | 7,506.64 | 1,871.52 | 435.61 | 102,340.94 | 7,189,041.02 | 1,007.45 | 116,242.27 |
| MINNESOTA | 39 | 788.10 | 0.00 | 165,139.76 | 15,674.97 | 3,864.62 | 291,564.48 | 100,910,649.85 | 76,477.51 | 558,019.52 |
| MISSISSIPPI | 12 | 40.08 | 0.00 | 72,576.62 | 7,070.45 | 5,116.84 | 131,099.06 | 77,762,405.03 | 10,493.60 | 226,396.65 |
| MISSOURI | 17 | 0.00 | 0.00 | 11,087.50 | 13,807.00 | 90.00 | 47,623.99 | 10,397,351.12 | 259.43 | 72,868.00 |
| MONTANA | 53 | 435,134.99 | 388,952.77 | 78,755.26 | 155,525.03 | 6,601.97 | 91,076.57 | 21,319,716.08 | 162,178.00 | 1,334,004.17 |
| NEBRASKA | 17 | 15,786.86 | 7,684.81 | 70,015.85 | 0.00 | 4,781.65 | 81,748.81 | 16,570,546.74 | 1,341.89 | 178,359.89 |
| NEVADA | 11 | 2,344,908.96 | 18,261.22 | 4.45 | 628.20 | 2,549.11 | 86,085.71 | 23,951,578.25 | 65,964.22 | 2,416,386.37 |
| NEW HAMPSHIRE | 5 | 0.00 | 0.00 | 1,094.00 | 0.00 | 1,856.60 | 15,941.48 | 12,486,625.96 | 55.21 | 18,847.29 |
| NEW JERSEY | 4 | 0.00 | 0.00 | 6.86 | 1.96 | 4,026.79 | 65,055.62 | 111,549,612.10 | 2,905.35 | 71,975.76 |
| NEW MEXICO | 10 | 15,766.28 | 57,215.48 | 0.00 | 438.57 | 220,300.00 | 90,697.96 | 5,317,667.89 | 733.67 | 385,051.89 |
| NEW YORK | 12 | 0.00 | 0.00 | 1,829.19 | 0.00 | 5,634.04 | 19,681.25 | 10,345,339.67 | 1,966.95 | 29,081.43 |
| NORTH CAROLINA | 12 | 0.00 | 0.00 | 50,964.86 | 11.58 | 757,790.65 | 127,026.69 | 34,363,305.52 | 9,802.40 | 425,595.98 |
| NORTH DAKOTA | 108 | 18,557.86 | 0.00 | 138,426.49 | 14,962.69 | 4,495.98 | 318,804.06 | 79,179,486.86 | 1,100,960.12 | 1,596,185.20 |
| OHIO | 5 | 77.15 | 0.00 | 0.00 | 0.00 | 2,445.62 | 5,754.14 | 3,981,998.55 | 508.20 | 8,874.87 |
| OKLAHOMA | 10 | 77,966.20 | 0.00 | 622.49 | 61,224.08 | 450.55 | 25,998.49 | 13,929,164.31 | 3,861.89 | 170,121.70 |
| OREGON | 28 | 267,494.20 | 4,908.08 | 65,078.95 | 7,826.80 | 1,443.47 | 275,669.10 | 46,331,951.30 | 844.77 | 572,965.55 |
| PENNSYLVANIA | 4 | 0.00 | 0.00 | 87.36 | 45.04 | 243.14 | 9,672.39 | 7,889,374.75 | 0.00 | 10,047.85 |
| RHODE ISLAND | 5 | 0.00 | 0.00 | 581.96 | 0.00 | 680.89 | 997.58 | 17,250,300.00 | 156.20 | 2,366.63 |
| SOUTH CAROLINA | 9 | 0.00 | 0.00 | 53,214.67 | 100.00 | 8,906.45 | 57,611.01 | 24,802,162.22 | 45,915.16 | 165,747.29 |
| SOUTH DAKOTA | 51 | 1,848.76 | 0.00 | 28,782.89 | 581.00 | 7,096.46 | 163,715.94 | 29,485,092.79 | 1,145,097.53 | 1,347,122.60 |
| TENNESSEE | 8 | 0.00 | 0.00 | 7,925.67 | 53,510.81 | 8.26 | 40,916.34 | 33,775,496.19 | 15,482.07 | 117,843.35 |
| TEXAS | 22 | 0.00 | 0.00 | 40,742.73 | 18,431.84 | 14,373.47 | 438,824.65 | 194,387,675.12 | 53,431.30 | 565,844.00 |
| UTAH | 9 | 65,780.81 | 0.00 | 2,302.91 | 0.00 | 4,285.43 | 34,778.23 | 4,168,528.72 | 4,717.28 | 112,144.66 |
| VERMONT | 4 | 0.00 | 0.00 | 0.00 | 0.00 | 344.56 | 12,797.87 | 7,529,647.37 | 86.00 | 33,230.18 |
| VIRGINIA | 14 | 0.00 | 0.00 | 5,994.55 | 0.00 | 53,794.95 | 69,490.65 | 76,854,069.89 | 4,572.15 | 133,652.08 |
| WASHINGTON | 39 | 40,488.42 | 2,182.11 | 34,874.66 | 187,347.02 | 1,291.87 | 70,151.82 | 38,316,896.78 | 7,634.20 | 343,954.14 |
| WEST VIRGINIA | 4 | 0.00 | 0.00 | 18.90 | 0.00 | 166.87 | 58,356.06 | 42,965,781.10 | 26.34 | 58,600.17 |
| WISCONSIN | 26 | 747.95 | 0.00 | 99,468.57 | 40,341.00 | 174.64 | 96,549.33 | 21,377,578.51 | 58.40 | 237,319.67 |
| WYOMING | 13 | 22,221.58 | 11,501.57 | 16,079.95 | 15,547.63 | 4,474.22 | 26,918.73 | 11,787,700.76 | 6,954.47 | 104,680.13 |
| AMERICAN SAMOA | 1 | 0.00 | 57,451.00 | 1,615.00 | 0.00 | 0.00 | 0.00 | 0.00 | 0.00 | 59,066.00 |
| BAKER ISLAND | 1 | 0.00 | 0.00 | 31,736.89 | 0.00 | 0.00 | 0.00 | 0.00 | 0.00 | 31,736.89 |
| GUAM | 1 | 0.00 | 0.00 | 777.10 | 0.00 | 0.00 | 0.00 | 0.00 | 22,456.00 | 23,249.10 |

TABLE 2 - SUMMARY BY STATES, ASSOCIATED GOVERNMENTS AND POSSESSIONS

| STATE | | RESERVED FROM PUBLIC DOMAIN | | ACQUIRED BY OTHER FEDERAL AGENCY | | DEVISE OR GIFT | PURCHASED | | AGREEMENT EASEMENT OR LEASE | TOTAL ACRES |
|---|---|---|---|---|---|---|---|---|---|---|
| | | SOLE OR PRIMARY | SECONDARY | SOLE OR PRIMARY | SECONDARY | | ACRES | COST ($) | | |
| HOWLAND ISLAND | 1 | 0.00 | 0.00 | 32,550.25 | 0.00 | 0.00 | 0.00 | 0.00 | 0.00 | 32,550.25 |
| JARVIS ISLAND | 1 | 0.00 | 0.00 | 37,519.17 | 0.00 | 0.00 | 0.00 | 0.00 | 0.00 | 37,519.17 |
| JOHNSTON ATOLL | 1 | 0.00 | 0.00 | 100.00 | 0.00 | 0.00 | 0.00 | 0.00 | 0.00 | 100.00 |
| KINGMAN REEF | 1 | 0.00 | 0.00 | 426,392.00 | 0.00 | 0.00 | 0.00 | 0.00 | 0.00 | 426,392.00 |
| MIDWAY ISLANDS | 1 | 0.00 | 0.00 | 298,156.50 | 282,885.00 | 0.00 | 0.00 | 0.00 | 0.00 | 581,991.50 |
| NAVASSA ISLAND | 1 | 0.00 | 0.00 | 564,950.00 | 0.00 | 0.00 | 0.00 | 0.00 | 0.00 | 564,950.00 |
| PALMYRA ATOLL | 1 | 0.00 | 0.00 | 303,963.00 | 0.00 | 0.00 | 415.75 | 8,900,000.00 | 2.30 | 304,381.05 |
| PUERTO RICO | 5 | 0.00 | 0.00 | 20,457.74 | 68.00 | 0.00 | 1,369.38 | 2,999,285.65 | 737.10 | 22,582.22 |
| VIRGIN ISLANDS | 3 | 0.00 | 0.00 | 45.15 | 0.00 | 0.00 | 545.94 | 3,757,570.00 | 0.00 | 591.09 |
| GRAND TOTAL | 911 | 81,403,589.50 | 671,861.13 | 3,312,792.76 | 1,289,147.48 | 720,249.14 | 4,052,636.92 | 1,976,242,040.56 | 5,625,058.03 | 95,675,284.35 |

| STATE | | RESERVED FROM PUBLIC DOMAIN | | ACQUIRED BY OTHER FEDERAL AGENCY | | DEVISE OR GIFT | PURCHASED | | AGREEMENT EASEMENT OR LEASE | TOTAL ACRES |
|---|---|---|---|---|---|---|---|---|---|---|
| | | SOLE OR PRIMARY | SECONDARY | SOLE OR PRIMARY | SECONDARY | | ACRES | COST ($) | | |
| ALABAMA | 3 | 0.00 | 0.00 | 7,758.68 | 0.00 | 0.00 | 1,858.01 | 3,066,413.00 | 0.00 | 9,616.69 |
| ALASKA | 6 | 0.00 | 0.00 | 0.00 | 0.00 | 0.00 | 1,139.44 | 1,157,000.00 | (.19) | 1,139.44 |
| ARIZONA | 1 | 0.00 | 0.00 | 0.00 | 0.00 | 0.00 | 49.88 | 152,000.00 | 0.00 | 49.88 |
| ARKANSAS | 7 | 0.00 | 0.00 | 0.00 | 0.00 | 0.00 | 927.58 | 1,667,534.00 | 0.00 | 927.58 |
| CALIFORNIA | 7 | 0.00 | 0.00 | 0.00 | 0.00 | 259.80 | 5,756.30 | 7,280,000.00 | 2,571.80 | 8,017.90 |
| COLORADO | 3 | 0.00 | 0.00 | 3,301.64 | 0.00 | 718.90 | 638.36 | 787,000.00 | 21.00 | 4,180.10 |
| CONNECTICUT | 1 | 0.00 | 0.00 | 0.00 | 0.00 | 0.00 | 52.80 | 6,000,000.00 | 0.00 | 52.80 |
| FLORIDA | 8 | 0.00 | 0.00 | (146.20) | 0.00 | 1.92 | 197.49 | 1,038,500.00 | 42.00 | 206.21 |
| IDAHO | 7 | 0.00 | 0.00 | 0.00 | 0.00 | 0.00 | 562.14 | 619,000.00 | 0.00 | 562.14 |
| ILLINOIS | 2 | 0.00 | 0.00 | 3,077.00 | 6,382.00 | 0.00 | 778.64 | 352,209.78 | 0.00 | 9,682.64 |
| INDIANA | 1 | 0.00 | 0.00 | 0.00 | 0.00 | 0.00 | 80.00 | 44,000.00 | 0.00 | 80.00 |
| IOWA | 2 | 0.00 | 0.00 | 0.00 | 0.00 | 0.00 | 358.17 | 768,758.75 | 0.00 | 358.17 |
| KENTUCKY | 1 | 0.00 | 0.00 | 0.00 | 0.00 | 0.00 | 468.07 | 585,650.00 | 0.00 | 468.07 |
| LOUISIANA | 5 | 0.00 | 0.00 | 0.00 | 0.00 | 0.00 | 9,676.55 | 9,328,095.00 | 3,846.74 | 13,523.29 |
| MAINE | 3 | 0.00 | 0.00 | 0.00 | 0.00 | 0.00 | 552.20 | 3,140,500.00 | 0.00 | 552.20 |
| MARYLAND | 1 | 0.00 | 0.00 | 0.00 | 0.00 | 0.00 | 486.00 | 166,560.00 | 0.00 | 486.00 |
| MASSACHUSETTS | 1 | 0.00 | 0.00 | 0.00 | 0.00 | 0.00 | 178.26 | 3,194,400.00 | 0.00 | 178.26 |
| MICHIGAN | 1 | 0.00 | 0.00 | 0.00 | 168.00 | 0.00 | 152.53 | 600,000.00 | 656.45 | 976.98 |
| MINNESOTA | 20 | 0.00 | 0.00 | 470.00 | 0.00 | 175.19 | 4,525.17 | 3,730,166.75 | 962.23 | 5,132.59 |
| MISSISSIPPI | 4 | 0.00 | 0.00 | 0.00 | 0.00 | 45.63 | 254.69 | 284,160.00 | 100.00 | 400.32 |
| MISSOURI | 1 | 0.00 | 0.00 | 0.00 | 0.00 | 0.00 | 1,809.00 | 7,610,700.00 | 0.00 | 1,809.00 |
| MONTANA | 15 | 0.00 | 0.00 | 0.00 | 0.00 | 51.00 | 850.30 | 185,000.00 | 4,767.73 | 5,717.46 |
| NEBRASKA | 1 | 0.00 | 0.00 | 0.00 | 0.00 | 0.00 | 28.94 | 158,000.00 | 0.00 | 28.94 |
| NEVADA | 3 | 26,498.19 | 0.00 | 4.45 | 0.00 | 0.00 | 267.40 | 955,500.00 | 0.00 | 36,770.34 |
| NEW HAMPSHIRE | 2 | 0.00 | 0.00 | 0.00 | 0.00 | 0.00 | 5,045.50 | 1,982,560.00 | 0.00 | 5,045.50 |
| NEW JERSEY | 1 | 0.00 | 0.00 | 0.00 | 0.00 | 0.00 | 222.64 | 5,848,500.00 | 0.00 | 222.64 |
| NORTH CAROLINA | 4 | 0.00 | 0.00 | 0.00 | 0.00 | 38.00 | 1,648.03 | 1,469,400.00 | (37.90) | 1,686.03 |
| NORTH DAKOTA | 21 | 0.00 | 0.00 | (8.48) | 0.00 | 160.00 | 16.61 | 5,300.00 | 29,990.59 | 30,257.22 |
| OKLAHOMA | 1 | 0.00 | 0.00 | 0.00 | 0.00 | 0.00 | 90.00 | 31,500.00 | 0.00 | 90.00 |
| OREGON | 5 | 0.00 | 0.00 | (165.00) | 0.00 | 63.95 | 417.90 | 424,528.00 | 10.00 | 326.85 |
| RHODE ISLAND | 2 | 0.00 | 0.00 | 0.00 | 0.00 | 0.00 | 187.42 | 1,600,800.00 | 0.00 | 187.42 |
| SOUTH CAROLINA | 3 | 0.00 | 0.00 | 0.00 | 0.00 | 43.72 | 2,745.82 | 4,985,584.00 | 0.00 | 2,789.54 |
| SOUTH DAKOTA | 77 | 0.00 | 0.00 | 0.00 | 0.00 | 1,126.71 | 103.46 | 86,190.00 | 45,547.56 | 47,022.77 |
| TENNESSEE | 2 | 0.00 | 0.00 | 0.00 | 0.00 | 0.00 | 877.37 | 1,964,868.00 | 0.00 | 877.37 |
| TEXAS | 6 | 0.00 | 0.00 | 0.00 | 0.00 | 631.85 | 32,185.04 | 15,175,341.49 | 68.36 | 32,865.25 |
| UTAH | 3 | 0.00 | 0.00 | 0.00 | 0.00 | 13.22 | 104.79 | 695,000.00 | 0.00 | 118.01 |
| VERMONT | 1 | 0.00 | 0.00 | 0.00 | 0.00 | 0.00 | 0.00 | 5,750.00 | 0.00 | 0.00 |
| VIRGINIA | 2 | 0.00 | 0.00 | 0.00 | 0.00 | 0.00 | 555.80 | 1,292,480.00 | 0.00 | 555.80 |
| WASHINGTON | 5 | 0.00 | 0.00 | (188.00) | 0.00 | 0.00 | 346.19 | 1,531,253.00 | 0.00 | 158.19 |
| WISCONSIN | 8 | 0.00 | 0.00 | 0.00 | 0.00 | 0.00 | 671.85 | 1,522,681.17 | .64 | 672.49 |
| WYOMING | 2 | 0.00 | 0.00 | 0.00 | 0.00 | 0.00 | 825.00 | 627,500.00 | 0.00 | 825.00 |
| MIDWAY ISLANDS | 1 | 0.00 | 0.00 | 0.00 | 282,835.00 | 0.00 | 0.00 | 0.00 | 0.00 | 282,835.00 |
| PUERTO RICO | 1 | 0.00 | 0.00 | 14,669.20 | 0.00 | 0.00 | 0.00 | 0.00 | 0.00 | 14,669.20 |
| VIRGIN ISLANDS | 1 | 0.00 | 0.00 | 0.00 | 0.00 | 0.00 | 20.00 | 574,900.00 | 0.00 | 20.00 |
| PALMYRA ATOLL | 1 | 0.00 | 0.00 | 0.00 | 0.00 | 0.00 | 415.75 | 8,900,000.00 | 2.30 | 418.05 |
| GRAND TOTAL | 195 | 26,498.19 | 0.00 | 26,718.49 | 289,385.00 | 2,779.87 | 73,874.66 | 91,638,066.94 | 88,569.35 | 510,316.88 |

TABLE 3 - NATIONAL WILDLIFE REFUGES

| STATE AND UNIT | RESERVED FROM PUBLIC DOMAIN | | ACQUIRED BY OTHER FEDERAL AGENCY | | DEVISE OR GIFT | PURCHASED | | AGREEMENT EASEMENT OR LEASE | TOTAL ACRES |
| --- | --- | --- | --- | --- | --- | --- | --- | --- | --- |
| | SOLE OR PRIMARY | SECONDARY | SOLE OR PRIMARY | SECONDARY | | ACRES | COST ($) | | |
| **ALABAMA** | | | | | | | | | |
| BON SECOUR | 0.00 | 0.00 | 32.34 | 0.00 | 155.03 | 6,092.93 | 21,456,494.00 | 575.00 | 6,855.52 |
| CAHABA RIVER | 0.00 | 0.00 | 0.00 | 0.00 | 0.00 | 2,977.09 | 7,139,413.00 | 0.00 | 2,977.09 |
| CHOCTAW | 0.00 | 0.00 | 0.00 | 4,218.00 | 0.00 | 0.00 | 0.00 | 0.00 | 4,218.00 |
| EUFAULA (1) | 0.00 | 0.00 | 0.00 | 7,979.00 | 0.00 | 74.19 | 70,000.00 | 0.00 | 7,953.19 |
| FERN CAVE | 0.00 | 0.00 | 0.00 | 0.00 | 0.00 | 199.23 | 110,000.00 | 0.00 | 199.23 |
| FSA INTEREST AL **  | 0.00 | 0.00 | 0.00 | 0.00 | 0.00 | 0.00 | 0.00 | 742.69 | 742.69 |
| GRAND BAY (27) | 0.00 | 0.00 | 0.00 | 0.00 | 895.86 | 1,822.00 | 710,613.00 | 0.00 | 2,717.86 |
| KEY CAVE | 0.00 | 0.00 | 0.00 | 0.00 | 0.00 | 1,060.00 | 0.00 | 0.00 | 1,060.00 |
| MOUNTAIN LONGLEAF | 0.00 | 0.00 | 7,758.68 | 0.00 | 0.00 | 0.00 | 0.00 | 0.00 | 7,758.68 |
| SAUTA CAVE | 0.00 | 0.00 | 0.00 | 0.00 | 0.00 | 264.00 | 275,000.00 | 0.00 | 264.00 |
| WATERCRESS DARTER | 0.00 | 0.00 | 0.00 | 0.00 | 0.00 | 24.52 | 250,850.00 | 0.00 | 24.52 |
| WHEELER | 0.00 | 0.00 | 8,322.98 | 25,474.62 | 183.66 | 349.38 | 149,700.00 | 0.00 | 34,430.66 |
| STATE TOTAL 11 | 0.00 | 0.00 | 16,114.00 | 37,621.62 | 1,214.59 | 12,715.54 | 78,432,070.00 | 1,317.69 | 69,181.24 |
| **ALASKA** | | | | | | | | | |
| ALASKA MARITIME | 3,361,527.44 | 65,495.00 | 0.00 | 0.00 | 0.00 | 17,055.02 | 7,677,891.61 | 26,989.53 | 3,465,026.77 |
| ALASKA PENINSULA | 3,456,905.00 | 0.00 | 0.00 | 0.00 | 74,325.17 | 47,195.41 | 360,100.00 | .34 | 3,584,420.87 |
| ARCTIC | 19,263,110.00 | 0.00 | 0.00 | 0.00 | 0.00 | 22,971.99 | 78,000.00 | .40 | 19,286,082.39 |
| BECHAROF | 1,200,000.00 | 0.00 | 0.00 | 0.00 | 0.00 | 20.33 | 239,300.00 | 0.00 | 1,200,020.33 |
| INNOKO | 3,850,000.00 | 0.00 | 0.00 | 0.00 | 0.00 | 479.99 | 176,501.00 | 1.03 | 3,850,481.02 |
| IZEMBEK | 302,201.00 | 898.00 | 0.00 | 0.00 | 7,981.78 | 0.00 | 0.00 | 0.00 | 311,075.78 |
| KANUTI | 1,430,000.00 | 0.00 | 0.00 | 0.00 | 0.00 | 159.91 | 68,000.00 | 0.00 | 1,430,159.91 |
| KENAI | 1,904,472.00 | 0.00 | 0.00 | 0.00 | 0.00 | 7,923.07 | 10,619,299.96 | 30.33 | 1,912,425.40 |
| KODIAK | 1,636,169.40 | 0.00 | 0.00 | 0.00 | 888.86 | 175,357.64 | 125,912,995.54 | 101,000.24 | 1,988,410.50 |
| KOYUKUK | 3,350,000.00 | 0.00 | 0.00 | 0.00 | 0.00 | 0.00 | 0.00 | .53 | 3,350,000.53 |
| NOWITNA | 1,560,000.00 | 0.00 | 0.00 | 0.00 | 0.00 | 0.00 | 0.00 | 0.00 | 1,560,000.00 |
| SELAWIK | 2,150,000.00 | 0.00 | 0.00 | 0.00 | 0.00 | 0.00 | 0.00 | 2.01 | 2,150,002.01 |
| TETLIN | 700,000.00 | 0.00 | 0.00 | 0.00 | 0.00 | 5.00 | 15,500.00 | 53.54 | 700,058.54 |
| TOGIAK | 4,097,430.00 | 0.00 | 0.00 | 0.00 | 0.00 | 2,026.66 | 2,567,000.00 | 1.28 | 4,099,457.94 |
| YUKON DELTA | 19,131,581.00 | 63.00 | 0.00 | 0.00 | 0.00 | 17,094.00 | 0.00 | 17,357.48 | 19,166,094.48 |
| YUKON FLATS | 8,630,000.00 | 0.00 | 0.00 | 0.00 | 0.00 | 639.75 | 294,000.00 | .53 | 8,630,640.51 |
| STATE TOTAL 16 | 76,243,175.84 | 66,453.00 | 0.00 | 0.00 | 45,185.25 | 260,747.71 | 177,998,587.60 | 145,437.04 | 76,779,198.82 |
| **ARIZONA** | | | | | | | | | |
| BILL WILLIAMS RIVER | 2,781.00 | 945.07 | 0.00 | 758.00 | 0.00 | 1,574.69 | 1,600,000.00 | 0.00 | 6,054.76 |
| BUENOS AIRES | 0.00 | 0.00 | 0.00 | 0.00 | 0.00 | 116,362.87 | 13,855,291.00 | 301.66 | 116,664.53 |
| CABEZA PRIETA | 860,000.00 | 0.00 | 0.00 | 0.00 | 0.00 | 41.32 | 18,500.00 | 0.00 | 860,041.32 |
| CIBOLA (2) | 3,577.92 | 0.00 | 4,212.93 | 623.38 | 0.00 | 191.81 | 382,000.00 | 0.00 | 8,606.04 |
| HAVASU (2) | 10,004.54 | 10,418.50 | 0.00 | 7,816.78 | 0.00 | 40.00 | 8,000.00 | 0.00 | 38,279.82 |
| IMPERIAL (2) | 0.00 | 15,861.27 | 0.00 | 1,304.87 | 0.00 | 643.62 | 201,724.00 | 0.00 | 17,809.76 |
| KOFA | 665,400.00 | 0.00 | 0.00 | 0.00 | 0.00 | 1,080.00 | 398,000.00 | 0.00 | 666,480.00 |
| LESLIE CANYON | 0.00 | 0.00 | 0.00 | 0.00 | 1,700.00 | 1,366.76 | 750,000.00 | 7,052.72 | 9,795.48 |
| SAN BERNARDINO | 0.00 | 0.00 | 0.00 | 0.00 | 0.00 | 2,367.87 | 880,600.00 | .70 | 2,368.57 |
| STATE TOTAL 9 | 1,541,763.46 | 27,222.84 | 4,212.93 | 12,301.25 | 1,700.00 | 123,066.94 | 17,541,915.00 | 7,355.08 | 1,718,100.29 |
| **ARKANSAS** | | | | | | | | | |
| BALD KNOB | 0.00 | 0.00 | 0.00 | 0.00 | 0.00 | 14,809.95 | 9,250,000.00 | 0.00 | 14,809.95 |
| BIG LAKE | 8,875.82 | 0.00 | 1,997.34 | 0.00 | 0.00 | 362.91 | 31,854.69 | .79 | 11,056.10 |
| CACHE RIVER | 0.00 | 0.00 | 6,051.79 | 0.00 | 787.12 | 50,968.50 | 49,194,012.42 | 0.00 | 57,896.61 |
| FELSENTHAL | 0.00 | 0.00 | 64,813.54 | 0.00 | 0.00 | 88.60 | 100,000.00 | 0.00 | 64,902.14 |
| FSA INTEREST AR **  | 0.00 | 0.00 | 3,161.47 | 0.00 | 0.00 | 0.00 | 0.00 | 297.20 | 3,458.67 |
| HOLLA BEND | 0.00 | 0.00 | 4,028.00 | 0.00 | 48.85 | 2,201.45 | 657,905.00 | .73 | 6,299.03 |
| LOGAN CAVE | 0.00 | 0.00 | 0.00 | 0.00 | 0.00 | 123.59 | 109,196.00 | 0.00 | 123.59 |
| OVERFLOW | 0.00 | 0.00 | 0.00 | 0.00 | 0.00 | 11,042.89 | 10,407,020.50 | 0.00 | 11,042.89 |

13

TABLE 5 - NATIONAL WILDLIFE REFUGES

| STATE AND UNIT | RESERVED FROM PUBLIC DOMAIN | | ACQUIRED BY OTHER FEDERAL AGENCY | | DEVISE OR GIFT | PURCHASED | | AGREEMENT EASEMENT OR LEASE | TOTAL ACRES |
|---|---|---|---|---|---|---|---|---|---|
| | SOLE OR PRIMARY | SECONDARY | SOLE OR PRIMARY | SECONDARY | | ACRES | COST ($) | | |
| **ARKANSAS** | | | | | | | | | |
| POND CREEK | 0.00 | 0.00 | 0.00 | E 700.00 | 1,933.11 | 24,182.70 | 0.00 | 0.00 | 26,815.81 |
| WAPANOCCA | 0.00 | 0.00 | 0.00 | 0.00 | 0.00 | 5,484.17 | 7,751,616.00 | 0.00 | 5,484.17 |
| WHITE RIVER | 6.00 | 0.00 | 84,243.02 | E 46.80 | 1,092.12 | 72,614.56 | 5,464,198.37 | 413.22 | 158,414.72 |
| STATE TOTAL 10 | 5,881.60 | 0.00 | 168,974.36 | 746.80 | 3,841.20 | 184,069.32 | 66,247,535.96 | 711.40 | 362,225.60 |
| **CALIFORNIA** | | | | | | | | | |
| ANTIOCH DUNES | 0.00 | 0.00 | 0.00 | 0.00 | 0.00 | 55.50 | 2,135,000.00 | 0.00 | 55.50 |
| BITTER CREEK | 0.00 | 0.00 | 0.00 | 0.00 | 40.00 | 14,056.70 | 4,779,600.00 | 0.00 | 14,096.70 |
| BLUE RIDGE | 0.00 | 0.00 | 0.00 | 0.00 | 0.00 | 897.08 | 662,500.00 | 0.00 | 897.08 |
| BUTTE SINK | 0.00 | 0.00 | 0.00 | 0.00 | 0.00 | 752.86 | 3,890,700.00 | 10,310.64 | 11,045.50 |
| CASTLE ROCK | 0.00 | 0.00 | 0.00 | 0.00 | 0.00 | 15.89 | 41,250.00 | 0.00 | 15.89 |
| CIBOLA 151 * | 1,255.00 | 0.00 | 7,094.52 | 0.00 | 600.00 | 0.00 | 0.00 | 297.00 | 4,246.52 |
| CLEAR LAKE | 0.00 | R 11,705.43 | 13,020.07 | 0.00 | 0.00 | 0.00 | 0.00 | 0.00 | 24,725.50 |
| COACHELLA VALLEY | 0.00 | 0.00 | 0.00 | 0.00 | 1,029.51 | 2,548.10 | 3,515,908.77 | 0.00 | 3,577.61 |
| COLUSA | 0.00 | 0.00 | 0.00 | 0.00 | .27 | 4,039.71 | 291,280.85 | 0.00 | 4,039.98 |
| DELEVAN | 0.00 | 0.00 | 0.00 | 0.00 | 0.00 | 5,796.54 | 7,545,739.00 | 0.00 | 5,796.54 |
| DON EDWARDS SAN FRAN. BAY | 0.00 | 0.00 | 57.26 | 0.00 | 449.34 | 24,807.46 | 42,916,134.00 | 4,678.83 | 29,992.89 |
| ELLICOTT SLOUGH | 0.00 | 0.00 | 0.00 | 0.00 | 0.00 | 144.44 | 971,000.00 | 55.11 | 199.55 |
| FARALLON | 91.00 | CG 180.00 | 0.00 | 0.00 | 0.00 | 0.00 | 0.00 | 0.00 | 211.00 |
| FSA INTEREST CA ** * | 0.00 | 0.00 | 60.00 | 0.00 | 0.00 | 0.00 | 0.00 | 0.00 | 60.00 |
| GRASSLANDS | 0.00 | 0.00 | 0.00 | 0.00 | 0.00 | 13,064.85 | 17,811,228.00 | 69,540.37 | 82,605.22 |
| GUADALUPE-NIPOMO DUNES | 0.00 | 0.00 | 0.00 | 0.00 | 2,555.00 | 0.00 | 0.00 | 0.00 | 2,555.00 |
| HAVASU (3) * | 10.00 | R 4,160.23 | 0.00 | M 3,065.11 | 0.00 | 0.00 | 0.00 | 0.00 | 7,235.34 |
| HOPPER MOUNTAIN | 0.00 | 0.00 | 0.00 | 0.00 | 0.00 | 2,471.00 | 840,000.00 | 0.00 | 2,471.00 |
| HUMBOLDT BAY | 0.00 | CG 1.00 | 0.00 | 0.00 | 485.48 | 2,455.24 | 5,274,610.00 | 0.00 | 2,941.72 |
| IMPERIAL (5) * | 0.00 | R 6,509.05 | 0.00 | M 1,449.14 | 0.00 | 0.00 | 0.00 | 0.00 | 7,958.19 |
| KERN | 0.00 | 0.00 | 0.00 | 0.00 | 0.00 | 10,618.17 | 579,912.00 | 0.00 | 10,618.17 |
| LOWER KLAMATH (4) | 39,515.72 | 0.00 | 0.00 | 0.00 | 447.87 | 4,330.55 | 3,870,125.00 | 0.00 | 44,294.14 |
| MARIN ISLANDS | 0.00 | 0.00 | 0.00 | 0.00 | 152.59 | 30.70 | 1,010,000.00 | 0.00 | 151.29 |
| MERCED | 0.00 | 0.00 | 0.00 | 0.00 | 0.00 | 5,803.84 | 2,180,000.00 | 1.76 | 5,805.58 |
| MODOC | 40.00 | 0.00 | 0.00 | 0.00 | 510.00 | 6,470.62 | 1,544,854.19 | .61 | 7,021.23 |
| NORTH CENTRAL VALLEY | 0.00 | 0.00 | 0.00 | 0.00 | 0.00 | 2,518.46 | 4,037,732.00 | 12,007.13 | 14,525.59 |
| PIXLEY | 0.00 | 0.00 | 4,521.05 | 0.00 | 170.00 | 1,693.54 | 1,459,998.00 | 4.55 | 6,389.11 |
| SACRAMENTO | 0.00 | 0.00 | 0.00 | 0.00 | 33.66 | 10,785.34 | 162,998.00 | 0.00 | 10,819.00 |
| SACRAMENTO RIVER | 0.00 | 0.00 | 0.00 | 0.00 | 157.25 | 9,065.75 | 79,453,370.85 | 1,484.41 | 10,506.69 |
| SALINAS RIVER | 0.00 | 0.00 | 563.61 | 0.00 | 0.00 | 0.00 | 0.00 | 5.87 | 367.48 |
| SAN DIEGO | 0.00 | 0.00 | 88.00 | 0.00 | 3,757.16 | 4,166.06 | 71,181,990.00 | 2,401.01 | 10,012.23 |
| SAN JOAQUIN RIVER | 0.00 | 0.00 | 0.00 | 0.00 | 0.00 | 6,778.49 | 21,345,808.00 | 2,946.97 | 9,725.46 |
| SAN LUIS | 8.00 | 0.00 | 14,760.00 | 700.00 | 0.00 | 7,422.41 | 7,171,095.00 | 705.00 | 22,895.41 |
| SAN PABLO BAY | 0.00 | 0.00 | 0.00 | 0.00 | 648.72 | 1,741.00 | 6,742,600.00 | 11,800.00 | 15,189.72 |
| SEAL BEACH | 0.00 | 0.00 | 0.00 | M 852.17 | 0.00 | 0.00 | 0.00 | 58.54 | 910.71 |
| SONNY BONO SALTON SEA | 0.00 | R 27,474.58 | 563.98 | 0.00 | 0.00 | 9,342.14 | 294,461.00 | 4,551.17 | 37,656.57 |
| STONE LAKES | 0.00 | 0.00 | 0.00 | 0.00 | 121.14 | 1,088.26 | 4,115,089.00 | 1,705.56 | 2,914.96 |
| SUTTER | 0.00 | 0.00 | 0.00 | 0.00 | 0.00 | 2,590.16 | 791,281.80 | 0.00 | 2,590.16 |
| SWEETWATER MARSH | 0.00 | 0.00 | 0.00 | 0.00 | 315.80 | 0.00 | 0.00 | 0.00 | 315.80 |
| TIJUANA SLOUGH | 0.00 | 0.00 | 0.00 | M 951.47 | 0.00 | 406.04 | 7,685,000.00 | 65.00 | 1,022.50 |
| TULE LAKE | 39,103.37 | 0.00 | 0.00 | 0.00 | 0.00 | 9.37 | 0.00 | 3.84 | 39,116.58 |
| WILLOW CREEK-LURLINE | 0.00 | 0.00 | 0.00 | 0.00 | 0.00 | 0.00 | 0.00 | 5,467.50 | 5,467.50 |
| STATE TOTAL 38 | 79,848.09 | 45,118.29 | 77,575.47 | 5,157.84 | 10,648.79 | 154,155.64 | 193,411,154.36 | 177,048.82 | 468,212.96 |
| **COLORADO** | | | | | | | | | |
| ALAMOSA | 86.29 | 0.00 | 816.40 | 0.00 | 218.90 | 10,904.78 | 2,377,465.16 | 0.00 | 12,026.37 |
| ARAPAHO | 4,792.54 | 0.00 | 0.00 | 0.00 | 0.00 | 18,451.44 | 4,188,486.00 | 0.00 | 23,243.87 |
| BACA | 0.00 | 0.00 | 3,501.84 | 0.00 | 0.00 | 0.00 | 0.00 | 0.00 | 5,501.84 |

14

TABLE 3 — NATIONAL WILDLIFE REFUGES

| STATE AND UNIT | RESERVED FROM PUBLIC DOMAIN | | ACQUIRED BY OTHER FEDERAL AGENCY | | DEVISE OR GIFT | PURCHASED | | AGREEMENT EASEMENT OR LEASE | TOTAL ACRES |
|---|---|---|---|---|---|---|---|---|---|
| | SOLE OR PRIMARY | SECONDARY | SOLE OR PRIMARY | SECONDARY | | ACRES | COST ($) | | |
| COLORADO | | | | | | | | | |
| BROWNS PARK | 6,794.30 | 0.00 | 0.00 | 0.00 | 0.00 | 5,355.53 | 642,976.00 | 1,305.47 | 13,455.30 |
| COLORADO RIVER (AG1)* | 0.00 | 0.00 | 17.64 | 0.00 | 0.00 | 0.00 | 0.00 | 182.31 | 199.95 |
| FSA INTEREST CO ** * | 0.00 | 0.00 | 0.00 | 0.00 | 0.00 | 0.00 | 0.00 | 298.00 | 298.00 |
| MONTE VISTA | 800.00 | 0.00 | 0.00 | 0.00 | 84.65 | 13,950.64 | 2,241,750.00 | 0.00 | 14,835.99 |
| ROCKY MOUNTAIN ARSENAL | 0.00 | 0.00 | 0.00 | 17,000.00 | 0.00 | 0.00 | 0.00 | 0.00 | 17,000.00 |
| TWO PONDS | 0.00 | 0.00 | 0.00 | 0.00 | 7.10 | 64.94 | 5,944,105.20 | 0.00 | 72.04 |
| STATE TOTAL 7 | 12,479.13 | 0.00 | 4,135.88 | 17,000.00 | 309.33 | 48,727.34 | 14,146,578.96 | 1,783.78 | 84,429.96 |
| CONNECTICUT | | | | | | | | | |
| STEWART B. MCKINNEY | 0.00 | 0.00 | 0.00 | 4.90 | 243.79 | 654.73 | 21,753,590.00 | 1.72 | 905.14 |
| STATE TOTAL 1 | 0.00 | 0.00 | 0.00 | 4.90 | 243.79 | 654.73 | 21,753,590.00 | 1.72 | 905.14 |
| DELAWARE | | | | | | | | | |
| BOMBAY HOOK | 0.00 | 0.00 | 541.50 | 0.00 | 0.00 | 15,436.26 | 1,637,288.60 | 80.00 | 16,057.76 |
| FSA INTEREST DE ** * | 0.00 | 0.00 | 0.00 | 0.00 | 0.00 | 0.00 | 0.00 | 2.60 | 2.60 |
| PRIME HOOK | 0.00 | 0.00 | 0.00 | 0.00 | 29.60 | 9,165.90 | 6,219,464.16 | 870.59 | 10,066.09 |
| STATE TOTAL 2 | 0.00 | 0.00 | 541.50 | 0.00 | 29.60 | 24,602.16 | 7,856,752.76 | 953.19 | 26,126.45 |
| FLORIDA | | | | | | | | | |
| ARCHIE CARR | 0.00 | 0.00 | 1.42 | 0.00 | 77.65 | 42.64 | 11,778,938.00 | 116.91 | 238.62 |
| ARTHUR R. MARSHALL | 0.00 | 0.00 | 0.00 | 0.00 | 0.00 | 2,549.77 | 118,511.97 | 141,404.00 | 143,954.77 |
| CALOOSAHATCHEE | 40.00 | 0.00 | 0.00 | 0.00 | 0.00 | 0.00 | 0.00 | 0.00 | 40.00 |
| CEDAR KEYS | 348.61 | 0.00 | 0.00 | 0.00 | 0.00 | 342.54 | 681,190.00 | 170.00 | 861.15 |
| CHASSAHOWITZKA | 320.56 | 0.00 | 0.00 | 0.00 | 0.00 | 30,522.35 | 496,746.12 | 0.00 | 30,842.91 |
| CROCODILE LAKE | 0.00 | 0.00 | 0.00 | 0.00 | 40.63 | 6,521.65 | 15,092,844.00 | 125.76 | 6,688.04 |
| CRYSTAL RIVER | 0.00 | 0.00 | 0.00 | 0.00 | 0.00 | 80.13 | 1,132,180.00 | 0.00 | 80.13 |
| EGMONT KEY | 328.30 | 0.00 | 0.00 | 0.00 | 0.00 | 0.00 | 0.00 | 0.00 | 328.30 |
| FLORIDA PANTHER | 0.00 | 0.00 | 0.00 | 0.00 | 594.00 | 25,935.04 | 10,232,916.68 | 0.00 | 26,529.04 |
| FSA INTEREST FL ** * | 0.00 | 0.00 | 95.54 | 0.00 | 0.00 | 0.00 | 0.00 | 2,881.79 | 2,977.33 |
| GREAT WHITE HERON | 770.40 | 0.00 | 244.95 | 0.00 | 288.24 | 3,181.99 | 3,158,327.77 | 186,287.05 | 192,787.63 |
| HOBE SOUND | 0.00 | 0.00 | 0.00 | 0.00 | 1,022.40 | 4.28 | 18,000.00 | 8.50 | 1,084.98 |
| ISLAND BAY | 20.24 | 0.00 | 0.00 | 0.00 | 0.00 | 0.00 | 0.00 | 0.00 | 20.24 |
| J. N. DING DARLING | 407.02 | 0.00 | 0.00 | 0.00 | 366.20 | 4,442.82 | 5,721,581.50 | 1,174.64 | 6,390.68 |
| KEY WEST | 1,545.17 | 754.00 | 0.00 | 0.00 | 0.00 | 0.00 | 0.00 | 206,209.00 | 208,508.17 |
| LAKE WALES RIDGE | 0.00 | 0.00 | 0.00 | 0.00 | 0.00 | 1,853.40 | 3,317,600.00 | 0.00 | 1,853.40 |
| LAKE WOODRUFF | 0.00 | 0.00 | 7.00 | 0.00 | 642.66 | 18,542.36 | 1,424,890.75 | 2,407.00 | 21,599.02 |
| LOWER SUWANNEE | 0.00 | 0.00 | 0.00 | 0.00 | 75.00 | 49,270.38 | 13,652,060.00 | 1,831.14 | 51,176.52 |
| MATLACHA PASS | 277.61 | 0.00 | 0.00 | 0.00 | 115.03 | 0.00 | 0.00 | 0.00 | 392.64 |
| MERRITT ISLAND | 0.00 | 0.00 | 0.00 | 138,262.70 | 0.00 | 925.70 | 1,333,689.00 | 1.00 | 139,189.40 |
| NATIONAL KEY DEER | 52.78 | 0.00 | 0.00 | 0.00 | 805.85 | 7,867.20 | 27,590,058.41 | 257.11 | 8,982.94 |
| OKEFENOKEE (1) | 0.00 | 0.00 | 0.00 | 0.00 | 0.00 | 3,678.14 | 52,686.00 | 46.34 | 3,724.48 |
| PASSAGE KEY | 36.37 | 0.00 | 0.00 | 0.00 | 0.00 | 0.00 | 0.00 | 27.50 | 63.87 |
| PELICAN ISLAND | 48.00 | 0.00 | 0.00 | 0.00 | 0.00 | 345.65 | 22,029,210.00 | 4,987.50 | 5,375.35 |
| PINE ISLAND | 175.17 | 0.00 | 0.00 | 0.00 | 0.00 | 427.07 | 2,434,000.00 | 0.00 | 602.24 |
| PINELLAS | 0.00 | 0.00 | 0.00 | 0.00 | 0.00 | 17.35 | 75,000.00 | 377.00 | 394.35 |
| ST. JOHNS | 0.00 | 0.00 | 0.00 | 0.00 | 2.50 | 6,254.95 | 2,678,325.64 | 0.00 | 6,257.45 |
| ST. MARKS | 95.70 | 0.00 | 31,729.47 | 0.00 | 383.64 | 35,080.50 | 1,748,811.41 | 444.29 | 67,691.01 |
| ST. VINCENT | 45.33 | 0.00 | 0.00 | 0.00 | 0.00 | 12,444.60 | 2,093,000.00 | 0.00 | 12,489.93 |
| TEN THOUSAND ISLANDS | 0.00 | 0.00 | 0.00 | 0.00 | 0.00 | 35,000.00 | 0.00 | 53.40 | 35,053.40 |
| STATE TOTAL 29 | 4,863.76 | 154.00 | 32,078.40 | 138,262.70 | 4,368.40 | 247,290.30 | 124,927,305.45 | 548,864.94 | 975,897.77 |
| GEORGIA | | | | | | | | | |
| BANKS LAKE | 0.00 | 0.00 | 490.00 | 0.00 | 0.00 | 3,069.00 | 756,000.00 | 0.00 | 3,559.00 |
| BLACKBEARD ISLAND | 0.00 | 0.00 | 4,858.64 | 0.00 | 0.00 | 959.00 | 0.00 | 0.00 | 5,817.64 |
| BOND SWAMP | 0.00 | 0.00 | 0.00 | 0.00 | 0.00 | 5,490.75 | 2,758,250.00 | 0.00 | 5,490.75 |

TABLE 5 — NATIONAL WILDLIFE REFUGES

| STATE AND UNIT | RESERVED FROM PUBLIC DOMAIN | | ACQUIRED BY OTHER FEDERAL AGENCY | | DEVISE OR GIFT | PURCHASED | | AGREEMENT EASEMENT OR LEASE | TOTAL ACRES |
|---|---|---|---|---|---|---|---|---|---|
| | SOLE OR PRIMARY | SECONDARY | SOLE OR PRIMARY | SECONDARY | | ACRES | COST ($) | | |
| **GEORGIA** | | | | | | | | | |
| TUFALA A (15) * | 0.00 | 0.00 | 0.00 E | 3,231.00 | 0.00 | 0.00 | 0.00 | 0.00 | 3,231.00 |
| FSA INTEREST GA ** * | 0.00 | 0.00 | 886.58 | 0.00 | 0.00 | 0.00 | 0.00 | 3,909.19 | 4,795.57 |
| HARRIS NECK | 0.00 | 0.00 | 2,686.94 | 0.00 | 0.00 | 66.41 | 450,000.00 | 70.57 | 2,823.92 |
| OKEFENOKEE (16) * | 0.00 | 0.00 | 1,800.44 | 0.00 | 15,403.65 | 574,157.97 | 1,780,185.17 | 0.00 | 791,401.99 |
| PIEDMONT | 0.00 | 0.00 | 34,238.22 | 0.00 | 0.00 | 10,717.46 | 44,000.00 | 11.30 | 34,966.98 |
| SAVANNAH (7) | 0.00 | 0.00 | 4,019.04 | 0.00 | 0.00 | 9,280.17 | 4,427,862.40 | 26.27 | 13,325.48 |
| WASSAW | 0.00 | 0.00 | 0.00 | 0.00 | 10,049.87 | 0.00 | 0.00 | 20.00 | 10,069.87 |
| WOLF ISLAND | 0.00 | 0.00 | 538.00 | 0.00 | 0.00 | 4,587.82 | 125,615.52 | 0.00 | 5,125.82 |
| STATE TOTAL 8 | 0.00 | 0.00 | 39,373.66 | 3,231.00 | 25,453.50 | 406,308.03 | 8,881,101.04 | 4,049.63 | 480,405.52 |
| **HAWAII** | | | | | | | | | |
| HAKALAU FOREST | 0.00 | 0.00 | 0.00 | 0.00 | 0.00 | 38,005.12 | 26,178,265.00 | 25.32 | 38,030.44 |
| HANALEI | 0.00 | 0.00 | 0.00 | 0.00 | 0.00 | 917.42 | 1,299,000.00 | 0.00 | 917.42 |
| HAWAIIAN ISLANDS | 254,418.10 | 0.00 | 0.00 | 0.00 | 0.00 | 0.00 | 0.00 | 0.00 | 254,418.10 |
| HULEIA | 0.00 | 0.00 | 0.00 | 0.00 | 0.00 | 240.17 | 527,625.00 | .96 | 241.11 |
| JAMES CAMPBELL | 0.00 | 0.00 | 0.00 | 0.00 | 0.00 | 0.00 | 0.00 | 165.51 | 165.51 |
| KAKAHAIA | 0.00 | 0.00 | 0.00 | 0.00 | 0.00 | 44.61 | 784,550.00 | 0.00 | 44.61 |
| KEALIA POND | 0.00 | 0.00 | 0.00 | 0.00 | 0.00 | 0.00 | 0.00 | 691.56 | 691.56 |
| KILAUEA POINT | 0.00 | 0.00 | 51.00 | 0.00 | 91.68 | 39.48 | 6,475,000.00 | 16.82 | 198.68 |
| OAHU FOREST | 0.00 | 0.00 | 0.00 | 0.00 | 0.00 | 4,524.66 | 3,620,000.00 | 44.90 | 4,569.36 |
| PEARL HARBOR | 0.00 | 0.00 | 37.37 N | 61.15 | 0.00 | 0.00 | 0.00 | 0.00 | 98.52 |
| STATE TOTAL 10 | 254,418.10 | 0.00 | 88.37 | 61.15 | 91.68 | 43,771.46 | 38,574,518.60 | 945.05 | 299,375.51 |
| **IDAHO** | | | | | | | | | |
| BEAR LAKE | 16,977.61 | 0.00 | 0.00 | 0.00 | 0.00 | 1,107.97 | 597,873.90 | 0.00 | 18,085.58 |
| CAMAS | 0.00 | 0.00 | 0.00 | 0.00 | 0.00 | 10,580.48 | 317,700.84 | 0.00 | 10,580.48 |
| DEER FLAT (4) | 290.54 R | 9,993.79 | 0.00 | 0.00 | 21.26 | 242.89 | 26,475.50 | 0.00 | 10,547.57 |
| FSA INTEREST ID ** * | 0.00 | 0.00 | 998.60 | 0.00 | 0.00 | 0.00 | 0.00 | 112.00 | 1,110.60 |
| GRAYS LAKE | 80.00 | 0.00 | 0.00 | 0.00 | 160.00 | 4,463.93 | 2,447,100.00 | 15,421.15 | 20,125.08 |
| KOOTENAI | 0.00 | 0.00 | 0.00 | 0.00 | 0.00 | 2,774.15 | 708,900.00 | .14 | 2,774.29 |
| MINIDOKA | 2,863.93 R | 16,766.87 | 0.00 R | 1,070.32 | 0.00 | 0.00 | 0.00 | 2.49 | 20,703.61 |
| STATE TOTAL 6 | 20,211.68 | 26,758.15 | 998.60 | 1,070.32 | 181.26 | 19,169.42 | 3,729,195.64 | 15,535.78 | 83,975.21 |
| **ILLINOIS** | | | | | | | | | |
| CHAUTAUQUA | 0.00 | 0.00 | 0.00 | 0.00 | 1,708.54 | 4,488.41 | 30,592.80 | 203.61 | 6,400.56 |
| CRAB ORCHARD | 0.00 | 0.00 | 42,507.58 | 0.00 | 0.00 | 1,580.94 | 456,105.50 | 0.00 | 43,888.52 |
| CYPRESS CREEK | 0.00 | 0.00 | 0.00 | 0.00 | 0.00 | 15,578.11 | 11,580,537.96 | 0.00 | 15,578.11 |
| EMIQUON | 0.00 | 0.00 | 0.00 | 0.00 | 0.00 | 2,154.94 | 4,145,400.00 | 0.00 | 2,154.94 |
| FSA INTEREST IL ** * | 0.00 | 0.00 | 335.40 | 0.00 | 0.00 | 0.00 | 0.00 | 0.00 | 335.40 |
| GREAT RIVER (8) | 0.00 | 0.00 | 0.00 E | 5,490.81 | 49.95 | 1,569.87 | 358,202.72 | 0.00 | 7,110.63 |
| MEREDOSIA | 0.00 | 0.00 | 0.00 | 0.00 | 2,141.49 | 1,259.31 | 1,336,790.00 | 0.00 | 3,400.80 |
| MIDDLE MISSISSIPPI RIVER (8) | 0.00 | 0.00 | 0.00 | 0.00 | 0.00 | 2,437.53 | 599,795.00 | 0.00 | 2,437.53 |
| PORT LOUISA (19) | 0.00 | 0.00 | 0.00 E | 1,466.00 | 0.00 | 4.60 | 11,900.00 | .29 | 1,470.89 |
| TWO RIVERS (8) | 0.00 | 0.00 | 0.00 E | 7,017.00 | 2.31 | 853.17 | 462,343.75 | 160.72 | 8,033.20 |
| UPPER MISSISSIPPI RIVER (5) | 65.15 | 0.00 | 1,344.63 E | 29,502.00 | 0.00 | 7,924.75 | 48,679.98 | .19 | 32,836.72 |
| STATE TOTAL 10 | 65.15 | 0.00 | 46,187.61 | 40,475.81 | 3,912.29 | 32,341.61 | 17,301,883.73 | 444.81 | 123,327.25 |
| **INDIANA** | | | | | | | | | |
| BIG OAKS | 0.00 | 0.00 | 0.00 A | 51,000.00 | 0.00 | 0.00 | 0.00 | 0.00 | 51,000.00 |
| FSA INTEREST IN ** * | 0.00 | 0.00 | 219.05 | 0.00 | 0.00 | 0.00 | 0.00 | 0.00 | 219.05 |
| MUSCATATUCK | 0.00 | 0.00 | 0.00 | 0.00 | 78.75 | 7,775.99 | 4,612,847.72 | 0.00 | 7,802.77 |
| PATOKA RIVER | 0.00 | 0.00 | 0.00 | 0.00 | 334.35 | 5,337.89 | 4,337,354.00 | 0.00 | 5,672.24 |
| STATE TOTAL 4 | 0.00 | 0.00 | 219.05 | 51,000.00 | 413.58 | 13,061.88 | 7,950,192.60 | 0.00 | 64,693.49 |

16

TABLE 5 - NATIONAL WILDLIFE REFUGES

| STATE AND UNIT | RESERVED FROM PUBLIC DOMAIN | | ACQUIRED BY OTHER FEDERAL AGENCY | | DEVISE OR GIFT | PURCHASED | | AGREEMENT EASEMENT OR LEASE | TOTAL ACRES |
| --- | --- | --- | --- | --- | --- | --- | --- | --- | --- |
| | SOLE OR PRIMARY | SECONDARY | SOLE OR PRIMARY | SECONDARY | | ACRES | COST ($) | | |
| **IOWA** | | | | | | | | | |
| DESOTO (10) | 0.00 | 0.00 | 0.00 | 0.00 | 0.00 | 3,499.16 | 735,409.30 | 3.61 | 3,502.77 |
| DRIFTLESS AREA | 0.00 | 0.00 | 0.00 | 0.00 | 0.00 | 776.84 | 429,718.50 | 0.00 | 776.84 |
| NEAL SMITH | 0.00 | 0.00 | 0.00 | 0.00 | 0.00 | 5,366.35 | 7,502,780.00 | 0.00 | 5,366.35 |
| HO. TALLGRASS PRAIRIE (A7) | 0.00 | 0.00 | 0.00 | 0.00 | 0.00 | 160.00 | 176,000.00 | 0.00 | 160.00 |
| PORT LOUISA (11)* | 0.00 | 0.00 | 0.00 | 10,423.94 | 80.00 | 12,119.44 | 2,680,549.54 | 0.00 | 22,623.38 |
| UNION SLOUGH | 0.00 | 0.00 | 0.00 | 0.00 | 0.00 | 2,845.24 | 710,404.49 | 70.70 | 2,915.94 |
| UPPER MISSISSIPPI RIVER (*3)* | 333.66 | 0.00 | 0.00 | 30,315.00 | .57 | 20,389.98 | 409,867.96 | 0.00 | 51,089.21 |
| STATE TOTAL 7 | 333.66 | 0.00 | 0.00 | 40,738.94 | 80.57 | 45,157.01 | 12,544,731.97 | 74.31 | 86,384.49 |
| **KANSAS** | | | | | | | | | |
| FLINT HILLS | 0.00 | 0.00 | 0.00 | 18,463.21 | 0.00 | 0.00 | 0.00 | .15 | 18,463.36 |
| FSA INTEREST KS ** * | 0.00 | 0.00 | 116.50 | 0.00 | 0.00 | 0.00 | 0.00 | 0.00 | 116.50 |
| KIRWIN | 0.00 | 0.00 | 0.00 | 10,778.00 | 0.00 | 0.00 | 0.00 | 0.00 | 10,778.00 |
| MARAIS DES CYGNES | 0.00 | 0.00 | 0.00 | 0.00 | 0.00 | 7,303.34 | 4,114,781.40 | 0.00 | 7,303.34 |
| QUIVIRA | 0.00 | 0.00 | 0.00 | 0.00 | 199.20 | 21,820.10 | 2,059,238.00 | 0.00 | 22,019.30 |
| STATE TOTAL 6 | 0.00 | 0.00 | 116.50 | 29,241.21 | 199.20 | 29,123.44 | 6,173,019.40 | .15 | 58,680.50 |
| **KENTUCKY** | | | | | | | | | |
| CLARKS RIVER | 0.00 | 0.00 | 0.00 | 0.00 | 0.00 | 7,081.68 | 6,404,409.00 | 0.00 | 7,081.68 |
| OHIO RIVER ISLANDS (58)* | 0.00 | 0.00 | 0.00 | 0.00 | 0.00 | 404.56 | 288,640.00 | 0.00 | 404.56 |
| REELFOOT (14) | 0.00 | 0.00 | 0.00 | 0.00 | 0.00 | 2,039.64 | 418,450.15 | 0.00 | 2,039.64 |
| STATE TOTAL 2 | 0.00 | 0.00 | 0.00 | 0.00 | 0.00 | 9,525.88 | 7,111,499.15 | 0.00 | 9,525.88 |
| **LOUISIANA** | | | | | | | | | |
| ATCHAFALAYA | 0.00 | 0.00 | 0.00 | 0.00 | 0.00 | 15,255.23 | 11,065,618.00 | 0.00 | 15,255.23 |
| BAYOU COCODRIE | 0.00 | 0.00 | 0.00 | 0.00 | 0.00 | 13,168.51 | 7,016,570.00 | 0.00 | 13,168.51 |
| BAYOU SAUVAGE | 0.00 | 0.00 | 0.00 | 0.00 | 0.00 | 22,264.43 | 10,992,000.00 | 0.00 | 22,264.43 |
| BAYOU TECHE | 0.00 | 0.00 | 0.00 | 0.00 | 0.00 | 9,073.50 | 2,234,000.00 | 0.00 | 9,073.50 |
| BIG BRANCH MARSH | 0.00 | 0.00 | 0.00 | 0.00 | 11,588.54 | 4,417.25 | 8,514,174.00 | 0.00 | 16,005.79 |
| BLACK BAYOU LAKE | 0.00 | 0.00 | 0.00 | 0.00 | 0.00 | 2,287.39 | 3,033,500.00 | 2,750.00 | 4,537.39 |
| BOGUE CHITTO (22) | 0.00 | 0.00 | 0.00 | 0.00 | 55.00 | 28,755.79 | 13,488,228.86 | 762.00 | 29,552.79 |
| BRETON | 9,047.00 | 0.00 | 0.00 | 0.00 | 0.00 | 0.00 | 0.00 | 0.00 | 9,047.00 |
| CAMERON PRAIRIE | 0.00 | 0.00 | 14,928.75 | 0.00 | 0.00 | 9,621.30 | 5,090,650.00 | 0.00 | 24,548.05 |
| CAT ISLAND | 0.00 | 0.00 | 0.00 | 0.00 | 15.40 | 2,288.51 | 6,474,472.00 | 0.00 | 9,378.91 |
| CATAHOULA | 0.00 | 0.00 | 0.00 | 0.00 | 0.00 | 14,909.61 | 2,191,497.25 | 10,000.00 | 24,909.61 |
| D'ARBONNE | 0.00 | 0.00 | 17,419.63 | 0.00 | 0.00 | 0.00 | 0.00 | 0.00 | 17,419.63 |
| DELTA | 1,607.65 | 7,897.50 | 10,088.42 | 0.00 | 0.00 | 34,462.73 | 233,324.17 | 0.00 | 48,799.10 |
| FSA INTEREST LA ** * | 0.00 | 0.00 | 8,445.51 | 0.00 | 0.00 | 0.00 | 0.00 | 5,580.44 | 14,025.95 |
| GRAND COTE | 0.00 | 0.00 | 0.00 | 0.00 | 0.00 | 5,997.00 | 1,776,000.00 | 80.00 | 6,077.00 |
| HANDY BRAKE | 0.00 | 0.00 | 465.70 | 0.00 | 0.00 | 0.00 | 0.00 | 35.00 | 500.70 |
| LACASSINE | 0.00 | 0.00 | 22,991.51 | 0.00 | 0.00 | 10,734.75 | 1,958,356.43 | 652.51 | 34,378.77 |
| LAKE OPHELIA | 0.00 | 0.00 | 13.70 | 0.00 | 0.00 | 17,341.46 | 7,570,080.00 | 200.00 | 17,555.16 |
| MANDALAY | 0.00 | 0.00 | 0.00 | 0.00 | 4,416.00 | 0.00 | 0.00 | 205.00 | 4,619.00 |
| RED RIVER | 0.00 | 0.00 | 0.00 | 0.00 | 0.00 | 4,112.93 | 4,445,900.00 | 1,102.86 | 5,215.79 |
| SABINE | 0.00 | 0.00 | 124,943.42 | 0.00 | 0.00 | 566.66 | 14,000.51 | 1,280.00 | 125,790.08 |
| SHELL KEYS | 8.00 | 0.00 | 0.00 | 0.00 | 0.00 | 0.00 | 0.00 | 0.00 | 8.00 |
| TENSAS RIVER | 0.00 | 0.00 | 53,174.58 | 0.00 | 528.85 | 12,498.57 | 3,356,070.00 | 195.17 | 66,395.17 |
| UPPER OUACHITA | 0.00 | 0.00 | 0.00 | 0.00 | 0.00 | 42,594.98 | 20,596,956.00 | 3,216.74 | 45,811.72 |
| STATE TOTAL 25 | 10,662.65 | 7,892.50 | 251,417.20 | 0.00 | 16,577.79 | 257,527.60 | 119,088,740.21 | 25,537.72 | 564,733.26 |
| **MAINE** | | | | | | | | | |
| AROOSTOOK | 0.00 | 0.00 | 4,458.50 | 0.00 | 0.00 | 196.57 | 62,120.00 | 0.00 | 4,655.07 |
| CROSS ISLAND | 0.00 | 0.00 | 0.00 | 0.00 | 1,738.40 | 164.70 | 0.00 | 0.00 | 1,903.10 |
| FRANKLIN ISLAND | 0.00 | 0.00 | 11.94 | 0.00 | 0.00 | 0.00 | 0.00 | 0.00 | 11.94 |
| FSA INTEREST ME ** * | 0.00 | 0.00 | 394.08 | 0.00 | 0.00 | 0.00 | 0.00 | 238.00 | 632.08 |

17

TABLE 6 - NATIONAL WILDLIFE REFUGES

| STATE AND UNIT | RESERVED FROM PUBLIC DOMAIN | | ACQUIRED BY OTHER FEDERAL AGENCY | | DEVISE OR GIFT | PURCHASED | | AGREEMENT EASEMENT OR LEASE | TOTAL ACRES |
|---|---|---|---|---|---|---|---|---|---|
| | SOLE OR PRIMARY | SECONDARY | SOLE OR PRIMARY | SECONDARY | | ACRES | COST ($) | | |
| **MAINE** | | | | | | | | | |
| LAKE UMBAGOG        (561)* | 0.00 | 0.00 | 0.00 | 0.00 | 24.52 | 4,525.06 | 7,916,420.00 | 0.00 | 4,549.58 |
| MOOSEHORN | 0.00 | 0.00 | 6,590.55 | 0.00 | 552.84 | 20,801.27 | 5,127,609.19 | 80.32 | 77,704.76 |
| PETIT MANAN | 0.00 | 0.00 | 108.42 | 0.00 | 1,650.02 | 5,685.46 | 5,361,694.00 | 274.96 | 5,686.86 |
| POND ISLAND | 0.00 | 0.00 | 10.00 | 0.00 | 0.00 | 0.00 | 0.00 | 0.00 | 10.00 |
| RACHEL CARSON | 0.00 | 0.00 | 0.00 | 0.00 | 581.11 | 4,450.77 | 17,972,406.75 | 150.54 | 5,182.42 |
| SEAL ISLAND | 0.00 | 0.00 | 65.00 | 0.00 | 0.00 | 0.00 | 0.00 | 0.00 | 65.00 |
| SUNKHAZE MEADOWS | 0.00 | 0.00 | 0.00 | 0.00 | 126.30 | 10,139.41 | 2,317,950.00 | 0.00 | 10,265.71 |
| STATE TOTAL        9 | 0.00 | 0.00 | 11,556.27 | 0.00 | 4,252.99 | 45,966.34 | 34,757,989.94 | 735.82 | 60,456.32 |
| **MARYLAND** | | | | | | | | | |
| BLACKWATER | 0.00 | 0.00 | 0.00 | 0.00 | 1,570.73 | 24,105.14 | 12,818,542.01 | 0.00 | 25,475.87 |
| CHINCOTEAGUE       (161)^ | 0.00 | 0.00 | 0.00 | 0.00 | 0.00 | 417.81 | 13,780.42 | 0.00 | 417.81 |
| EASTERN NECK | 0.00 | 0.00 | 0.00 | 0.00 | 0.00 | 2,386.27 | 1,606,145.09 | 0.00 | 2,786.27 |
| FSA INTEREST MD    ** ^ | 0.00 | 0.00 | 0.00 | 0.00 | 0.00 | 0.00 | 0.00 | 67.94 | 67.94 |
| MARTIN             (16)^ | 0.00 | 0.00 | 0.00 | 0.00 | 2,569.86 | 1,853.57 | 61,027.00 | 0.00 | 4,423.43 |
| PATUXENT | 0.00 | 0.00 | 11,852.10 | 0.00 | 0.00 | 988.83 | 1,310,786.71 | .27 | 12,841.20 |
| SUSQUEHANNA | 0.00 | 0.00 | 3.79 | 0.00 | 0.00 | 0.00 | 0.00 | 0.00 | 3.79 |
| STATE TOTAL        5 | 0.00 | 0.00 | 11,855.89 | 0.00 | 4,140.59 | 29,651.62 | 15,810,081.75 | 68.21 | 45,576.31 |
| **MASSACHUSETTS** | | | | | | | | | |
| ASSABET RIVER | 0.00 | 0.00 | 2,229.20 | 0.00 | 0.00 | 0.00 | 0.00 | 0.00 | 2,229.20 |
| GREAT MEADOWS | 0.00 | 0.00 | 0.00 | 0.00 | 786.55 | 3,547.95 | 11,804,900.90 | 27.33 | 3,899.81 |
| MASHPEE | 0.00 | 0.00 | 0.00 | 0.00 | 3.00 | 284.40 | 2,810,000.00 | 54.75 | 341.65 |
| MASSASOIT | 0.00 | 0.00 | 0.00 | 0.00 | 0.00 | 198.11 | 605,432.00 | 0.00 | 198.11 |
| MONOMOY | 0.00 | 0.00 | 2.10 | 0.00 | 0.00 | 2,699.75 | 140,465.00 | 0.00 | 2,701.85 |
| NANTUCKET | 0.00 | 0.00 | 24.00 | 0.00 | 0.00 | 0.00 | 0.00 | 0.00 | 24.00 |
| NOMANS LAND ISLAND | 0.00 | 0.00 | 628.00 | 0.00 | 0.00 | 0.00 | 0.00 | 0.00 | 628.00 |
| OXBOW | 0.00 | 0.00 | 1,547.55 | 0.00 | 4.29 | 125.40 | 3,410,000.00 | 0.00 | 1,677.02 |
| PARKER RIVER | 0.00 | 0.00 | 1.90 | 0.00 | 0.00 | 4,850.61 | 557,740.84 | 0.00 | 4,852.51 |
| SILVIO O. CONTE    (47)^ | 0.00 | 0.00 | 0.00 | 0.00 | 3.80 | 211.93 | 1,647,210.00 | 0.00 | 215.73 |
| THACHER ISLAND | 0.00 | 0.00 | 22.00 | 0.00 | 0.00 | 0.00 | 0.00 | 0.00 | 22.00 |
| STATE TOTAL        10 | 0.00 | 0.00 | 4,454.55 | 0.00 | 795.62 | 11,718.15 | 21,014,748.74 | 81.58 | 16,549.86 |
| **MICHIGAN** | | | | | | | | | |
| DETROIT RIVER | 504.47 | 0.00 | 0.00 | A 168.00 | 42.51 | 157.55 | 600,000.00 | 656.45 | 1,515.96 |
| FSA INTEREST MI    ** ^ | 0.00 | 0.00 | 94.00 | 0.00 | 0.00 | 0.00 | 0.00 | 0.00 | 94.00 |
| HARBOR ISLAND | 0.00 | 0.00 | 0.00 | 0.00 | 0.00 | 695.00 | 197,000.00 | 0.00 | 695.00 |
| HURON | 22.50 | 0.00 | 124.35 | 0.00 | 0.00 | 0.00 | 0.00 | 0.00 | 146.85 |
| KIRTLANDS WARBLER | 0.00 | 0.00 | 0.00 | 0.00 | 0.00 | 6,684.46 | 5,574,466.40 | 0.00 | 6,684.46 |
| MICHIGAN ISLANDS | 11.94 | (C) 121.70 | 229.70 | 0.00 | 234.05 | 0.00 | 0.00 | 0.00 | 597.39 |
| SENEY | 2,660.60 | 0.00 | 7,058.99 | 0.00 | 0.00 | 85,525.62 | 177,178.95 | 0.00 | 95,244.81 |
| SHIAWASSEE | 0.00 | 0.00 | 0.00 | 0.00 | 52.21 | 8,960.54 | 2,470,575.67 | 350.00 | 9,362.75 |
| STATE TOTAL        7 | 2,999.51 | 121.70 | 7,506.66 | 168.00 | 338.77 | 102,018.15 | 6,971,441.02 | 1,006.45 | 114,139.22 |
| **MINNESOTA** | | | | | | | | | |
| AGASSIZ | 6.00 | 0.00 | 60,091.88 | 0.00 | 0.00 | 954.30 | 43,726.04 | 448.75 | 61,500.93 |
| BIG STONE | 0.00 | 0.00 | 10,540.45 | F 254.20 | 0.00 | 725.50 | 639,200.00 | 0.00 | 11,520.15 |
| CRANE MEADOWS | 0.00 | 0.00 | 0.00 | 0.00 | 20.00 | 1,667.50 | 1,755,986.00 | 0.00 | 1,687.50 |
| FSA INTEREST MN    ** ^ | 0.00 | 0.00 | 2,561.80 | 0.00 | 0.00 | 0.00 | 0.00 | 0.00 | 2,561.80 |
| HAMDEN SLOUGH | 0.00 | 0.00 | 0.00 | 0.00 | 0.00 | 3,136.45 | 1,882,872.00 | 73.40 | 3,209.85 |
| MILLE LACS | .60 | 0.00 | 0.00 | 0.00 | 0.00 | 0.00 | 0.00 | 0.00 | .60 |
| MINNESOTA VALLEY | 0.00 | 0.00 | 566.98 | 0.00 | 1,500.51 | 7,347.20 | 19,912,155.63 | 1,701.18 | 10,715.87 |
| NO. TALLGRASS PRAIRIE (191)* | 0.00 | 0.00 | 0.00 | 0.00 | 0.00 | 984.99 | 860,775.00 | 348.37 | 1,333.36 |
| RICE LAKE | 0.00 | 0.00 | 9,831.57 | 0.00 | 0.00 | 6,640.71 | 295,529.77 | 0.00 | 16,472.28 |
| RYDELL | 0.00 | 0.00 | 0.00 | 0.00 | 2,070.00 | 0.00 | 0.00 | 0.00 | 2,070.00 |

18

TABLE 3 - NATIONAL WILDLIFE REFUGES

| STATE AND UNIT | RESERVED FROM PUBLIC DOMAIN | | ACQUIRED BY OTHER FEDERAL AGENCY | | DEVISE OR GIFT | PURCHASED | | AGREEMENT EASEMENT OR LEASE | TOTAL ACRES |
|---|---|---|---|---|---|---|---|---|---|
| | SOLE OR PRIMARY | SECONDARY | SOLE OR PRIMARY | SECONDARY | | ACRES | COST ($) | | |
| **MINNESOTA** | | | | | | | | | |
| SHERBURNE | 0.00 | 0.00 | 0.00 | 0.00 | 0.00 | 29,677.84 | 3,296,341.05 | 0.00 | 29,677.84 |
| TAMARAC | 40.00 | 0.00 | 0.00 | 0.00 | 0.00 | 35,151.38 | 612,159.96 | 0.00 | 35,191.38 |
| UPPER MISSISSIPPI RIVER (150)* | 241.56 | 0.00 | 0.00 | 15,420.77 | 149.18 | 17,776.26 | 567,904.80 | 92.97 | 33,680.74 |
| STATE TOTAL    10 | 288.16 | 0.00 | 33,390.44 | 15,474.77 | 1,559.67 | 104,062.14 | 29,052,927.22 | 2,804.67 | 209,820.90 |
| **MISSISSIPPI** | | | | | | | | | |
| BOGUE CHITTO (120)* | 0.00 | 0.00 | 0.00 | 0.00 | 0.00 | 6,949.08 | 6,695,784.00 | 0.00 | 6,949.08 |
| COLDWATER RIVER | 0.00 | 0.00 | 94.36 | 0.00 | 0.00 | 2,374.10 | 1,450,450.00 | 0.00 | 2,468.56 |
| DAHOMEY | 0.00 | 0.00 | 0.00 | 0.00 | 162.00 | 8,744.80 | 4,900,000.00 | 260.00 | 9,166.80 |
| FSA INTEREST MS ** * | 0.00 | 0.00 | 21,755.38 | 0.00 | 0.00 | 0.00 | 0.00 | 6,940.71 | 28,696.09 |
| GRAND BAY (5)* | 0.00 | 0.00 | 0.00 | 0.00 | 4,456.63 | 2,774.08 | 2,322,545.00 | 0.00 | 7,230.71 |
| HILLSIDE | 0.00 | 0.00 | 15,383.13 | 0.00 | 22.74 | 3,645.52 | 2,879,100.00 | 0.00 | 19,051.39 |
| MATHEWS BRAKE | 0.00 | 0.00 | 0.00 | 0.00 | 0.00 | 2,418.74 | 1,091,446.00 | 0.00 | 2,418.74 |
| MISSISSIPPI SANDHILL CRANE | 0.00 | 0.00 | 0.00 | 0.00 | 157.78 | 18,001.50 | 21,115,501.00 | 1,679.28 | 19,838.56 |
| MORGAN BRAKE | 0.00 | 0.00 | 0.00 | 0.00 | 111.83 | 7,241.28 | 4,517,482.20 | 0.00 | 7,373.11 |
| NOXUBEE | 40.08 | 0.00 | 35,344.86 | 0.00 | 80.00 | 11,585.26 | 145,413.05 | 0.00 | 47,049.19 |
| PANTHER SWAMP | 0.00 | 0.00 | 0.00 | 7,070.49 | 0.00 | 27,359.80 | 15,015,725.00 | 841.51 | 35,271.85 |
| ST. CATHERINE CREEK | 0.00 | 0.00 | 0.00 | 0.00 | 0.00 | 24,429.29 | 12,925,167.00 | 502.10 | 24,931.39 |
| TALLAHATCHIE | 0.00 | 0.00 | 0.00 | 0.00 | 0.00 | 2,324.14 | 1,551,000.00 | 470.00 | 2,794.14 |
| YAZOO | 0.00 | 0.00 | 0.00 | 0.00 | 0.00 | 13,022.98 | 2,760,803.78 | 0.00 | 13,022.98 |
| STATE TOTAL    13 | 40.08 | 0.00 | 72,576.62 | 7,070.49 | 5,010.98 | 131,070.66 | 77,760,615.03 | 10,693.60 | 228,262.89 |
| **MISSOURI** | | | | | | | | | |
| BIG MUDDY | 0.00 | 0.00 | 442.00 | 1,900.00 | 0.00 | 8,212.21 | 4,878,105.00 | 1.68 | 9,955.89 |
| CLARENCE CANNON | 0.00 | 0.00 | 0.00 | 0.00 | 0.00 | 1,749.98 | 1,175,584.25 | 0.00 | 3,749.98 |
| FSA INTEREST MO ** * | 0.00 | 0.00 | 1,673.04 | 0.00 | 0.00 | 0.00 | 0.00 | 111.62 | 1,784.68 |
| GREAT RIVER (11)* | 0.00 | 0.00 | 0.00 | 0.00 | 0.00 | 2,107.93 | 999,500.00 | 0.00 | 2,107.93 |
| MIDDLE MISSISSIPPI RIVER (11)* | 0.00 | 0.00 | 0.00 | 0.00 | 0.00 | 1,704.17 | 1,916,805.00 | 0.00 | 1,704.17 |
| MINGO | 0.00 | 0.00 | 0.00 | 0.00 | 0.00 | 21,676.06 | 317,365.82 | 69.80 | 21,745.86 |
| OZARK CAVEFISH | 0.00 | 0.00 | 0.00 | 0.00 | 0.00 | 41.80 | 117,000.00 | 0.00 | 41.80 |
| PILOT KNOB | 0.00 | 0.00 | 0.00 | 0.00 | 90.00 | 0.00 | 0.00 | 0.00 | 90.00 |
| SQUAW CREEK | 0.00 | 0.00 | 3,049.10 | 0.00 | 0.00 | 4,300.96 | 575,941.87 | 64.83 | 7,414.89 |
| SWAN LAKE | 0.00 | 0.00 | 5,923.42 | 0.00 | 0.00 | 5,569.55 | 355,195.19 | 0.00 | 11,492.97 |
| TWO RIVERS (11)* | 0.00 | 0.00 | 0.00 | 232.00 | 0.00 | 0.00 | 0.00 | 0.00 | 232.00 |
| STATE TOTAL    7 | 0.00 | 0.00 | 11,007.56 | 1,932.00 | 90.00 | 47,362.66 | 10,346,303.15 | 347.93 | 60,370.17 |
| **MONTANA** | | | | | | | | | |
| BENTON LAKE | 12,254.92 | 0.00 | 0.00 | 0.00 | 0.00 | 147.64 | 5,315.00 | 76.88 | 12,479.44 |
| BLACK COULEE | 640.00 | 0.00 | 0.00 | 0.00 | 0.00 | 0.00 | 0.00 | 668.88 | 1,308.88 |
| BLACKFOOT VALLEY | 0.00 | 0.00 | 0.00 | 0.00 | 0.00 | 0.00 | 0.00 | 10,420.22 | 10,420.22 |
| BOWDOIN | 14,796.58 | 0.00 | 640.00 | 0.00 | 0.00 | 0.00 | 0.00 | 115.39 | 15,551.97 |
| CHARLES M. RUSSELL | 358,196.42 | 300,901.05 | 5,574.02 | 147,599.11 | 56.37 | 10,875.87 | 2,626,780.00 | 6,346.50 | 912,348.32 |
| CREEDMAN COULEE | 80.00 | 0.00 | 0.00 | 0.00 | 0.00 | 0.00 | 0.00 | 2,648.00 | 2,728.00 |
| FSA INTEREST MT ** * | 0.00 | 0.00 | 270.62 | 0.00 | 0.00 | 0.00 | 0.00 | 240.00 | 510.62 |
| HAILSTONE | 0.00 | 160.00 | 0.00 | 0.00 | 0.00 | 0.00 | 0.00 | 760.00 | 920.00 |
| HALFBREED LAKE | 0.00 | 0.00 | 0.00 | 0.00 | 0.00 | 3,279.02 | 291,000.00 | 1,039.22 | 4,318.24 |
| HEWITT LAKE | 0.00 | 400.00 | 520.49 | 0.00 | 0.00 | 0.00 | 0.00 | 660.43 | 1,580.92 |
| LAKE MASON | 17.59 | 0.00 | 6,981.65 | 0.00 | 0.00 | 4,756.60 | 18,500.00 | 5,558.68 | 16,814.52 |
| LAKE THIBADEAU | 19.42 | 0.00 | 0.00 | 0.00 | 0.00 | 0.00 | 0.00 | 5,849.06 | 5,868.48 |
| LAMESTEER | 0.00 | 0.00 | 0.00 | 0.00 | 0.00 | 0.00 | 0.00 | 800.00 | 800.00 |
| LEE METCALF | 0.00 | 0.00 | 0.00 | 0.00 | 0.00 | 2,792.52 | 868,080.00 | 0.00 | 2,792.52 |
| LOST TRAIL | 0.00 | 0.00 | 0.00 | 0.00 | 3,112.00 | 4,693.20 | 1,738,205.00 | 1,029.04 | 8,834.24 |
| MEDICINE LAKE | 1,520.99 | 0.00 | 27,419.81 | 0.00 | 7.44 | 2,515.26 | 25,480.00 | 26.71 | 31,484.01 |
| NATIONAL BISON RANGE | 0.00 | 0.00 | 18,479.50 | 0.00 | 0.00 | 320.34 | 177,900.00 | 0.00 | 18,799.84 |

19

TABLE 5 - NATIONAL WILDLIFE REFUGES

| STATE AND UNIT | RESERVED FROM PUBLIC DOMAIN | | ACQUIRED BY OTHER FEDERAL AGENCY | | DEVISE OR GIFT | PURCHASED | | AGREEMENT EASEMENT OR LEASE | TOTAL ACRES |
|---|---|---|---|---|---|---|---|---|---|
| | SOLE OR PRIMARY | SECONDARY | SOLE OR PRIMARY | SECONDARY | | ACRES | COST ($) | | |
| **MONTANA** | | | | | | | | | |
| NINE-PIPE | 0.00 | 0.00 | 0.00 | 0.00 | 0.00 | 0.00 | 0.00 | 4,027.68 | 4,027.68 |
| PABLO | 0.00 | 0.00 | 0.00 | 0.00 | 0.00 | 0.00 | 0.00 | 2,473.52 | 2,473.52 |
| RED ROCK LAKES | 9,718.51 | 564.28 | 29,483.58 | 0.00 | 540.00 | 5,961.54 | 7,656,879.00 | 8,664.79 | 56,932.70 |
| SWAN RIVER | 0.00 | 0.00 | 0.00 | 0.00 | 0.00 | 1,568.81 | 901,645.00 | 0.00 | 1,568.81 |
| UL BEND | 29,678.22 | 6,897.46 | 1,299.79 | 7,929.90 | 0.00 | 9,688.19 | 577,280.00 | 560.00 | 56,049.56 |
| WAR HORSE | 0.00 | 0.00 | 3,192.24 | 0.00 | 0.00 | 0.00 | 0.00 | 0.00 | 3,192.24 |
| **STATE TOTAL 77** | 626,402.45 | 586,952.77 | 96,661.70 | 155,329.01 | 3,511.01 | 48,036.99 | 10,178,534.00 | 49,514.60 | 1,166,466.53 |
| **NEBRASKA** | | | | | | | | | |
| BOYER CHUTE | 0.00 | 0.00 | 0.00 | 0.00 | 1,953.80 | 1,375.36 | 3,644,940.93 | 0.00 | 3,329.21 |
| CRESCENT LAKE | 265.87 | 0.00 | 240.00 | 0.00 | 0.00 | 45,457.99 | 328,115.00 | 31.49 | 45,995.35 |
| DESOTO (191)* | 0.00 | 0.00 | 0.00 | 0.00 | 0.00 | 4,324.20 | 761,275.70 | 0.00 | 4,324.20 |
| FORT NIOBRARA | 14,778.12 | 0.00 | 2,584.31 | 0.00 | 8.05 | 1,962.45 | 34,309.32 | 0.00 | 19,132.93 |
| FSA INTEREST NE | 0.00 | 0.00 | 688.70 | 0.00 | 0.00 | 0.00 | 0.00 | 1,409.02 | 2,092.72 |
| JOHN W. & LOUISE SEIER | 0.00 | 0.00 | 0.00 | 0.00 | 2,400.00 | 0.00 | 0.00 | 0.00 | 2,400.00 |
| KARL E. MUNDT (20)* | 0.00 | 0.00 | 0.00 | 0.00 | 19.39 | 0.00 | 0.00 | 0.00 | 19.39 |
| NORTH PLATTE | 742.99 | 2,684.61 | 0.00 | 0.00 | 0.00 | 45.53 | 27,500.00 | 0.00 | 3,473.25 |
| VALENTINE | 0.00 | 0.00 | 65,114.00 | 0.00 | 0.00 | 6,509.84 | 78,572.00 | 1,524.25 | 73,058.09 |
| **STATE TOTAL 6** | 15,786.86 | 2,684.61 | 68,421.61 | 0.00 | 4,501.29 | 59,786.67 | 4,669,757.44 | 2,764.76 | 153,804.72 |
| **NEVADA** | | | | | | | | | |
| ANAHO ISLAND | 247.73 | 0.00 | 0.00 | 0.00 | 0.00 | 0.00 | 0.00 | 0.00 | 247.73 |
| ASH MEADOWS | 0.00 | 0.00 | 0.00 | 0.00 | 0.00 | 13,999.54 | 4,462,600.00 | 582.00 | 13,741.54 |
| DESERT | 1,614,556.49 | 0.00 | 4.45 | 0.00 | 1.45 | 760.00 | 992,800.00 | 0.00 | 1,615,321.39 |
| FALLON | 0.00 | 17,901.94 | 0.00 | 0.00 | 0.00 | 0.00 | 0.00 | 0.00 | 17,901.94 |
| MOAPA VALLEY | 0.00 | 0.00 | 0.00 | 0.00 | 0.00 | 104.26 | 2,060,000.00 | 0.00 | 104.26 |
| PAHRANAGAT | 1,466.39 | 0.00 | 0.00 | 0.00 | 0.00 | 3,915.60 | 500,000.00 | .75 | 5,382.74 |
| RUBY LAKE | 7,565.53 | 120.00 | 0.00 | 0.00 | 0.00 | 31,600.57 | 708,457.25 | 0.00 | 39,286.10 |
| SHELDON (4) | 544,276.82 | 80.00 | 0.00 | 0.00 | 2,535.66 | 25,983.67 | 582,502.00 | 0.00 | 572,876.15 |
| STILLWATER | 76,799.00 | 0.00 | 0.00 | 0.00 | 0.00 | 10,556.93 | 15,515,039.00 | 26.41 | 87,142.34 |
| **STATE TOTAL 9** | 2,244,908.96 | 18,101.94 | 4.45 | 0.00 | 2,537.11 | 86,060.37 | 25,919,378.25 | 609.16 | 2,352,023.99 |
| **NEW HAMPSHIRE** | | | | | | | | | |
| GREAT BAY | 0.00 | 0.00 | 1,054.00 | 0.00 | 0.00 | 33.18 | 1,268,560.00 | 28.90 | 1,116.08 |
| JOHN HAY | 0.00 | 0.00 | 0.00 | 0.00 | 164.60 | 0.00 | 0.00 | .30 | 164.90 |
| LAKE UMBAGOG (37) | 0.00 | 0.00 | 0.00 | 0.00 | 0.00 | 12,180.06 | 9,974,571.00 | 6.01 | 12,186.07 |
| SILVIO O. CONTE (431)* | 0.00 | 0.00 | 0.00 | 0.00 | 0.00 | 3,680.82 | 934,792.96 | 0.00 | 3,680.82 |
| WAPACK | 0.00 | 0.00 | 0.00 | 0.00 | 1,672.00 | 0.00 | 0.00 | 0.00 | 1,672.00 |
| **STATE TOTAL 4** | 0.00 | 0.00 | 1,054.00 | 0.00 | 1,836.60 | 15,894.06 | 12,177,623.96 | 35.21 | 18,819.89 |
| **NEW JERSEY** | | | | | | | | | |
| CAPE MAY | 0.00 | 0.00 | 0.00 | 0.00 | 0.00 | 10,517.70 | 25,086,855.22 | 490.80 | 11,008.50 |
| EDWIN B. FORSYTHE | 0.00 | 0.00 | 0.00 | 0.00 | 1,153.59 | 42,178.62 | 45,857,409.85 | 2,415.03 | 45,743.24 |
| GREAT SWAMP | 0.00 | 0.00 | 0.00 | 0.00 | 2,872.20 | 4,708.64 | 19,080,308.05 | 1.52 | 7,582.36 |
| SUPAWNA MEADOWS | 0.00 | 0.00 | 6.86 | 1.96 | 0.00 | 7,885.93 | 1,297,644.00 | 0.00 | 2,894.75 |
| WALLKILL RIVER (159)* | 0.00 | 0.00 | 0.00 | 0.00 | 0.00 | 4,744.93 | 21,227,855.00 | 0.00 | 4,744.93 |
| **STATE TOTAL 4** | 0.00 | 0.00 | 6.86 | 1.96 | 4,025.79 | 65,035.82 | 111,949,612.10 | 2,905.35 | 71,975.78 |
| **NEW MEXICO** | | | | | | | | | |
| BITTER LAKE | 12,395.71 | 0.00 | 0.00 | 0.00 | 0.00 | 14,212.93 | 845,804.00 | 0.00 | 26,608.64 |
| BOSQUE DEL APACHE | 140.00 | 0.00 | 0.00 | 0.00 | 0.00 | 56,850.31 | 125,311.00 | 200.79 | 57,191.10 |
| GRULLA (172) | 3,230.55 | 0.00 | 0.00 | 0.00 | 0.00 | 0.00 | 0.00 | 0.00 | 3,230.55 |
| LAS VEGAS | 0.00 | 0.00 | 0.00 | 0.00 | 0.00 | 8,672.08 | 2,121,150.00 | 0.00 | 8,672.08 |
| MAXWELL | 0.00 | 0.00 | 0.00 | 468.52 | 0.00 | 2,791.89 | 428,570.79 | 468.52 | 3,698.93 |
| SAN ANDRES | 0.00 | 57,215.48 | 0.00 | 0.00 | 0.00 | 0.00 | 0.00 | 0.00 | 57,215.48 |

20

TABLE 5 - NATIONAL WILDLIFE REFUGES

| STATE AND UNIT | RESERVED FROM PUBLIC DOMAIN | | ACQUIRED BY OTHER FEDERAL AGENCY | | DEVISE OR GIFT | PURCHASED | | AGREEMENT EASEMENT OR LEASE | TOTAL ACRES |
|---|---|---|---|---|---|---|---|---|---|
| | SOLE OR PRIMARY | SECONDARY | SOLE OR PRIMARY | SECONDARY | | ACRES | COST ($) | | |
| NEW MEXICO SEVILLETA | 0.00 | 0.00 | 0.00 | 0.00 | 220,200.00 | 9,411.07 | 1,545,765.00 | 62.50 | 229,673.57 |
| STATE TOTAL 7 | 75,766.28 | 57,215.48 | 0.00 | 438.52 | 220,200.00 | 89,958.08 | 5,099,400.79 | 731.67 | 584,290.01 |
| NEW YORK AMAGANSETT | 0.00 | 0.00 | 55.84 | 0.00 | 0.00 | 0.00 | 0.00 | 0.00 | 55.84 |
| CONSCIENCE POINT | 0.00 | 0.00 | 0.00 | 0.00 | 60.40 | 0.00 | 0.00 | 0.00 | 60.40 |
| ELIZABETH A. MORTON | 0.00 | 0.00 | 0.00 | 0.00 | 187.19 | 0.00 | 0.00 | 0.00 | 187.19 |
| FSA INTEREST NY ** * | 0.00 | 0.00 | 1,178.45 | 0.00 | 0.00 | 0.00 | 0.00 | 1,535.65 | 2,714.10 |
| IROQUOIS | 0.00 | 0.00 | 0.00 | 0.00 | 0.00 | 10,824.61 | 1,261,819.86 | 3.45 | 10,828.06 |
| MONTEZUMA | 0.00 | 0.00 | 0.00 | 0.00 | 12.31 | 8,036.88 | 2,449,050.01 | 407.85 | 8,457.04 |
| OYSTER BAY | 0.00 | 0.00 | 0.00 | 0.00 | 3,204.08 | 0.00 | 0.00 | 0.00 | 3,204.08 |
| SEATUCK | 0.00 | 0.00 | 0.00 | 0.00 | 209.23 | 0.00 | 0.00 | 0.00 | 209.23 |
| SHAWANGUNK GRASSLANDS | 0.00 | 0.00 | 566.53 | 0.00 | 0.00 | 0.00 | 0.00 | 0.00 | 566.53 |
| TARGET ROCK | 0.00 | 0.00 | 0.00 | 0.00 | 80.09 | 0.00 | 0.00 | 0.00 | 80.09 |
| WALLKILL RIVER (40) | 0.00 | 0.00 | 0.00 | 0.00 | 0.00 | 147.09 | 756,960.00 | 0.00 | 147.09 |
| WERTHEIM | 0.00 | 0.00 | 25.95 | 0.00 | 1,870.74 | 672.67 | 6,377,489.80 | 0.00 | 2,569.36 |
| STATE TOTAL 11 | 0.00 | 0.00 | 1,806.77 | 0.00 | 5,624.04 | 19,681.25 | 10,345,319.67 | 1,946.95 | 29,059.01 |
| NORTH CAROLINA ALLIGATOR RIVER | 0.00 | 0.00 | 0.00 | 0.00 | 125,359.00 | 26,901.81 | 5,688,267.00 | 0.00 | 152,260.81 |
| CEDAR ISLAND | 0.00 | 0.00 | 31.60 | 0.00 | 1,966.15 | 12,484.77 | 347,171.21 | 0.00 | 14,482.32 |
| CURRITUCK | 0.00 | 0.00 | 0.00 | 0.00 | 0.00 | 4,098.88 | 6,696,048.00 | 3,930.78 | 8,029.66 |
| FSA INTEREST NC ** * | 0.00 | 0.00 | 565.49 | 0.00 | 0.00 | 0.00 | 0.00 | 5,868.55 | 6,434.04 |
| GREAT DISMAL SWAMP (16) | 0.00 | 0.00 | 0.00 | 0.00 | 10,957.00 | 15,152.70 | 7,682,534.47 | 0.00 | 26,109.70 |
| MACKAY ISLAND (16) | 0.00 | 0.00 | 0.00 | 0.00 | 541.88 | 6,302.88 | 1,485,506.95 | 0.00 | 7,344.76 |
| MATTAMUSKEET | 0.00 | 0.00 | 49,925.05 | 0.00 | 0.00 | 252.04 | 1,285.33 | 3.09 | 50,180.18 |
| PEA ISLAND | 0.00 | 0.00 | 54.65 | 11.38 | 0.00 | 5,787.97 | 40,401.86 | 0.00 | 5,854.20 |
| PEE DEE | 0.00 | 0.00 | 0.00 | 0.00 | 0.00 | 8,458.94 | 2,561,851.76 | 0.00 | 8,458.94 |
| POCOSIN LAKES | 0.00 | 0.00 | 0.00 | 0.00 | 97,736.29 | 12,360.35 | 1,682,157.99 | 0.00 | 110,106.64 |
| ROANOKE RIVER | 0.00 | 0.00 | 0.00 | 0.00 | 0.00 | 19,477.80 | 10,015,258.00 | 0.00 | 19,477.80 |
| SWANQUARTER | 0.00 | 0.00 | 0.00 | 0.00 | 910.33 | 15,500.76 | 61,000.95 | 0.00 | 16,411.09 |
| STATE TOTAL 11 | 0.00 | 0.00 | 50,556.79 | 11.38 | 237,770.65 | 126,948.90 | 34,261,308.52 | 9,802.40 | 425,110.12 |
| NORTH DAKOTA APPERT LAKE | 0.00 | 0.00 | 0.00 | 0.00 | 0.00 | 0.00 | 0.00 | 907.75 | 907.75 |
| ARDOCH | 0.00 | 0.00 | 0.00 | 0.00 | 14.72 | 298.41 | 1,751.00 | 2,583.00 | 7,696.13 |
| ARROWWOOD | 4.26 | 0.00 | 11,348.72 | 0.00 | 4.84 | 2,097.51 | 46,906.58 | 2,589.01 | 15,942.86 |
| AUDUBON | 0.00 | 0.00 | 0.00 | 14,739.19 | 0.00 | 0.00 | 0.00 | 0.00 | 14,739.19 |
| BONE HILL | 0.00 | 0.00 | 0.00 | 0.00 | 0.00 | 0.00 | 0.00 | 640.00 | 640.00 |
| BRUMBA | 0.00 | 0.00 | 0.00 | 0.00 | 0.00 | 0.00 | 0.00 | 1,977.48 | 1,977.48 |
| BUFFALO LAKE | 23.80 | 0.00 | 0.00 | 0.00 | 0.00 | 0.00 | 0.00 | 1,539.92 | 1,563.72 |
| CAMP LAKE | 0.00 | 0.00 | 0.00 | 0.00 | 0.00 | 0.00 | 0.00 | 584.70 | 584.70 |
| CAMFIELD LAKE | 0.00 | 0.00 | 0.00 | 0.00 | 0.00 | 3.10 | 100.00 | 310.13 | 313.23 |
| CHASE LAKE | 0.00 | 0.00 | 0.00 | 0.00 | 0.00 | 4,449.47 | 25,611.00 | 0.00 | 4,449.47 |
| COTTONWOOD LAKE | 0.00 | 0.00 | 0.00 | 0.00 | 0.00 | 0.00 | 0.00 | 1,015.47 | 1,015.47 |
| DAKOTA LAKE | 0.00 | 0.00 | 0.00 | 0.00 | 0.00 | 0.00 | 0.00 | 2,799.78 | 2,799.78 |
| DAKOTA TALLGRASS PRAIRIE (20) | 0.00 | 0.00 | 0.00 | 0.00 | 0.00 | 0.00 | 0.00 | 5,852.86 | 5,852.86 |
| DES LACS | 100.25 | 0.00 | 13,257.02 | 0.00 | 30.00 | 721.82 | 6,675.60 | 5,478.07 | 19,547.14 |
| FLORENCE LAKE | 0.00 | 0.00 | 0.00 | 0.00 | 0.00 | 1,468.40 | 31,485.00 | 419.80 | 1,888.20 |
| FSA INTEREST ND ** * | 0.00 | 0.00 | 0.00 | 0.00 | 0.00 | 0.00 | 0.00 | 6,591.40 | 6,591.40 |
| HALF-WAY LAKE | 0.00 | 0.00 | 0.00 | 0.00 | 0.00 | 0.00 | 0.00 | 160.00 | 160.00 |
| HIDDENWOOD | 0.00 | 0.00 | 0.00 | 0.00 | 0.00 | 0.00 | 0.00 | 568.35 | 568.35 |
| HOBART LAKE | 9.40 | 0.00 | 0.00 | 0.00 | 0.00 | 756.49 | 5,165.00 | 1,831.71 | 2,077.10 |
| HUTCHINSON LAKE | 0.00 | 0.00 | 0.00 | 0.00 | 0.00 | 0.00 | 0.00 | 478.90 | 478.90 |

TABLE 5 - NATIONAL WILDLIFE REFUGES

| STATE AND UNIT | RESERVED FROM PUBLIC DOMAIN | | ACQUIRED BY OTHER FEDERAL AGENCY | | DEVISE OR GIFT | PURCHASED | | AGREEMENT EASEMENT OR LEASE | TOTAL ACRES |
|---|---|---|---|---|---|---|---|---|---|
| | SOLE OR PRIMARY | SECONDARY | SOLE OR PRIMARY | SECONDARY | | ACRES | COST ($) | | |
| **NORTH DAKOTA** | | | | | | | | | |
| J. CLARK SALYER | 520.66 | 0.00 | 56,702.29 | 0.00 | 2.59 | 21,669.05 | 608,862.80 | 690.52 | 79,373.11 |
| JOHNSON LAKE | 0.00 | 0.00 | 0.00 | 0.00 | 4.49 | 0.00 | 0.00 | 2,003.42 | 2,007.91 |
| KELLYS SLOUGH | 680.00 | 0.00 | 0.00 | 0.00 | 0.00 | 0.00 | 0.00 | 589.50 | 1,269.50 |
| LAKE ALICE | 0.00 | 0.00 | 160.00 | 0.00 | 2.18 | 8,349.86 | 2,195,584.00 | 3,588.50 | 12,095.54 |
| LAKE GEORGE | 29.20 | 0.00 | 0.00 | 0.00 | 0.00 | 0.00 | 0.00 | 3,089.61 | 3,118.81 |
| LAKE ILO | 0.00 | 0.00 | 0.00 | 0.00 | 10.71 | 3,166.50 | 116,422.98 | 875.91 | 4,033.12 |
| LAKE NETTIE | 0.00 | 0.00 | 0.00 | 0.00 | 0.00 | 4,460.60 | 148,245.00 | 634.30 | 5,094.90 |
| LAKE OTIS | 0.00 | 0.00 | 0.00 | 0.00 | 0.00 | 0.00 | 0.00 | 320.00 | 320.00 |
| LAKE PATRICIA | 0.00 | 0.00 | 0.00 | 0.00 | 0.00 | 0.00 | 0.00 | 800.25 | 800.25 |
| LAKE ZAHL | 40.00 | 0.00 | 0.00 | 0.00 | 0.00 | 3,178.98 | 55,275.00 | 604.21 | 3,823.19 |
| LAMBS LAKE | 0.00 | 0.00 | 0.00 | 0.00 | 0.00 | 0.00 | 0.00 | 1,206.67 | 1,206.67 |
| LITTLE GOOSE | 0.00 | 0.00 | 0.00 | 0.00 | 0.00 | 0.00 | 0.00 | 288.41 | 288.41 |
| LONG LAKE | 1,170.34 | 0.00 | 0.00 | 0.00 | 0.00 | 12,748.82 | 107,180.00 | 8,589.34 | 22,495.50 |
| LORDS LAKE | 0.00 | 0.00 | 0.00 | 0.00 | 0.00 | 0.00 | 0.00 | 1,915.29 | 1,915.29 |
| LOST LAKE | 0.00 | 0.00 | 0.00 | 0.00 | 0.00 | 0.00 | 0.00 | 960.21 | 960.21 |
| LOSTWOOD | 255.60 | 0.00 | 25,395.86 | 0.00 | 0.00 | 3,304.53 | 73,255.00 | 0.00 | 28,903.99 |
| MAPLE RIVER | 0.00 | 0.00 | 0.00 | 0.00 | 0.00 | 0.00 | 0.00 | 712.00 | 712.00 |
| MCLEAN | 0.00 | 0.00 | 0.00 | 0.00 | 0.00 | 344.00 | 12,516.00 | 416.00 | 760.00 |
| NORTH DAKOTA | 0.00 | 0.00 | 0.00 | 0.00 | 0.00 | 0.00 | 0.00 | 41,660.04 | 41,660.04 |
| PLEASANT LAKE | 0.00 | 0.00 | 0.00 | 0.00 | 0.00 | 0.00 | 0.00 | 897.80 | 897.80 |
| PRETTY ROCK | 0.00 | 0.00 | 0.00 | 0.00 | 0.00 | 0.00 | 0.00 | 800.00 | 800.00 |
| RABB LAKE | 0.00 | 0.00 | 0.00 | 0.00 | 0.00 | 0.00 | 0.00 | 260.80 | 260.80 |
| ROCK LAKE | 0.00 | 0.00 | 0.00 | 0.00 | 0.00 | 0.00 | 0.00 | 5,505.96 | 5,505.96 |
| ROSE LAKE | 0.00 | 0.00 | 0.00 | 0.00 | 0.00 | 0.00 | 0.00 | 856.50 | 856.50 |
| SCHOOL SECTION LAKE | 0.00 | 0.00 | 0.00 | 0.00 | 0.00 | 0.00 | 0.00 | 297.50 | 297.50 |
| SHELL LAKE | 0.00 | 0.00 | 0.00 | 0.00 | 0.00 | 785.20 | 38,902.00 | 1,124.90 | 1,910.10 |
| SHEYENNE LAKE | 0.00 | 0.00 | 0.00 | 0.00 | 0.00 | 0.00 | 0.00 | 797.30 | 797.30 |
| SIBLEY LAKE | 0.00 | 0.00 | 0.00 | 0.00 | 0.00 | 0.00 | 0.00 | 1,077.40 | 1,077.40 |
| SILVER LAKE | 0.00 | 0.00 | 0.00 | 0.00 | 0.00 | 0.00 | 0.00 | 3,347.64 | 3,347.64 |
| SLADE | 0.00 | 0.00 | 0.00 | 0.00 | 3,000.20 | 0.00 | 0.00 | 0.00 | 3,000.20 |
| SNYDER LAKE | 0.00 | 0.00 | 0.00 | 0.00 | 0.00 | 0.00 | 0.00 | 1,550.18 | 1,550.18 |
| SPRINGWATER | 0.00 | 0.00 | 0.00 | 0.00 | 0.00 | 0.00 | 0.00 | 640.00 | 640.00 |
| STEWART LAKE | 0.00 | 0.00 | 0.00 | 0.00 | 1.99 | 656.01 | 92,200.00 | 1,591.40 | 2,250.40 |
| STONEY SLOUGH | 0.00 | 0.00 | 0.00 | 0.00 | 0.00 | 0.00 | 0.00 | 880.00 | 880.00 |
| STORM LAKE | 0.00 | 0.00 | 0.00 | 0.00 | 0.00 | 1.70 | 161.00 | 684.20 | 685.90 |
| STUMP LAKE | 27.39 | 0.00 | 0.00 | 0.00 | 0.00 | 0.00 | 0.00 | 0.00 | 27.39 |
| SULLYS HILL | 1,673.85 | 0.00 | 0.00 | 0.00 | 0.00 | 0.00 | 0.00 | 1.29 | 1,675.14 |
| SUNBURST LAKE | 0.00 | 0.00 | 0.00 | 0.00 | 0.00 | 0.00 | 0.00 | 527.51 | 527.51 |
| TEWAUKON | 1.48 | 0.00 | 0.00 | 0.00 | 0.00 | 6,856.65 | 460,124.00 | 1,505.49 | 8,363.62 |
| TOMAHAWK | 0.00 | 0.00 | 0.00 | 0.00 | 0.00 | 0.00 | 0.00 | 440.00 | 440.00 |
| UPPER SOURIS | 160.17 | 0.00 | 28,758.43 | 0.00 | 7.36 | 3,199.99 | 41,720.00 | 216.30 | 32,302.75 |
| WHITE LAKE | 0.00 | 0.00 | 0.00 | 0.00 | 0.00 | 1,040.00 | 28,800.00 | 0.00 | 1,040.00 |
| WILD RICE LAKE | 0.00 | 0.00 | 0.00 | 0.00 | 0.00 | 0.00 | 0.00 | 778.80 | 778.80 |
| WILLOW LAKE | 0.00 | 0.00 | 0.00 | 0.00 | .69 | 0.00 | 0.00 | 2,619.69 | 2,620.38 |
| WINTERING RIVER | 0.00 | 0.00 | 0.00 | 0.00 | 0.00 | 0.00 | 0.00 | 259.26 | 259.26 |
| WOOD LAKE | 0.00 | 0.00 | 0.00 | 0.00 | 0.00 | 0.00 | 0.00 | 280.00 | 280.00 |
| STATE TOTAL 65 | 4,444.40 | 0.00 | 111,502.52 | 14,749.79 | 3,079.77 | 76,912.09 | 1,797,887.76 | 129,729.01 | 542,406.78 |
| **OHIO** | | | | | | | | | |
| CEDAR POINT | 0.00 | 0.00 | 0.00 | 0.00 | 2,445.42 | 0.00 | 0.00 | 4.35 | 2,449.77 |
| OTTAWA | 0.00 | 0.00 | 0.00 | 0.00 | 0.00 | 5,754.14 | 5,951,504.55 | 790.85 | 6,544.99 |
| WEST SISTER ISLAND | 77.13 | 0.00 | 0.00 | 0.00 | 0.00 | 0.00 | 0.00 | 3.00 | 80.13 |
| STATE TOTAL 3 | 77.13 | 0.00 | 0.00 | 0.00 | 2,445.42 | 5,754.14 | 5,951,504.55 | 798.70 | 9,074.89 |

TABLE 5 - NATIONAL WILDLIFE REFUGES

| STATE AND UNIT | RESERVED FROM PUBLIC DOMAIN | | ACQUIRED BY OTHER FEDERAL AGENCY | | DEVISE OR GIFT | PURCHASED | | AGREEMENT EASEMENT OR LEASE | TOTAL ACRES |
|---|---|---|---|---|---|---|---|---|---|
| | SOLE OR PRIMARY | SECONDARY | SOLE OR PRIMARY | SECONDARY | | ACRES | COST ($) | | |
| **OKLAHOMA** | | | | | | | | | |
| DEEP FORK | 0.00 | 0.00 | 0.00 | 0.00 | 0.00 | 8,476.51 | 7,063,800.00 | 0.00 | 8,476.51 |
| LITTLE RIVER | 0.00 | 0.00 | 0.00 | 0.00 | 0.00 | 15,400.04 | 10,701,445.51 | 0.00 | 15,400.04 |
| OPTIMA | 0.00 | 0.00 | 0.00 | 4,442.81 | 0.00 | 0.00 | 0.00 | 0.00 | 4,332.81 |
| OZARK PLATEAU | 0.00 | 0.00 | 755.00 | 0.00 | 425.00 | 2,398.04 | 957,145.00 | 408.53 | 3,636.57 |
| SALT PLAINS | 19,574.09 | 0.00 | 0.00 | 11,569.79 | 30.95 | 1,117.59 | 30,857.00 | 29.81 | 32,057.12 |
| SEQUOYAH | 0.00 | 0.00 | 0.00 | 20,800.00 | 0.00 | 0.00 | 0.00 | 0.00 | 20,800.00 |
| TISHOMINGO | 0.00 | 0.00 | 0.00 | 16,464.18 | 0.00 | 0.00 | 0.00 | 0.00 | 16,464.18 |
| WASHITA | 0.00 | 0.00 | 0.00 | 8,061.81 | 0.00 | 13.56 | 6,780.00 | 0.00 | 8,075.37 |
| WICHITA MOUNTAINS | 58,452.11 | 0.00 | 567.49 | 0.00 | 0.00 | 0.00 | 0.00 | 0.00 | 59,019.60 |
| **STATE TOTAL** 9 | 77,946.70 | 0.00 | 622.49 | 61,224.06 | 450.95 | 25,765.54 | 18,410,047.51 | 453.34 | 166,462.20 |
| **OREGON** | | | | | | | | | |
| ANKENY | 0.00 | 0.00 | 0.00 | 0.00 | 0.00 | 2,796.33 | 869,600.00 | 0.00 | 2,796.33 |
| BANDON MARSH | 0.00 | 0.00 | 0.00 | 0.00 | 34.26 | 827.50 | 1,701,025.00 | 0.00 | 861.76 |
| BASKETT SLOUGH | 0.00 | 0.00 | 0.00 | 0.00 | 0.00 | 2,492.33 | 341,985.00 | 0.00 | 2,492.33 |
| BEAR VALLEY | 0.00 | 0.00 | 0.00 | 0.00 | 0.00 | 4,198.08 | 3,298,034.00 | 2.18 | 4,200.26 |
| CAPE MEARES | 138.51 | 0.00 | 0.00 | 0.00 | 0.00 | 0.00 | 0.00 | 0.00 | 138.51 |
| COLD SPRINGS | 90.00 | 1,748.15 | 0.00 | 951.00 | 0.00 | 506.88 | 2,780.00 | 0.00 | 3,116.88 |
| DEER FLAT (21)* | 162.44 | 0.00 | 0.00 | 0.00 | 0.00 | 0.00 | 0.00 | 0.00 | 162.44 |
| FSA INTEREST OR *** | 0.00 | 0.00 | 299.70 | 0.00 | 0.00 | 0.00 | 0.00 | 338.05 | 637.75 |
| HART MOUNTAIN | 188,855.79 | 1,951.76 | 637.95 | 0.00 | 606.14 | 62,671.92 | 2,814,274.59 | 0.00 | 269,929.56 |
| JULIA BUTLER HANSEN (28) | 0.00 | 0.00 | 0.00 | 0.00 | 156.03 | 4,347.74 | 7,150,510.00 | 249.61 | 2,753.38 |
| KLAMATH MARSH | 0.00 | 0.00 | 0.00 | 0.00 | 0.00 | 40,884.96 | 11,921,507.00 | 0.00 | 40,884.96 |
| LEWIS AND CLARK | 0.00 | 0.00 | 4,350.14 | 0.00 | 347.08 | 2,850.84 | 469,250.00 | 4.00 | 7,631.85 |
| LOWER KLAMATH (2) * | 6,550.63 | 0.00 | 0.00 | 0.00 | 67.50 | 0.00 | 0.00 | 0.00 | 6,618.13 |
| MALHEUR | 57,898.45 | 0.00 | 33,929.86 | 0.00 | 340.00 | 15,027.47 | 3,239,576.60 | 50.95 | 107,126.94 |
| MCKAY CREEK | 28.50 | 0.00 | 0.00 | 1,813.00 | 0.00 | 0.00 | 0.00 | 0.00 | 1,836.50 |
| NESTUCCA BAY | 0.00 | 0.00 | 0.00 | 0.00 | 27.50 | 646.04 | 1,566,903.00 | 0.00 | 693.54 |
| OREGON ISLANDS | 925.06 | 0.00 | 0.00 | 0.00 | .41 | 151.82 | 4,990,000.00 | 2.32 | 1,079.61 |
| SHELDON (15)* | 0.00 | 0.00 | 0.00 | 0.00 | 0.00 | 627.48 | 4,079.00 | 0.00 | 627.48 |
| STEITZ BAY | 0.00 | 0.00 | 0.00 | 0.00 | 42.05 | 420.12 | 1,603,400.00 | 57.22 | 519.57 |
| THREE ARCH ROCKS | 15.00 | 0.00 | 0.00 | 0.00 | 0.00 | 0.00 | 0.00 | 0.00 | 15.00 |
| TUALATIN RIVER | 0.00 | 0.00 | 0.00 | 0.00 | 42.50 | 1,168.80 | 8,350,558.12 | 62.20 | 1,273.50 |
| UMATILLA (28) | 0.00 | 648.57 | 1,949.40 | 7,082.00 | 0.00 | 27.60 | 55,000.00 | 0.00 | 8,907.57 |
| UPPER KLAMATH | 10,888.81 | 0.00 | 0.00 | 0.00 | 0.00 | 4,070.85 | 123,476.00 | 0.00 | 14,966.16 |
| WILLIAM L. FINLEY | 0.00 | 0.00 | 0.00 | 0.00 | 0.00 | 5,665.96 | 2,480,800.00 | 7.15 | 5,673.11 |
| **STATE TOTAL** 30 | 360,274.72 | 4,048.28 | 44,047.05 | 9,826.80 | 1,446.47 | 725,342.73 | 48,534,991.50 | 755.66 | 564,956.71 |
| **PENNSYLVANIA** | | | | | | | | | |
| ERIE | 0.00 | 0.00 | 0.00 | 0.00 | 0.00 | 8,777.21 | 1,595,755.64 | 0.00 | 8,777.21 |
| JOHN HEINZ | 0.00 | 0.00 | 67.26 | 0.00 | 243.14 | 662.77 | 8,146,763.80 | 0.00 | 993.17 |
| OHIO RIVER ISLANDS (34)* | 0.00 | 0.00 | 0.00 | 0.00 | 0.00 | 55.20 | 82,500.00 | 0.00 | 55.20 |
| **STATE TOTAL** 2 | 0.00 | 0.00 | 67.26 | 0.00 | 243.14 | 9,495.18 | 9,825,019.44 | 0.00 | 9,825.58 |
| **RHODE ISLAND** | | | | | | | | | |
| BLOCK ISLAND | 0.00 | 0.00 | 26.30 | 0.00 | 0.00 | 82.62 | 5,505,000.00 | 20.00 | 128.92 |
| JOHN H. CHAFEE | 0.00 | 0.00 | 0.00 | 0.00 | 41.39 | 528.51 | 5,541,700.00 | 0.00 | 569.90 |
| NINIGRET | 0.00 | 0.00 | 198.64 | 0.00 | 0.00 | 449.33 | 5,518,000.00 | .67 | 648.61 |
| SACHUEST POINT | 0.00 | 0.00 | 157.00 | 0.00 | 62.80 | 22.10 | 0.00 | 0.00 | 241.90 |
| TRUSTOM POND | 0.00 | 0.00 | 0.00 | 0.00 | 516.70 | 115.02 | 885,600.00 | 145.58 | 777.30 |
| **STATE TOTAL** 5 | 0.00 | 0.00 | 381.94 | 0.00 | 630.89 | 997.58 | 17,250,300.00 | 156.20 | 2,366.63 |
| **SOUTH CAROLINA** | | | | | | | | | |
| ACE BASIN | 0.00 | 0.00 | 0.00 | 0.00 | 0.00 | 11,843.10 | 17,716,540.70 | 652.00 | 12,515.10 |
| CAPE ROMAIN | 0.00 | 0.00 | 5,242.56 | 0.00 | 8,540.14 | 77,306.16 | 58,768.18 | 41,180.00 | 66,268.86 |

TABLE 5 - NATIONAL WILDLIFE REFUGES

| STATE AND UNIT | RESERVED FROM PUBLIC DOMAIN | | ACQUIRED BY OTHER FEDERAL AGENCY | | DEVISE OR GIFT | PURCHASED | | AGREEMENT EASEMENT OR LEASE | TOTAL ACRES |
|---|---|---|---|---|---|---|---|---|---|
| | SOLE OR PRIMARY | SECONDARY | SOLE OR PRIMARY | SECONDARY | | ACRES | COST ($) | | |
| **SOUTH CAROLINA** | | | | | | | | | |
| CAROLINA SANDHILLS | 0.00 | 0.00 | 44,106.73 | 0.00 | 0.00 | 1,341.70 | 42,852.75 | 0.00 | 45,348.43 |
| FSA INTEREST SC     ** * | 0.00 | 0.00 | 200.30 | 0.00 | 0.00 | 0.00 | 0.00 | 1,229.74 | 1,430.04 |
| PINCKNEY ISLAND | 0.00 | 0.00 | 0.00 | 0.00 | 1,524.70 | 0.00 | 0.00 | 2,728.00 | 4,052.70 |
| SANTEE | 0.00 | 0.00 | 0.00 | 0.00 | 0.00 | 4,415.26 | 569,958.57 | 8,070.00 | 12,485.26 |
| SAVANNAH        (1) * | 0.00 | 0.00 | 5,454.88 | 0.00 | 57.10 | 9,315.09 | 1,667,508.54 | 24.50 | 15,011.37 |
| TYBEE | 0.00 | 0.00 | 0.00 | 100.00 | 0.00 | 0.00 | 0.00 | 0.00 | 100.00 |
| WACCAMAW | 0.00 | 0.00 | 0.00 | 0.00 | 870.50 | 8,404.38 | 10,257,485.00 | 1.12 | 9,276.00 |
| STATE TOTAL     7 | 0.00 | 0.00 | 55,184.27 | 100.00 | 5,772.44 | 37,513.71 | 24,788,085.82 | 44,715.16 | 165,485.58 |
| **SOUTH DAKOTA** | | | | | | | | | |
| BEAR BUTTE | 0.00 | 0.00 | 0.00 | 0.00 | 0.00 | 0.00 | 0.00 | 574.20 | 574.20 |
| DAKOTA TALLGRASS PRAIRIE (44)* | 0.00 | 0.00 | 0.00 | 0.00 | 0.00 | 0.00 | 0.00 | 41,752.82 | 41,752.82 |
| FSA INTEREST SD     ** * | 0.00 | 0.00 | 0.00 | 0.00 | 0.00 | 0.00 | 0.00 | 151.20 | 151.20 |
| KARL E. MUNDT     (10) | 0.00 | 0.00 | 0.00 | 0.00 | 738.82 | 0.00 | 0.00 | 305.00 | 1,043.82 |
| LACREEK | 0.00 | 0.00 | 6,807.47 | 0.00 | 225.11 | 9,579.75 | 788,491.00 | 445.00 | 16,893.33 |
| LAKE ANDES | 0.00 | 0.00 | 120.76 | 0.00 | 0.00 | 817.84 | 92,522.00 | 4,701.55 | 5,639.43 |
| SAND LAKE | 80.00 | 0.00 | 17,449.24 | 0.00 | 0.00 | 3,970.58 | 164,922.00 | 320.57 | 21,820.19 |
| WAUBAY | 0.00 | 0.00 | 3,965.97 | 0.00 | 0.00 | 684.77 | 21,656.00 | 90.58 | 4,740.22 |
| STATE TOTAL     8 | 80.00 | 0.00 | 28,542.69 | 0.00 | 963.93 | 14,661.74 | 1,069,573.00 | 48,140.65 | 92,377.21 |
| **TENNESSEE** | | | | | | | | | |
| CHICKASAW | 0.00 | 0.00 | 0.00 | 0.00 | 0.00 | 18,765.05 | 19,844,678.00 | 5,387.90 | 24,152.95 |
| CROSS CREEKS | 0.00 | 0.00 | 6,327.77 | 2,442.00 | 0.00 | 91.72 | 26,250.00 | 0.00 | 8,861.49 |
| FSA INTEREST TN     ** * | 0.00 | 0.00 | 112.98 | 0.00 | 0.00 | 0.00 | 0.00 | 572.41 | 685.39 |
| HATCHIE | 0.00 | 0.00 | 0.00 | 0.00 | 0.00 | 11,556.10 | 1,862,529.29 | 0.00 | 11,556.10 |
| LAKE ISOM | 0.00 | 0.00 | 1,485.12 | 0.00 | 0.00 | 360.84 | 27,290.72 | 0.00 | 1,845.96 |
| LOWER HATCHIE | 0.00 | 0.00 | 0.00 | 0.00 | 8.26 | 9,019.28 | 11,485,626.00 | 1,872.96 | 10,900.50 |
| REELFOOT     (22) * | 0.00 | 0.00 | 0.00 | 0.00 | 0.00 | 563.43 | 279,531.78 | 7,847.31 | 8,410.74 |
| TENNESSEE | 0.00 | 0.00 | 0.00 | 50,830.30 | 0.00 | 527.67 | 747,147.10 | 1.49 | 51,359.46 |
| STATE TOTAL     8 | 0.00 | 0.00 | 7,925.87 | 53,272.30 | 8.26 | 40,884.09 | 33,770,802.89 | 15,682.07 | 117,772.59 |
| **TEXAS** | | | | | | | | | |
| ANAHUAC | 0.00 | 0.00 | 0.00 | 0.00 | 552.57 | 33,660.97 | 15,671,965.67 | 83.09 | 34,296.25 |
| ARANSAS | 0.00 | 0.00 | 19,014.19 | 0.00 | 7,567.92 | 62,936.97 | 17,166,816.80 | 24,895.00 | 114,412.08 |
| ATTWATER PRAIRIE CHICKEN | 0.00 | 0.00 | 0.00 | 0.00 | 2,648.50 | 8,304.50 | 8,740,029.66 | 0.00 | 10,957.80 |
| BALCONES CANYONLANDS | 0.00 | 0.00 | 0.00 | 0.00 | 0.00 | 18,277.04 | 22,716,561.66 | 1,615.18 | 19,892.22 |
| BIG BOGGY | 0.00 | 0.00 | 0.00 | 0.00 | 0.00 | 4,216.29 | 2,457,398.19 | 309.88 | 4,526.17 |
| BRAZORIA | 0.00 | 0.00 | 0.00 | 0.00 | 25.00 | 44,220.20 | 14,664,168.26 | 168.68 | 44,413.88 |
| BUFFALO LAKE | 0.00 | 0.00 | 7,663.93 | 0.00 | 0.00 | 0.00 | 0.00 | .25 | 7,664.18 |
| CADDO LAKE | 0.00 | 0.00 | 0.00 | 7,172.00 | 0.00 | 0.00 | 0.00 | 0.00 | 7,172.00 |
| FSA INTEREST TX     ** * | 0.00 | 0.00 | 1,878.13 | 0.00 | 0.00 | 0.00 | 0.00 | 0.00 | 1,878.13 |
| GRULLA     (17) * | 0.00 | 0.00 | 0.00 | 0.00 | 0.00 | 4.97 | 5,000.00 | 0.00 | 4.97 |
| HAGERMAN | 0.00 | 0.00 | 0.00 | 11,519.84 | 0.00 | 0.00 | 0.00 | 0.00 | 11,519.84 |
| LAGUNA ATASCOSA | 0.00 | 0.00 | 8,486.00 | 0.00 | 0.00 | 78,718.82 | 13,090,515.84 | 113.10 | 86,817.92 |
| LITTLE SANDY | 0.00 | 0.00 | 0.00 | 0.00 | 0.00 | 0.00 | 0.00 | 3,802.00 | 3,802.00 |
| LOWER RIO GRANDE VALLEY | 0.00 | 0.00 | 44.18 | 0.00 | 1,642.41 | 75,577.45 | 68,648,797.50 | 10,979.81 | 88,044.05 |
| MCFADDIN | 0.00 | 0.00 | 0.00 | 0.00 | 0.00 | 48,431.82 | 10,719,900.00 | 7,748.88 | 56,180.70 |
| MOODY | 0.00 | 0.00 | 0.00 | 0.00 | 0.00 | 0.00 | 0.00 | 3,516.67 | 3,516.67 |
| MULESHOE | 0.00 | 0.00 | 3,454.30 | 0.00 | 0.00 | 2,154.80 | 25,740.00 | 0.00 | 5,609.10 |
| SAN BERNARD | 0.00 | 0.00 | 0.00 | 0.00 | 1,816.73 | 34,040.76 | 11,925,577.56 | 127.00 | 35,984.49 |
| SANTA ANA | 0.00 | 0.00 | 0.00 | 0.00 | 37.06 | 2,049.91 | 205,516.00 | .53 | 2,087.50 |
| TEXAS POINT | 0.00 | 0.00 | 0.00 | 0.00 | 0.00 | 8,952.02 | 1,719,000.00 | 0.00 | 8,952.02 |
| TRINITY RIVER | 0.00 | 0.00 | 0.00 | 0.00 | 0.00 | 17,758.34 | 10,977,576.00 | 0.00 | 17,758.54 |
| STATE TOTAL     19 | 0.00 | 0.00 | 40,742.73 | 18,691.84 | 14,077.99 | 458,824.65 | 194,387,675.12 | 53,358.25 | 565,470.47 |

TABLE 5 - NATIONAL WILDLIFE REFUGES

| STATE AND UNIT | RESERVED FROM PUBLIC DOMAIN | | ACQUIRED BY OTHER FEDERAL AGENCY | | DIVEST OR GIFT | PURCHASED | | AGREEMENT EASEMENT OR LEASE | TOTAL ACRES |
|---|---|---|---|---|---|---|---|---|---|
| | SOLE OR PRIMARY | SECONDARY | SOLE OR PRIMARY | SECONDARY | | ACRES | COST ($) | | |
| **UTAH** | | | | | | | | | |
| BEAR RIVER | 43,442.89 | 0.00 | 0.00 | 0.00 | 4,285.43 | 25,968.43 | 3,583,119.47 | 46.64 | 73,763.39 |
| COLORADO RIVER (66) | 0.00 | 0.00 | 0.00 | 0.00 | 0.00 | 0.00 | 0.00 | 553.00 | 553.00 |
| FISH SPRINGS | 14,217.42 | 0.00 | 0.00 | 0.00 | 0.00 | 3,774.82 | 95,325.00 | 0.00 | 17,992.24 |
| FSA INTEREST UT ** * | 0.00 | 0.00 | 0.00 | 0.00 | 0.00 | 0.00 | 0.00 | 280.84 | 280.84 |
| OURAY | 3,111.08 | 0.00 | 161.68 | 0.00 | 0.00 | 5,014.98 | 487,084.25 | 3,970.50 | 12,258.24 |
| STATE TOTAL 4 | 60,771.39 | 0.00 | 161.68 | 0.00 | 4,285.43 | 34,778.23 | 4,165,528.72 | 4,850.98 | 104,847.71 |
| **VERMONT** | | | | | | | | | |
| FSA INTEREST VT ** * | 0.00 | 0.00 | 0.00 | 0.00 | 0.00 | 0.00 | 0.00 | 71.00 | 71.00 |
| MISSISQUOI | 0.00 | 0.00 | 0.00 | 0.00 | 264.50 | 6,256.98 | 291,154.27 | 0.00 | 6,521.48 |
| SILVIO O. CONTE (41) | 0.00 | 0.00 | 0.00 | 0.00 | 81.86 | 26,452.25 | 6,892,383.10 | 0.00 | 26,534.11 |
| STATE TOTAL 2 | 0.00 | 0.00 | 0.00 | 0.00 | 346.36 | 32,709.23 | 7,183,517.37 | 71.00 | 33,126.59 |
| **VIRGINIA** | | | | | | | | | |
| BACK BAY | 0.00 | 0.00 | 0.00 | 0.00 | 2.56 | 8,893.36 | 22,157,866.08 | 0.00 | 8,895.72 |
| CHINCOTEAGUE (23) | 0.00 | 0.00 | 0.00 | 0.00 | 1,434.85 | 11,579.60 | 8,316,579.16 | 600.00 | 13,614.45 |
| EASTERN SHORE OF VIRGINIA | 0.00 | 0.00 | 175.35 | 0.00 | 70.35 | 872.32 | 4,882,444.00 | 5.27 | 1,123.27 |
| FEATHERSTONE | 0.00 | 0.00 | 0.00 | 0.00 | 161.92 | 163.90 | 656,800.00 | 0.00 | 325.82 |
| FISHERMAN ISLAND | 0.00 | 0.00 | 1,078.20 | 0.00 | 0.00 | 871.30 | 1,800,000.00 | 0.00 | 1,949.50 |
| FSA INTEREST VA ** * | 0.00 | 0.00 | 0.00 | 0.00 | 0.00 | 0.00 | 0.00 | 133.70 | 133.70 |
| GREAT DISMAL SWAMP (24)* | 0.00 | 0.00 | 27.14 | 0.00 | 49,097.01 | 35,968.96 | 17,198,270.15 | 0.00 | 85,093.11 |
| JAMES RIVER | 0.00 | 0.00 | 0.00 | 0.00 | 0.00 | 4,199.58 | 6,966,072.00 | 0.00 | 4,199.58 |
| MACKAY ISLAND (24)* | 0.00 | 0.00 | 0.00 | 0.00 | 0.00 | 874.40 | 26,865.75 | 0.00 | 874.40 |
| MARTIN (25)* | 0.00 | 0.00 | 0.00 | 0.00 | 143.62 | 0.00 | 0.00 | 0.00 | 143.62 |
| MASON NECK | 0.00 | 0.00 | 0.00 | 0.00 | 0.00 | 1,487.72 | 7,285,457.50 | 789.06 | 2,276.78 |
| NANSEMOND | 0.00 | 0.00 | 422.99 | 0.00 | 0.00 | 0.00 | 11,350.00 | 0.00 | 422.99 |
| OCCOQUAN BAY | 0.00 | 0.00 | 642.07 | 0.00 | 0.00 | 0.00 | 0.00 | 0.00 | 642.07 |
| PLUM TREE ISLAND | 0.00 | 0.00 | 3,275.60 | 0.00 | 19.08 | 711.00 | 105,500.00 | 0.00 | 5,501.68 |
| PRESQUILE | 0.00 | 0.00 | 0.00 | 0.00 | 1,328.92 | 0.00 | 0.00 | 0.00 | 1,328.92 |
| RAPPAHANNOCK RIVER | 0.00 | 0.00 | 0.00 | 0.00 | 1,358.84 | 3,925.78 | 8,647,815.75 | 44.12 | 5,328.74 |
| WALLOPS ISLAND | 0.00 | 0.00 | 373.00 | 0.00 | 0.00 | 0.00 | 0.00 | 3,000.00 | 3,373.00 |
| STATE TOTAL 18 | 0.00 | 0.00 | 5,994.33 | 0.00 | 53,594.95 | 69,045.92 | 76,634,201.39 | 4,572.15 | 135,207.33 |
| **WASHINGTON** | | | | | | | | | |
| COLUMBIA | 10,978.11 R | 1,387.11 | 0.00 R | 1,274.89 | 0.00 | 15,062.09 | 456,001.04 | 894.07 | 29,596.27 |
| CONBOY LAKE | 0.00 | 0.00 | 0.00 | 0.00 | 0.00 | 6,249.59 | 2,797,910.00 | 718.39 | 6,987.68 |
| COPALIS | 60.80 | 0.00 | 0.00 | 0.00 | 0.00 | 0.00 | 0.00 | 0.00 | 60.80 |
| DUNGENESS | 202.50 OG | 52.50 | 0.00 | 0.00 | 128.86 | 84.22 | 756,300.00 | 324.84 | 772.92 |
| FLATTERY ROCKS | 125.00 | 0.00 | 0.00 | 0.00 | 0.00 | 0.00 | 0.00 | 0.00 | 125.00 |
| FRANZ LAKE | 0.00 | 0.00 | 0.00 | 0.00 | 0.00 | 550.33 | 1,143,700.00 | 1.40 | 551.73 |
| FSA INTEREST WA ** * | 0.00 | 0.00 | 466.43 | 0.00 | 0.00 | 0.00 | 0.00 | 499.49 | 965.92 |
| GRAYS HARBOR | 0.00 | 0.00 | 0.00 | 0.00 | 0.00 | 1,407.77 | 1,039,800.00 | 63.61 | 1,471.38 |
| JULIA BUTLER HANSEN (4) * | 0.00 | 0.00 | 0.00 | 0.00 | 0.00 | 2,888.78 | 1,980,321.00 | 155.66 | 3,044.44 |
| LITTLE PEND OREILLE | 8,790.40 | 0.00 | 27,359.33 | 0.00 | 0.00 | 6,443.84 | 626,425.00 | 0.00 | 42,593.57 |
| MCNARY | 0.00 | 0.00 | 3,106.71 E | 11,895.00 | 5.49 | 422.26 | 122,485.00 | 30.00 | 15,459.46 |
| NISQUALLY | 0.00 | 0.00 | 486.25 | 0.00 | 121.19 | 3,272.65 | 8,943,849.57 | 32.20 | 3,912.29 |
| PIERCE | 0.00 | 0.00 | 0.00 | 0.00 | 319.00 | 10.38 | 125,000.00 | 0.00 | 329.38 |
| PROTECTION ISLAND | 0.00 | 0.00 | 0.00 | 0.00 | 1.42 | 317.89 | 3,624,095.00 | 340.00 | 659.31 |
| QUILLAYUTE NEEDLES | 300.20 | 0.00 | 0.00 | 0.00 | 0.00 | 0.00 | 0.00 | 0.00 | 300.20 |
| RIDGEFIELD | 0.00 | 0.00 | 0.00 | 0.00 | 24.99 | 5,190.97 | 5,314,600.00 | 1.74 | 5,217.70 |
| SADDLE MOUNTAIN | 0.00 NR | 440.00 | 0.00 NR | 161,045.95 | 0.00 | 0.00 | 0.00 | 0.00 | 161,485.95 |
| SAN JUAN ISLANDS | 448.55 | 0.00 | 0.00 | 0.00 | 0.00 | 0.00 | 0.00 | 0.00 | 448.55 |
| STEIGERWALD LAKE | 0.00 | 0.00 | 632.44 | 0.00 | 0.00 | 413.58 | 2,784,000.00 | 0.00 | 1,046.02 |
| TOPPENISH | 0.00 | 0.00 | 0.00 | 0.00 | 0.00 | 1,977.55 | 715,137.00 | 1.29 | 1,978.84 |

TABLE 4 - NATIONAL WILDLIFE REFUGES

| STATE AND UNIT | RESERVED FROM PUBLIC DOMAIN | | ACQUIRED BY OTHER FEDERAL AGENCY | | DEVISE OR GIFT | PURCHASED | | AGREEMENT EASEMENT OR LEASE | TOTAL ACRES |
|---|---|---|---|---|---|---|---|---|---|
| | SOLE OR PRIMARY | SECONDARY | SOLE OR PRIMARY | SECONDARY | | ACRES | COST ($) | | |
| **WASHINGTON** | | | | | | | | | |
| TURNBULL | 0.00 | 0.00 | 0.00 | 0.00 | 0.00 | 15,656.29 | 888,880.46 | 875.78 | 16,532.07 |
| UMATILLA (4) * | 0.00 | 102.50 | 1,445.85 | 14,927.00 | 0.00 | 0.00 | 0.00 | 200.50 | 14,675.85 |
| WILLAPA | 2,058.90 | 0.00 | 1,445.85 | 0.00 | 635.00 | 9,697.54 | 6,199,010.74 | 3,122.81 | 15,514.25 |
| STATE TOTAL 20 | 22,764.44 | 1,962.11 | 33,516.99 | 187,322.82 | 1,285.75 | 69,885.54 | 47,298,464.75 | 7,261.46 | 575,979.12 |
| **WEST VIRGINIA** | | | | | | | | | |
| CANAAN VALLEY | 0.00 | 0.00 | 0.00 | 0.00 | 6.60 | 15,228.56 | 41,184,994.00 | 18.97 | 15,254.15 |
| FSA INTEREST WV ** * | 0.00 | 0.00 | 0.00 | 0.00 | 0.00 | 0.00 | 0.00 | 8.37 | 8.37 |
| OHIO RIVER ISLANDS (15) | 0.00 | 0.00 | 18.90 | 0.00 | 160.27 | 2,288.50 | 4,829,242.10 | 1.00 | 2,448.67 |
| STATE TOTAL 2 | 0.00 | 0.00 | 18.90 | 0.00 | 166.87 | 17,497.06 | 35,014,236.10 | 28.34 | 17,711.19 |
| **WISCONSIN** | | | | | | | | | |
| FOX RIVER | 0.00 | 0.00 | 0.00 | 0.00 | 0.00 | 924.88 | 499,553.07 | 0.00 | 924.88 |
| FSA INTEREST WI ** * | 0.00 | 0.00 | 920.00 | 0.00 | 0.00 | 0.00 | 0.00 | 0.00 | 920.00 |
| GRAVEL ISLAND | 27.00 | 0.00 | 0.00 | 0.00 | 0.00 | 0.00 | 0.00 | 0.00 | 27.00 |
| GREEN BAY | 2.00 | 0.00 | 0.00 | 0.00 | 0.00 | 0.00 | 0.00 | 0.00 | 2.00 |
| HORICON | 0.00 | 0.00 | 0.00 | 0.00 | 5.44 | 21,366.05 | 791,987.42 | 33.83 | 21,405.32 |
| NECEDAH | 30.18 | 0.00 | 43,288.42 | 0.00 | 0.00 | 382.26 | 75,194.26 | 0.00 | 43,499.86 |
| TRIMPEALEAU | 0.00 | 0.00 | 0.00 | 0.00 | 0.00 | 6,198.83 | 425,492.50 | 0.00 | 6,198.83 |
| UPPER MISSISSIPPI RIVER (25) * | 693.57 | 0.00 | 4.25 | 40,341.00 | 119.18 | 48,345.16 | 956,916.27 | 2.50 | 89,467.66 |
| WHITTLESEY CREEK | 0.00 | 0.00 | 0.00 | 0.00 | 50.02 | 69.07 | 273,000.00 | 0.00 | 119.09 |
| STATE TOTAL 7 | 714.75 | 0.00 | 44,207.65 | 40,341.00 | 174.64 | 77,286.75 | 3,469,823.47 | 36.33 | 162,760.62 |
| **WYOMING** | | | | | | | | | |
| BAMFORTH * | 701.75 | 0.00 | 0.00 | 0.00 | 0.00 | 784.80 | 6,368.00 | 0.00 | 1,166.03 |
| COKEVILLE MEADOWS | 0.00 | 0.00 | 0.00 | 0.00 | 0.00 | 6,465.82 | 3,105,412.76 | 2,793.50 | 9,259.32 |
| FSA INTEREST WY ** * | 0.00 | 0.00 | 0.00 | 0.00 | 0.00 | 0.00 | 0.00 | 3,132.75 | 3,132.75 |
| HUTTON LAKE | 152.85 | 0.00 | 0.00 | 0.00 | 0.00 | 1,815.49 | 7,943.00 | 0.00 | 1,968.34 |
| MORTENSON LAKE | 0.00 | 0.00 | 0.00 | 0.00 | 0.00 | 1,927.34 | 571,000.00 | 0.00 | 1,927.34 |
| NATIONAL ELK | 4,676.55 | 0.00 | 0.00 | 0.00 | 4,474.23 | 15,626.55 | 7,884,177.00 | 1.01 | 24,778.31 |
| PATHFINDER | 2,294.84 | 11,501.57 | 0.00 | 3,010.49 | 0.00 | 0.00 | 0.00 | 0.00 | 16,806.90 |
| SEEDSKADEE | 10,124.29 | 0.00 | 16,079.93 | 0.00 | 0.00 | 0.00 | 0.00 | 1,026.00 | 27,230.22 |
| STATE TOTAL 7 | 17,669.74 | 11,501.57 | 16,079.93 | 3,010.49 | 4,474.77 | 26,600.00 | 11,372,900.76 | 6,953.26 | 86,269.21 |
| **AMERICAN SAMOA** | | | | | | | | | |
| ROSE ATOLL | 0.00 | 37,453.00 | 1,613.00 | 0.00 | 0.00 | 0.00 | 0.00 | 0.00 | 39,066.00 |
| STATE TOTAL 1 | 0.00 | 37,453.00 | 1,613.00 | 0.00 | 0.00 | 0.00 | 0.00 | 0.00 | 39,066.00 |
| **BAKER ISLAND** | | | | | | | | | |
| BAKER ISLAND | 0.00 | 0.00 | 31,756.89 | 0.00 | 0.00 | 0.00 | 0.00 | 0.00 | 31,756.89 |
| STATE TOTAL 1 | 0.00 | 0.00 | 31,756.89 | 0.00 | 0.00 | 0.00 | 0.00 | 0.00 | 31,756.89 |
| **GUAM** | | | | | | | | | |
| GUAM | 0.00 | 0.00 | 772.10 | 0.00 | 0.00 | 0.00 | 0.00 | 22,456.00 | 23,228.10 |
| STATE TOTAL 1 | 0.00 | 0.00 | 772.10 | 0.00 | 0.00 | 0.00 | 0.00 | 22,456.00 | 23,228.10 |
| **HOWLAND ISLAND** | | | | | | | | | |
| HOWLAND ISLAND | 0.00 | 0.00 | 32,550.25 | 0.00 | 0.00 | 0.00 | 0.00 | 0.00 | 32,550.25 |
| STATE TOTAL 1 | 0.00 | 0.00 | 32,550.25 | 0.00 | 0.00 | 0.00 | 0.00 | 0.00 | 32,550.25 |
| **JARVIS ISLAND** | | | | | | | | | |
| JARVIS ISLAND | 0.00 | 0.00 | 37,519.17 | 0.00 | 0.00 | 0.00 | 0.00 | 0.00 | 37,519.17 |
| STATE TOTAL 1 | 0.00 | 0.00 | 37,519.17 | 0.00 | 0.00 | 0.00 | 0.00 | 0.00 | 37,519.17 |
| **JOHNSTON ATOLL** | | | | | | | | | |
| JOHNSTON ISLAND | 0.00 | 0.00 | 100.00 | 0.00 | 0.00 | 0.00 | 0.00 | 0.00 | 100.00 |
| STATE TOTAL 1 | 0.00 | 0.00 | 100.00 | 0.00 | 0.00 | 0.00 | 0.00 | 0.00 | 100.00 |

TABLE 3 - NATIONAL WILDLIFE REFUGES

| STATE AND UNIT | RESERVED FROM PUBLIC DOMAIN | | ACQUIRED BY OTHER FEDERAL AGENCY | | DEVEST OR GIFT | PURCHASED | | AGREEMENT EASEMENT OR LEASE | TOTAL ACRES |
|---|---|---|---|---|---|---|---|---|---|
| | SOLE OR PRIMARY | SECONDARY | SOLE OR PRIMARY | SECONDARY | | ACRES | COST ($) | | |
| KINGMAN REEF | | | | | | | | | |
| KINGMAN REEF | 0.00 | 0.00 | 426,392.00 | 0.00 | 0.00 | 0.00 | 0.00 | 0.00 | 426,392.00 |
| STATE TOTAL 1 | 0.00 | 0.00 | 426,392.00 | 0.00 | 0.00 | 0.00 | 0.00 | 0.00 | 426,392.00 |
| MIDWAY ISLANDS | | | | | | | | | |
| MIDWAY ATOLL | 0.00 | 0.00 | 298,156.50 | 282,835.00 | 0.00 | 0.00 | 0.00 | 0.00 | 580,991.50 |
| STATE TOTAL 1 | 0.00 | 0.00 | 298,156.50 | 282,835.00 | 0.00 | 0.00 | 0.00 | 0.00 | 580,991.50 |
| NAVASSA ISLAND | | | | | | | | | |
| NAVASSA ISLAND | 0.00 | 0.00 | 364,950.00 | 0.00 | 0.00 | 0.00 | 0.00 | 0.00 | 364,950.00 |
| STATE TOTAL 1 | 0.00 | 0.00 | 364,950.00 | 0.00 | 0.00 | 0.00 | 0.00 | 0.00 | 364,950.00 |
| PALMYRA ATOLL | | | | | | | | | |
| PALMYRA ATOLL | 0.00 | 0.00 | 503,963.00 | 0.00 | 0.00 | 415.75 | 8,900,000.00 | 2.30 | 504,381.05 |
| STATE TOTAL 1 | 0.00 | 0.00 | 503,963.00 | 0.00 | 0.00 | 415.75 | 8,900,000.00 | 2.30 | 504,381.05 |
| PUERTO RICO | | | | | | | | | |
| CABO ROJO | 0.00 | 0.00 | 587.33 | 0.00 | 0.00 | 1,269.38 | 2,999,265.63 | 0.00 | 1,856.71 |
| CULEBRA | 0.00 | 0.00 | 1,478.35 | 68.00 | 0.00 | 0.00 | 0.00 | 14.21 | 1,560.56 |
| DESECHEO | 0.00 | 0.00 | 360.00 | 0.00 | 0.00 | 0.00 | 0.00 | 0.00 | 360.00 |
| LAGUNA CARTAGENA | 0.00 | 0.00 | 262.86 | 0.00 | 0.00 | 0.00 | 0.00 | 772.89 | 1,035.75 |
| VIEQUES | 0.00 | 0.00 | 17,769.20 | 0.00 | 0.00 | 0.00 | 0.00 | 0.00 | 17,769.20 |
| STATE TOTAL 5 | 0.00 | 0.00 | 20,457.74 | 68.00 | 0.00 | 1,269.38 | 2,999,265.63 | 787.10 | 22,582.22 |
| VIRGIN ISLANDS | | | | | | | | | |
| BUCK ISLAND | 0.00 | 0.00 | 45.15 | 0.00 | 0.00 | 0.00 | 0.00 | 0.00 | 45.15 |
| GREEN CAY | 0.00 | 0.00 | 0.00 | 0.00 | 0.00 | 13.77 | 250,000.00 | 0.00 | 13.77 |
| SANDY POINT | 0.00 | 0.00 | 0.00 | 0.00 | 0.00 | 532.17 | 3,507,370.00 | 0.00 | 532.17 |
| STATE TOTAL 3 | 0.00 | 0.00 | 45.15 | 0.00 | 0.00 | 545.94 | 3,757,370.00 | 0.00 | 591.09 |
| GRAND TOTAL 542 | 81,527,927.21 | 690,838.04 | 3,744,158.02 | 7,229,726.53 | 705,688.51 | 4,140,126.03 | 1,770,263,754.96 | 1,303,625.66 | 92,541,558.18 |

(1) ALSO IN GEORGIA
(2) ALSO IN CALIFORNIA
(3) ALSO IN ARIZONA
(4) ALSO IN OREGON
(5) ALSO IN ALABAMA
(6) ALSO IN FLORIDA
(7) ALSO IN SOUTH CAROLINA
(8) ALSO IN MISSOURI
(9) ALSO IN IOWA, MINNESOTA AND WISCONSIN
(10) ALSO IN NEBRASKA
(11) ALSO IN ILLINOIS
(12) ALSO IN TEXAS
(13) ALSO IN ILLINOIS, MINNESOTA, AND WISCONSIN
(14) ALSO IN TENNESSEE
(15) ALSO IN NEVADA
(16) ALSO IN VIRGINIA
(17) ALSO IN NEW MEXICO
(18) ALSO IN ILLINOIS, IOWA, AND WISCONSIN
(19) ALSO IN IOWA
(20) ALSO IN SOUTH DAKOTA
(21) ALSO IN IDAHO
(22) ALSO IN KENTUCKY
(23) ALSO IN MARYLAND
(24) ALSO IN NORTH CAROLINA
(25) ALSO IN ILLINOIS, IOWA, AND MINNESOTA
(26) ALSO IN WASHINGTON
(27) ALSO IN MISSISSIPPI
(28) ALSO IN LOUISIANA
(33) ALSO IN ILLINOIS AND IOWA
(34) ALSO IN WEST VIRGINIA AND KENTUCKY
(35) ALSO IN PENNSYLVANIA AND KENTUCKY
(36) ALSO IN NEW HAMPSHIRE
(37) ALSO IN MAINE
(38) ALSO IN WEST VIRGINIA AND PENNSYLVANIA
(39) ALSO IN NEW YORK
(40) ALSO IN NEW JERSEY
(41) ALSO IN MASSACHUSETTS AND NEW HAMPSHIRE
(42) ALSO IN VERMONT AND NEW HAMPSHIRE
(43) ALSO IN VERMONT AND MASSACHUSETTS
(44) ALSO IN NORTH DAKOTA
(45) ALSO IN UTAH
(46) ALSO IN COLORADO
(47) ALSO IN MINNESOTA

A    - DEPARTMENT OF THE ARMY
BIA  - BUREAU OF INDIAN AFFAIRS, DEPARTMENT OF THE INTERIOR
C    - DEPARTMENT OF COMMERCE
CG   - COAST GUARD, DEPARTMENT OF HOMELAND SECURITY
E    - CORPS OF ENGINEERS, DEPARTMENT OF THE ARMY
F    - FOREST SERVICE, DEPARTMENT OF AGRICULTURE
FA   - FEDERAL AVIATION ADMINISTRATION, DEPARTMENT OF TRANSPORTATION
FSA  - FARM SERVICE AGENCY (FORMERLY FARMERS HOME ADMINISTRATION, DEPARTMENT OF AGRICULTURE)
GS   - GEOLOGICAL SURVEY, DEPARTMENT OF THE INTERIOR
I    - OFFICE OF INSULAR AFFAIRS, DEPARTMENT OF THE INTERIOR
LM   - BUREAU OF LAND MANAGEMENT, DEPARTMENT OF THE INTERIOR
N    - DEPARTMENT OF THE NAVY
NA   - NATIONAL AERONAUTICS AND SPACE ADMINISTRATION
NR   - NUCLEAR REGULATORY COMMISSION
R    - BUREAU OF RECLAMATION, DEPARTMENT OF THE INTERIOR
T    - TENNESSEE VALLEY AUTHORITY

(#) - COUNTED IN ANOTHER STATE
**  - SUMMARY BY STATE OF ALL OTHER ACRES, BOTH FEE AND LESS THAN FEE, ACQUIRED FROM THE
       FSA (FORMERLY FARMERS HOME ADMINISTRATION), NOT REPORTED WITHIN AN EXISTING PROJECT.
       SUMMARY MAY CONTAIN ONE OR MORE OWNERSHIPS.  FSA INTEREST STATE SUMMARY ACRES ARE
       INCLUDED IN THE TOTAL ACRES FOR EACH STATE BUT ARE NOT COUNTED AS SEPARATE UNITS IN
       THE NATIONAL WILDLIFE REFUGE STATE TOTALS.

TABLE 4 - WATERFOWL PRODUCTION AREA COUNTIES

| STATE AND UNIT | RESERVED FROM PUBLIC DOMAIN | | ACQUIRED BY OTHER FEDERAL AGENCY | | DEVISE OR GIFT | PURCHASED | | AGREEMENT EASEMENT OR LEASE | TOTAL ACRES |
|---|---|---|---|---|---|---|---|---|---|
| | SOLE OR PRIMARY | SECONDARY | SOLE OR PRIMARY | SECONDARY | | ACRES | COST ($) | | |
| **IDAHO** | | | | | | | | | |
| OXFORD SLOUGH | 0.00 | 0.00 | 0.00 | 0.00 | 0.00 | 1,878.41 | 550,000.00 | 0.00 | 1,878.41 |
| UNO TOTAL 1 | 0.00 | 0.00 | 0.00 | 0.00 | 0.00 | 1,878.41 | 550,000.00 | 0.00 | 1,878.41 |
| STATE TOTAL 1 | 0.00 | 0.00 | 0.00 | 0.00 | 0.00 | 1,878.41 | 550,000.00 | 0.00 | 1,878.41 |
| **IOWA** | | | | | | | | | |
| IOWA WMD BOONE | 0.00 | 0.00 | 0.00 | 0.00 | 0.00 | 391.33 | 399,600.00 | 0.00 | 391.33 |
| BUENA VISTA | 0.00 | 0.00 | 0.00 | 0.00 | 0.00 | 69.09 | 169,000.00 | 0.00 | 69.09 |
| CERRO GORDO | 0.00 | 0.00 | 0.00 | 0.00 | 0.00 | 2,494.25 | 2,882,677.82 | 5.70 | 2,499.95 |
| CLAY | 0.00 | 0.00 | 0.00 | 0.00 | 0.00 | 867.93 | 1,146,206.85 | 0.00 | 867.93 |
| DICKINSON | 0.00 | 0.00 | 0.00 | 0.00 | .65 | 4,896.82 | 5,867,147.00 | 98.00 | 4,994.47 |
| EMMET | 0.00 | 0.00 | 0.00 | 0.00 | 0.00 | 1,653.84 | 2,081,075.00 | 58.00 | 1,711.84 |
| GREENE | 0.00 | 0.00 | 0.00 | 0.00 | 0.00 | 669.05 | 1,280,700.00 | 0.00 | 669.05 |
| GUTHRIE | 0.00 | 0.00 | 0.00 | 0.00 | 0.00 | 185.53 | 295,840.00 | 0.00 | 185.53 |
| HANCOCK | 0.00 | 0.00 | 0.00 | 0.00 | 0.00 | 802.70 | 545,480.26 | 7.00 | 809.70 |
| KOSSUTH | 0.00 | 0.00 | 0.00 | 0.00 | 0.00 | 2,715.08 | 3,955,194.98 | 25.00 | 2,236.08 |
| OSCEOLA | 0.00 | 0.00 | 0.00 | 0.00 | 0.00 | 0.00 | 0.00 | 41.00 | 41.00 |
| PALO ALTO | 0.00 | 0.00 | 0.00 | 0.00 | 0.00 | 627.56 | 744,092.65 | 282.00 | 909.56 |
| POCAHONTAS | 0.00 | 0.00 | 0.00 | 0.00 | 0.00 | 225.76 | 465,000.00 | 0.00 | 225.76 |
| POLK | 0.00 | 0.00 | 0.00 | 0.00 | 0.00 | 110.00 | 241,500.00 | 0.00 | 110.00 |
| SAC | 0.00 | 0.00 | 0.00 | 0.00 | 0.00 | 296.52 | 665,880.00 | 0.00 | 296.52 |
| WINNEBAGO | 0.00 | 0.00 | 0.00 | 0.00 | 0.00 | 1,025.15 | 1,130,300.31 | 103.00 | 1,128.15 |
| WORTH | 0.00 | 0.00 | 0.00 | 0.00 | 0.00 | 1,491.84 | 1,088,529.87 | 18.00 | 1,509.84 |
| WRIGHT | 0.00 | 0.00 | 0.00 | 0.00 | 0.00 | 1,528.09 | 2,238,023.00 | 0.00 | 1,528.09 |
| WMD TOTAL 18 | 0.00 | 0.00 | 0.00 | 0.00 | .65 | 19,543.54 | 25,140,041.74 | 637.70 | 20,181.89 |
| STATE TOTAL 18 | 0.00 | 0.00 | 0.00 | 0.00 | .65 | 19,543.54 | 25,140,041.74 | 637.70 | 20,181.89 |
| **MAINE** | | | | | | | | | |
| CARLTON POND | 0.00 | 0.00 | 0.00 | 0.00 | 0.00 | 1,068.21 | 18,276.08 | 0.00 | 1,068.21 |
| WMD TOTAL 1 | 0.00 | 0.00 | 0.00 | 0.00 | 0.00 | 1,068.21 | 18,276.08 | 0.00 | 1,068.21 |
| STATE TOTAL 1 | 0.00 | 0.00 | 0.00 | 0.00 | 0.00 | 1,068.21 | 18,276.08 | 0.00 | 1,068.21 |
| **MICHIGAN** | | | | | | | | | |
| MICHIGAN WMD JACKSON | 0.00 | 0.00 | 0.00 | 0.00 | 0.00 | 160.00 | 170,000.00 | 0.00 | 160.00 |
| VAN BUREN | 0.00 | 0.00 | 0.00 | 0.00 | 0.00 | 77.08 | 45,600.00 | 0.00 | 77.08 |
| WMD TOTAL 2 | 0.00 | 0.00 | 0.00 | 0.00 | 0.00 | 237.08 | 215,600.00 | 0.00 | 237.08 |
| STATE TOTAL 2 | 0.00 | 0.00 | 0.00 | 0.00 | 0.00 | 237.08 | 215,600.00 | 0.00 | 237.08 |
| **MINNESOTA** | | | | | | | | | |
| BIG STONE WMD LINCOLN | 0.00 | 0.00 | 0.00 | 0.00 | 0.00 | 754.36 | 475,650.00 | 517.37 | 1,271.65 |
| LYON | 0.00 | 0.00 | 0.00 | 0.00 | 0.00 | 1,553.56 | 1,219,720.00 | 335.80 | 1,889.36 |
| WMD TOTAL 2 | 0.00 | 0.00 | 0.00 | 0.00 | 0.00 | 2,307.82 | 1,695,370.00 | 853.17 | 3,160.99 |
| DETROIT LAKES WMD BECKER | 0.00 | 0.00 | 0.00 | 0.00 | 4.33 | 12,395.63 | 1,744,020.56 | 2,012.14 | 14,412.10 |
| CLAY | 0.00 | 0.00 | 0.00 | 0.00 | 0.00 | 10,385.89 | 2,979,545.18 | 3,338.42 | 13,724.31 |
| MAHNOMEN | 0.00 | 0.00 | 0.00 | 0.00 | 0.00 | 5,399.55 | 864,568.90 | 4,947.00 | 10,346.55 |
| NORMAN | 0.00 | 0.00 | 0.00 | 0.00 | 0.00 | 1,120.00 | 400,000.00 | 0.00 | 1,120.00 |
| POLK | 0.00 | 0.00 | 0.00 | 0.00 | 0.00 | 12,441.29 | 2,540,752.06 | 1,743.80 | 14,185.09 |
| WMD TOTAL 5 | 0.00 | 0.00 | 0.00 | 0.00 | 4.33 | 41,742.16 | 10,506,877.90 | 12,041.36 | 53,787.65 |

TABLE 6 — WATERFOWL PRODUCTION AREA COUNTIES

| STATE AND UNIT | RESERVED FROM PUBLIC DOMAIN | | ACQUIRED BY OTHER FEDERAL AGENCY | | DEVISE OR GIFT | PURCHASED | | AGREEMENT EASEMENT OR LEASE | TOTAL ACRES |
|---|---|---|---|---|---|---|---|---|---|
| | SOLE OR PRIMARY | SECONDARY | SOLE OR PRIMARY | SECONDARY | | ACRES | COST ($) | | |
| **MINNESOTA** | | | | | | | | | |
| FERGUS FALLS WMD DOUGLAS | 0.00 | 0.00 | 0.00 | 0.00 | 5.00 | 9,604.07 | 1,916,515.20 | 6,185.41 | 15,789.48 |
| GRANT | 0.00 | 0.00 | 0.00 | 0.00 | 0.00 | 10,050.63 | 7,669,506.17 | 3,624.56 | 13,675.39 |
| OTTER TAIL | 0.00 | 0.00 | 0.00 | 0.00 | 52.19 | 20,804.48 | 6,879,052.26 | 14,085.43 | 34,942.10 |
| WILKIN | 0.00 | 0.00 | 0.00 | 0.00 | 0.00 | 2,443.28 | 900,064.35 | 309.00 | 2,742.28 |
| WMD TOTAL 4 | 0.00 | 0.00 | 0.00 | 0.00 | 52.19 | 42,942.64 | 12,365,139.93 | 24,154.40 | 67,149.23 |
| LITCHFIELD WMD AITKIN | 0.00 | 0.00 | 0.00 | 0.00 | 0.00 | 69.86 | 28,000.00 | 0.00 | 69.86 |
| KANDIYOHI | 0.00 | 0.00 | 0.00 | 0.00 | 0.00 | 13,562.86 | 5,611,562.68 | 4,264.85 | 17,827.68 |
| MCLEOD | 0.00 | 0.00 | 0.00 | 0.00 | 0.00 | 951.66 | 1,136,793.00 | 739.27 | 1,690.93 |
| MEEKER | 0.00 | 0.00 | 0.00 | 0.00 | 0.00 | 4,708.99 | 4,972,224.10 | 2,258.14 | 6,967.13 |
| RENVILLE | 0.00 | 0.00 | 0.00 | 0.00 | 0.00 | 1,455.03 | 1,840,340.00 | 0.00 | 1,455.03 |
| STEARNS | 0.00 | 0.00 | 0.00 | 0.00 | 0.00 | 9,065.71 | 2,710,733.57 | 1,779.71 | 10,845.42 |
| TODD | 0.00 | 0.00 | 0.00 | 0.00 | 0.00 | 802.85 | 385,672.20 | 16.00 | 818.85 |
| WRIGHT | 0.00 | 0.00 | 0.00 | 0.00 | 0.00 | 2,500.92 | 2,527,520.90 | 437.50 | 2,938.42 |
| WMD TOTAL 8 | 0.00 | 0.00 | 0.00 | 0.00 | 0.00 | 33,119.87 | 18,213,546.75 | 9,491.43 | 42,611.32 |
| MINNESOTA VALLEY WMD BLUE EARTH | 0.00 | 0.00 | 0.00 | 0.00 | 0.00 | 1,207.09 | 1,776,450.00 | 78.70 | 1,285.79 |
| CARVER | 0.00 | 0.00 | 0.00 | 0.00 | 0.00 | 219.00 | 321,000.00 | 47.57 | 266.57 |
| DAKOTA | 0.00 | 0.00 | 0.00 | 0.00 | 0.00 | 73.90 | 201,747.00 | .05 | 73.95 |
| LESUEUR | 0.00 | 0.00 | 0.00 | 0.00 | 0.00 | 413.79 | 549,254.50 | 209.15 | 622.94 |
| RICE | 0.00 | 0.00 | 0.00 | 0.00 | 0.00 | 412.10 | 631,999.35 | 473.74 | 885.84 |
| SCOTT | 0.00 | 0.00 | 0.00 | 0.00 | 0.00 | 40.00 | 129,200.00 | 164.21 | 204.21 |
| SIBLEY | 0.00 | 0.00 | 0.00 | 0.00 | 43.48 | 862.40 | 1,079,789.73 | 253.25 | 1,159.13 |
| STEELE | 0.00 | 0.00 | 0.00 | 0.00 | 0.00 | 630.11 | 655,744.00 | 0.00 | 630.11 |
| WASECA | 0.00 | 0.00 | 0.00 | 0.00 | 0.00 | 348.78 | 408,000.00 | 0.00 | 348.78 |
| WMD TOTAL 9 | 0.00 | 0.00 | 0.00 | 0.00 | 43.48 | 4,107.17 | 5,650,684.58 | 1,226.67 | 5,377.52 |
| MORRIS WMD BIG STONE | 0.00 | 0.00 | 0.00 | 0.00 | 0.00 | 11,508.96 | 2,294,645.85 | 8,207.43 | 19,716.39 |
| CHIPPEWA | 0.00 | 0.00 | 0.00 | 0.00 | 0.00 | 744.10 | 177,050.00 | 57.00 | 801.10 |
| LAC QUI PARLE | 0.00 | 0.00 | 0.00 | 0.00 | 0.00 | 4,007.42 | 986,028.73 | 1,657.07 | 5,664.49 |
| POPE | 0.00 | 0.00 | 0.00 | 0.00 | 80.00 | 12,884.11 | 2,473,445.07 | 8,920.08 | 21,884.19 |
| STEVENS | 0.00 | 0.00 | 0.00 | 0.00 | 0.00 | 9,567.88 | 3,479,202.84 | 1,206.00 | 10,773.88 |
| SWIFT | 0.00 | 0.00 | 0.00 | 0.00 | 0.00 | 7,601.12 | 1,804,950.17 | 1,865.87 | 9,466.99 |
| TRAVERSE | 0.00 | 0.00 | 0.00 | 0.00 | 0.00 | 4,105.55 | 1,469,588.63 | 1,443.61 | 5,549.16 |
| YELLOW MEDICINE | 0.00 | 0.00 | 0.00 | 0.00 | 0.00 | 959.58 | 709,483.50 | 235.09 | 1,194.67 |
| WMD TOTAL 8 | 0.00 | 0.00 | 0.00 | 0.00 | 80.00 | 50,898.72 | 15,338,574.57 | 23,592.15 | 74,570.87 |
| TAMARAC WMD CASS | 0.00 | 0.00 | 0.00 | 0.00 | 0.00 | 0.00 | 0.00 | 43.00 | 43.00 |
| CLEARWATER | 0.00 | 0.00 | 0.00 | 0.00 | 0.00 | 0.00 | 0.00 | 864.00 | 864.00 |
| WMD TOTAL 2 | 0.00 | 0.00 | 0.00 | 0.00 | 0.00 | 0.00 | 0.00 | 907.00 | 907.00 |
| WINDOM WMD COTTONWOOD | 0.00 | 0.00 | 0.00 | 0.00 | 0.00 | 2,945.14 | 1,580,033.85 | 192.85 | 3,137.99 |
| FARIBAULT | 0.00 | 0.00 | 0.00 | 0.00 | 0.00 | 830.06 | 800,991.80 | 129.37 | 959.43 |
| FREEBORN | 0.00 | 0.00 | 0.00 | 0.00 | 154.95 | 1,651.99 | 1,853,367.25 | 143.26 | 1,910.18 |
| JACKSON | 0.00 | 0.00 | 0.00 | 0.00 | 0.00 | 4,169.56 | 2,599,810.78 | 482.09 | 4,552.65 |
| MARTIN | 0.00 | 0.00 | 0.00 | 0.00 | 0.00 | 70.89 | 45,369.60 | 271.65 | 342.54 |
| MURRAY | 0.00 | 0.00 | 0.00 | 0.00 | 0.00 | 2,158.05 | 7,601,977.00 | 21.00 | 2,179.05 |
| NOBLES | 0.00 | 0.00 | 0.00 | 0.00 | 0.00 | 541.65 | 580,802.00 | 26.00 | 567.65 |
| ROCK | 0.00 | 0.00 | 0.00 | 0.00 | 0.00 | 0.00 | 0.00 | 11.00 | 11.00 |
| WATONWAN | 0.00 | 0.00 | 0.00 | 0.00 | 0.00 | 56.65 | 31,157.50 | 168.42 | 225.07 |
| WMD TOTAL 9 | 0.00 | 0.00 | 0.00 | 0.00 | 154.95 | 12,383.99 | 10,109,520.46 | 1,346.64 | 13,885.56 |

TABLE 4 - WATERFOWL PRODUCTION AREA COUNTIES

| STATE AND UNIT | RESERVED FROM PUBLIC DOMAIN | | ACQUIRED BY OTHER FEDERAL AGENCY | | DEVISE OR GIFT | PURCHASED | | AGREEMENT EASEMENT OR LEASE | TOTAL ACRES |
|---|---|---|---|---|---|---|---|---|---|
| | SOLE OR PRIMARY | SECONDARY | SOLE OR PRIMARY | SECONDARY | | ACRES | COST ($) | | |
| **MINNESOTA** | | | | | | | | | |
| WINDOM WMD | | | | | | | | | |
| STATE TOTAL 47 | 0.00 | 0.00 | 0.00 | 0.00 | 514.95 | 167,507.35 | 71,877,722.61 | 75,612.84 | 261,430.12 |
| **MONTANA** | | | | | | | | | |
| BENTON LAKE WMD | | | | | | | | | |
| CASCADE | 0.00 | 0.00 | 0.00 | 0.00 | 0.00 | 727.46 | 299,606.00 | 78.00 | 805.46 |
| CHOUTEAU | 0.00 | 0.00 | 0.00 | 0.00 | 0.00 | 2,136.13 | 588,543.00 | 501.00 | 2,637.13 |
| GLACIER | 0.00 | 0.00 | 0.00 | 0.00 | 0.00 | 94.20 | 17,698.00 | 9,978.33 | 10,072.53 |
| HILL | 0.00 | 0.00 | 0.00 | 0.00 | 378.95 | 0.00 | 0.00 | 918.00 | 1,296.95 |
| LEWIS AND CLARK | 0.00 | 0.00 | 0.00 | 0.00 | 0.00 | 0.00 | 0.00 | 1,845.50 | 1,845.50 |
| LIBERTY | 0.00 | 0.00 | 0.00 | 0.00 | 0.00 | 0.00 | 0.00 | 426.00 | 426.00 |
| PONDERA | 0.00 | 0.00 | 0.00 | 0.00 | 0.00 | 640.00 | 95,000.00 | 8,487.01 | 9,127.01 |
| POWELL | 0.00 | 0.00 | 0.00 | 0.00 | 1,612.07 | 2,644.60 | 588,854.00 | 22,808.41 | 27,065.08 |
| TETON | 0.00 | 0.00 | 0.00 | 0.00 | 0.00 | 1,486.05 | 178,264.00 | 5,100.46 | 6,586.51 |
| TOOLE | 0.00 | 0.00 | 0.00 | 0.00 | 0.00 | 4,610.48 | 1,003,964.00 | 12,166.37 | 16,776.85 |
| WMD TOTAL 10 | 0.00 | 0.00 | 0.00 | 0.00 | 2,181.00 | 17,156.97 | 3,156,098.00 | 62,111.08 | 76,631.00 |
| BOWDOIN WMD | | | | | | | | | |
| BLAINE | 0.00 | 0.00 | 0.00 | 0.00 | 0.00 | 2,425.26 | 167,340.00 | 2,972.20 | 5,407.46 |
| PHILLIPS | 0.00 | 0.00 | 0.00 | 0.00 | 51.00 | 6,877.83 | 1,571,863.00 | 24,218.55 | 31,147.38 |
| VALLEY | 0.00 | 0.00 | 0.00 | 0.00 | 0.00 | 0.00 | 0.00 | 201.00 | 201.00 |
| WMD TOTAL 3 | 0.00 | 0.00 | 0.00 | 0.00 | 51.00 | 9,313.09 | 1,589,203.00 | 27,391.75 | 36,755.84 |
| CHARLES M. RUSSELL WMD | | | | | | | | | |
| GOLDEN VALLEY | 0.00 | 0.00 | 0.00 | 0.00 | 0.00 | 760.27 | 76,427.00 | 160.00 | 920.27 |
| MUSSELSHELL | 0.00 | 0.00 | 0.00 | 0.00 | 0.00 | 532.45 | 144,001.00 | 160.00 | 692.45 |
| PETROLEUM | 0.00 | 0.00 | 0.00 | 0.00 | 0.00 | 40.00 | 23,800.00 | 0.00 | 40.00 |
| STILLWATER | 0.00 | 0.00 | 0.00 | 0.00 | 0.00 | 1,828.10 | 207,625.00 | .58 | 1,828.48 |
| YELLOWSTONE | 0.00 | 0.00 | 0.00 | 0.00 | 0.00 | 486.42 | 33,600.00 | 0.00 | 486.42 |
| WMD TOTAL 5 | 0.00 | 0.00 | 0.00 | 0.00 | 0.00 | 3,647.24 | 586,453.00 | 320.38 | 3,967.62 |
| NORTHEAST MONTANA WMD | | | | | | | | | |
| DANIELS | 0.00 | 0.00 | 0.00 | 0.00 | 7.85 | 1,080.58 | 97,889.00 | 1,011.32 | 2,099.75 |
| ROOSEVELT | 0.00 | 0.00 | 0.00 | 0.00 | 0.00 | 179.20 | 14,000.00 | 7,402.42 | 7,581.62 |
| SHERIDAN | 59.10 | 0.00 | 0.00 | 0.00 | 0.00 | 10,491.58 | 1,244,091.08 | 10,211.16 | 20,761.84 |
| WMD TOTAL 3 | 59.10 | 0.00 | 0.00 | 0.00 | 7.85 | 11,751.36 | 1,355,700.08 | 18,644.90 | 30,443.21 |
| NORTHWEST MONTANA WMD | | | | | | | | | |
| FLATHEAD | 0.00 | 0.00 | 0.00 | 0.00 | 507.92 | 4,410.31 | 2,746,518.00 | 0.00 | 5,218.23 |
| LAKE | 0.00 | 0.00 | 0.00 | 0.00 | 0.00 | 3,238.36 | 2,306,855.00 | 4,185.69 | 7,454.05 |
| WMD TOTAL 2 | 0.00 | 0.00 | 0.00 | 0.00 | 507.92 | 7,650.67 | 4,533,373.00 | 4,185.69 | 12,652.28 |
| STATE TOTAL 23 | 59.10 | 0.00 | 0.00 | 0.00 | 3,047.77 | 44,689.28 | 11,152,827.08 | 112,653.80 | 160,429.95 |
| **NEBRASKA** | | | | | | | | | |
| RAINWATER BASIN WMD | | | | | | | | | |
| ADAMS | 0.00 | 0.00 | 0.00 | 0.00 | 163.00 | 231.56 | 290,000.00 | 160.00 | 554.56 |
| CLAY | 0.00 | 0.00 | 1,052.19 | 0.00 | 0.00 | 5,308.14 | 2,648,258.86 | 4.25 | 6,364.58 |
| FILLMORE | 0.00 | 0.00 | 0.00 | 0.00 | 0.00 | 3,537.60 | 1,631,453.00 | 8.60 | 3,546.20 |
| FRANKLIN | 0.00 | 0.00 | 0.00 | 0.00 | 157.36 | 1,625.96 | 402,698.00 | 0.00 | 1,783.32 |
| GOSPER | 0.00 | 0.00 | 0.00 | 0.00 | 0.00 | 1,451.50 | 283,928.00 | 0.00 | 1,451.50 |
| HALL | 0.00 | 0.00 | 448.70 | 0.00 | 0.00 | 378.77 | 433,000.00 | 0.00 | 649.47 |
| HAMILTON | 0.00 | 0.00 | 160.00 | 0.00 | 70.00 | 880.00 | 1,271,250.00 | 4.00 | 1,126.00 |
| KEARNEY | 0.00 | 0.00 | 0.00 | 0.00 | 0.00 | 2,874.43 | 667,681.00 | 175.50 | 3,049.93 |
| PHELPS | 0.00 | 0.00 | 0.00 | 0.00 | 0.00 | 4,595.14 | 3,973,111.00 | 0.00 | 4,595.14 |
| POLK FSA | 0.00 | 0.00 | 0.00 | 0.00 | 0.00 | 0.00 | 0.00 | 140.78 | 140.78 |
| SALINE FSA | 0.00 | 0.00 | 61.55 | 0.00 | 0.00 | 0.00 | 0.00 | 43.00 | 104.55 |
| SEWARD | 0.00 | 0.00 | 0.00 | 0.00 | 0.00 | 471.14 | 309,010.45 | 0.00 | 471.14 |

31

| STATE AND UNIT | RESERVED FROM PUBLIC DOMAIN | | ACQUIRED BY OTHER FEDERAL AGENCY | | DEVISE OR GIFT | PURCHASED | | AGREEMENT EASEMENT OR LEASE | TOTAL ACRES |
|---|---|---|---|---|---|---|---|---|---|
| | SOLE OR PRIMARY | SECONDARY | SOLE OR PRIMARY | SECONDARY | | ACRES | COST ($) | | |
| **NEBRASKA** | | | | | | | | | |
| RAINWATER BASIN WMD | | | | | | | | | |
| YORK &ast; | 0.00 | 0.00 | 0.00 | 0.00 | 0.00 | 879.20 | 419,429.00 | 41.00 | 970.20 |
| WMD TOTAL 11 | 0.00 | 0.00 | 1,594.74 | 0.00 | 400.36 | 21,983.44 | 11,509,814.50 | 577.13 | 24,555.17 |
| STATE TOTAL 11 | 0.00 | 0.00 | 1,594.84 | 0.00 | 400.36 | 21,983.44 | 11,509,814.50 | 577.13 | 24,555.17 |
| **NORTH DAKOTA** | | | | | | | | | |
| ARROWWOOD WMD | | | | | | | | | |
| EDDY &ast; | 29.84 | 0.00 | 0.00 | 0.00 | 0.00 | 4,627.21 | 498,001.00 | 12,227.13 | 16,884.18 |
| FOSTER | 0.00 | 0.00 | 0.00 | 0.00 | 0.00 | 1,487.07 | 96,568.00 | 6,828.00 | 8,315.07 |
| WMD TOTAL 2 | 29.84 | 0.00 | 0.00 | 0.00 | 0.00 | 6,114.28 | 594,569.00 | 19,055.13 | 25,199.25 |
| AUDUBON WMD | | | | | | | | | |
| HETTINGER | 0.00 | 0.00 | 1,202.60 | 0.00 | 0.00 | 0.00 | 0.00 | 0.00 | 1,202.60 |
| MCLEAN | 515.00 | 0.00 | 7,600.91 | 0.00 | 199.00 | 4,048.29 | 420,234.00 | 29,199.59 | 41,542.79 |
| SHERIDAN &ast; | 229.20 | 0.00 | 3,990.65 | 0.00 | 334.49 | 7,663.03 | 468,427.00 | 42,989.84 | 55,207.21 |
| WARD | 120.00 | 0.00 | 0.00 | 0.00 | 0.00 | 5,848.09 | 489,211.00 | 44,980.31 | 50,968.40 |
| WMD TOTAL 4 | 864.20 | 0.00 | 12,794.16 | 0.00 | 495.49 | 17,559.41 | 1,477,872.00 | 117,169.74 | 148,921.00 |
| CHASE LAKE PRAIRIE PROJECT WMD | | | | | | | | | |
| STUTSMAN &ast; | 251.66 | 0.00 | 1,562.69 | 0.00 | 0.00 | 26,462.64 | 1,867,016.00 | 52,211.42 | 80,488.41 |
| WELLS &ast; | 0.00 | 0.00 | 2,935.40 | 0.00 | 0.00 | 7,661.43 | 1,188,559.00 | 13,666.40 | 24,263.23 |
| WMD TOTAL 7 | 251.66 | 0.00 | 4,498.09 | 0.00 | 0.00 | 34,124.07 | 7,655,575.00 | 65,877.82 | 104,751.64 |
| CROSBY WMD | | | | | | | | | |
| BURKE | 0.00 | 0.00 | 0.00 | 0.00 | 0.00 | 3,544.79 | 180,068.00 | 41,636.98 | 45,180.77 |
| DIVIDE | 1,344.83 | 0.00 | 0.00 | 0.00 | 0.00 | 9,444.62 | 474,790.00 | 34,647.09 | 45,336.54 |
| WILLIAMS &ast; | 520.00 | 0.00 | 0.00 | 0.00 | 0.00 | 4,163.17 | 278,057.00 | 8,384.00 | 13,067.17 |
| WMD TOTAL 3 | 1,864.83 | 0.00 | 0.00 | 0.00 | 0.00 | 17,151.96 | 932,915.00 | 84,867.67 | 103,584.48 |
| DEVILS LAKE WMD | | | | | | | | | |
| BENSON &ast; | 1,660.85 | 0.00 | 252.15 | 0.00 | 0.00 | 7,372.64 | 607,908.00 | 40,240.25 | 49,453.89 |
| CAVALIER &ast; | 0.00 | 0.00 | 775.71 | 0.00 | 0.00 | 10,129.12 | 1,354,471.00 | 13,910.00 | 24,762.83 |
| GRAND FORKS | 18.50 | 0.00 | 0.00 | 0.00 | 21.77 | 6,195.27 | 1,279,208.85 | 1,505.90 | 7,741.24 |
| NELSON &ast; | 0.00 | 0.00 | 340.91 | 0.00 | 0.00 | 3,203.23 | 174,341.00 | 38,319.70 | 41,863.84 |
| PEMBINA &ast; | 0.00 | 0.00 | 0.00 | 0.00 | 0.00 | 2,258.56 | 718,678.00 | 391.50 | 2,649.86 |
| RAMSEY &ast; | 132.10 | 0.00 | 1,119.45 | 0.00 | 0.00 | 8,225.00 | 1,144,252.00 | 29,116.00 | 38,592.53 |
| TOWNER &ast; | 14.50 | 0.00 | 829.39 | 0.00 | 801.05 | 3,847.02 | 494,146.00 | 25,089.00 | 30,569.96 |
| WALSH &ast; | 5.50 | 0.00 | 507.52 | 0.00 | 0.00 | 1,395.19 | 98,128.00 | 9,096.61 | 10,882.82 |
| WMD TOTAL 8 | 1,858.75 | 0.00 | 3,655.11 | 0.00 | 877.87 | 42,564.05 | 5,771,132.85 | 157,668.74 | 206,518.97 |
| J. CLARK SALYER WMD | | | | | | | | | |
| BOTTINEAU &ast; | 7.40 | 0.00 | 210.30 | 0.00 | 0.00 | 2,571.47 | 750,763.00 | 29,602.14 | 32,191.31 |
| MCHENRY &ast; | 995.59 | 0.00 | 0.00 | 0.00 | 0.00 | 4,868.80 | 374,404.50 | 43,184.64 | 49,067.03 |
| PIERCE &ast; | 3,276.00 | 0.00 | 1,054.56 | 0.00 | 1.20 | 8,417.74 | 922,115.00 | 41,620.61 | 54,370.11 |
| RENVILLE | 0.00 | 0.00 | 0.00 | 0.00 | 0.00 | 311.09 | 25,523.00 | 15,467.60 | 15,778.69 |
| ROLETTE | 105.96 | 0.00 | 0.00 | 0.00 | 0.00 | 5,694.08 | 758,347.00 | 20,510.01 | 26,310.00 |
| WMD TOTAL 5 | 4,382.95 | 0.00 | 1,264.86 | 0.00 | 1.20 | 21,663.13 | 2,280,152.50 | 150,385.00 | 177,717.14 |
| KULM WMD | | | | | | | | | |
| DICKEY &ast; | 506.75 | 0.00 | 0.00 | 0.00 | 0.00 | 9,755.40 | 1,150,814.00 | 37,972.34 | 48,014.49 |
| LA MOURE &ast; | 0.00 | 0.00 | 634.89 | 0.00 | 0.00 | 4,799.96 | 505,095.00 | 14,076.70 | 19,511.55 |
| LOGAN &ast; | 825.00 | 0.00 | 160.03 | 0.00 | 0.00 | 11,228.24 | 1,006,948.00 | 41,913.11 | 54,134.38 |
| MCINTOSH &ast; | 297.58 | 0.00 | 0.00 | 0.00 | 9.60 | 17,373.48 | 1,568,845.00 | 50,023.90 | 47,704.56 |
| WMD TOTAL 4 | 1,629.33 | 0.00 | 794.92 | 0.00 | 9.60 | 43,157.08 | 4,231,674.00 | 123,986.05 | 169,364.98 |
| LONG LAKE WMD | | | | | | | | | |
| BURLEIGH &ast; | 850.10 | 0.00 | 794.69 | 0.00 | 0.00 | 9,611.44 | 1,949,844.00 | 51,165.76 | 62,421.99 |
| EMMONS &ast; | 480.00 | 0.00 | 0.00 | 0.00 | 0.00 | 5,155.29 | 174,321.75 | 11,800.60 | 17,415.89 |
| KIDDER &ast; | 1,799.79 | 0.00 | 0.00 | 0.00 | 0.00 | 5,633.88 | 454,437.00 | 67,602.01 | 75,035.68 |

TABLE 4 - WATERFOWL PRODUCTION AREA COUNTIES

| STATE AND UNIT | | RESERVED FROM PUBLIC DOMAIN | | ACQUIRED BY OTHER FEDERAL AGENCY | | DEVISE OR GIFT | PURCHASED | | AGREEMENT EASEMENT OR LEASE | TOTAL ACRES |
|---|---|---|---|---|---|---|---|---|---|---|
| | | SOLE OR PRIMARY | SECONDARY | SOLE OR PRIMARY | SECONDARY | | ACRES | COST ($) | | |
| NORTH DAKOTA | | | | | | | | | | |
| LONG LAKE WMD | | | | | | | | | | |
| WMD TOTAL | 3 | 3,099.89 | 0.00 | 794.69 | 0.00 | 0.00 | 18,380.61 | 2,562,624.75 | 110,568.57 | 132,843.56 |
| LOSTWOOD WMD | | | | | | | | | | |
| MOUNTRAIL | * | 467.52 | 0.00 | 400.00 | 0.00 | 0.00 | 10,155.10 | 940,661.00 | 48,670.80 | 59,693.42 |
| WMD TOTAL | 1 | 467.52 | 0.00 | 400.00 | 0.00 | 0.00 | 10,155.10 | 940,661.00 | 48,670.80 | 59,693.42 |
| TEWAUKON WMD | | | | | | | | | | |
| RANSOM | | 0.00 | 0.00 | 0.00 | 0.00 | 0.00 | 4,315.02 | 617,357.00 | 73,805.46 | 78,120.50 |
| RICHLAND | | 0.00 | 0.00 | 0.00 | 0.00 | 0.00 | 5,992.25 | 938,052.00 | 6,051.40 | 12,043.65 |
| SARGENT | * | 0.00 | 0.00 | 405.71 | 0.00 | 0.00 | 3,537.46 | 305,439.00 | 71,005.06 | 74,948.25 |
| WMD TOTAL | 3 | 0.00 | 0.00 | 405.71 | 0.00 | 0.00 | 13,844.73 | 1,860,848.00 | 50,861.98 | 65,112.40 |
| VALLEY CITY WMD | | | | | | | | | | |
| BARNES | * | 1.26 | 0.00 | 338.63 | 0.00 | 15.61 | 6,661.68 | 998,087.00 | 18,999.70 | 26,016.88 |
| CASS | | 0.00 | 0.00 | 0.00 | 0.00 | 0.00 | 5,489.89 | 678,344.00 | 1,759.90 | 5,199.79 |
| GRIGGS | | 158.05 | 0.00 | 0.00 | 0.00 | 0.00 | 3,069.46 | 373,990.00 | 16,742.00 | 19,969.51 |
| STEELE | | 0.00 | 0.00 | 0.00 | 0.00 | 0.00 | 3,249.25 | 398,941.00 | 4,383.30 | 7,632.55 |
| TRAILL | | 0.00 | 0.00 | 0.00 | 0.00 | 0.00 | 719.25 | 75,109.00 | 254.00 | 953.25 |
| WMD TOTAL | 5 | 159.31 | 0.00 | 338.63 | 0.00 | 15.61 | 17,139.93 | 2,573,075.00 | 42,118.90 | 59,771.98 |
| STATE TOTAL | 40 | 14,089.78 | 0.00 | 24,924.17 | 0.00 | 1,547.73 | 241,891.97 | 25,381,999.10 | 971,250.18 | 7,258,478.82 |
| SOUTH DAKOTA | | | | | | | | | | |
| HURON WMD | | | | | | | | | | |
| BEADLE | * | 0.00 | 0.00 | 240.00 | 0.00 | 70.19 | 7,756.45 | 1,651,212.69 | 35,683.75 | 43,250.39 |
| BUFFALO | | 0.00 | 0.00 | 0.00 | 0.00 | 916.52 | 0.00 | 0.00 | 1,543.61 | 2,260.15 |
| HAND | * | 80.00 | 0.00 | 0.00 | 0.00 | 259.00 | 3,671.31 | 580,260.35 | 49,728.52 | 53,713.83 |
| HUGHES | | 0.00 | 0.00 | 0.00 | 0.00 | 0.00 | 456.99 | 62,800.00 | 744.50 | 1,200.49 |
| HYDE | * | 0.00 | 0.00 | 0.00 | 0.00 | 1,441.36 | 0.00 | 0.00 | 28,119.06 | 29,560.42 |
| JERAULD | * | 40.00 | 0.00 | 0.00 | 0.00 | 320.00 | 1,430.40 | 217,041.00 | 21,121.33 | 22,911.73 |
| SANBORN | * | 0.00 | 0.00 | 0.00 | 0.00 | 0.00 | 93.00 | 5,250.00 | 36,399.75 | 36,492.75 |
| SULLY | * | 0.00 | 0.00 | 0.00 | 0.00 | 0.00 | 266.48 | 5,993.00 | 5,809.51 | 6,075.99 |
| WMD TOTAL | 8 | 120.00 | 0.00 | 240.00 | 0.00 | 2,967.07 | 13,173.63 | 2,546,557.04 | 176,945.03 | 195,465.73 |
| LACREEK WMD | | | | | | | | | | |
| HAAKON FSA | ** * | 0.00 | 0.00 | 0.00 | 0.00 | 0.00 | 0.00 | 0.00 | 1,806.10 | 1,806.10 |
| JONES FSA | ** * | 0.00 | 0.00 | 0.00 | 0.00 | 0.00 | 0.00 | 0.00 | 232.00 | 232.00 |
| STANLEY FSA | ** * | 0.00 | 0.00 | 0.00 | 0.00 | 0.00 | 0.00 | 0.00 | 1,404.80 | 1,404.80 |
| WMD TOTAL | 0 | 0.00 | 0.00 | 0.00 | 0.00 | 0.00 | 0.00 | 0.00 | 3,442.90 | 3,442.90 |
| LAKE ANDES WMD | | | | | | | | | | |
| AURORA | * | 0.00 | 0.00 | 0.00 | 0.00 | 0.00 | 4,716.03 | 622,316.00 | 33,243.52 | 37,959.60 |
| BON HOMME | * | 0.00 | 0.00 | 0.00 | 0.00 | 0.00 | 1,174.17 | 525,624.90 | 752.73 | 1,426.90 |
| BRULE | | 0.00 | 0.00 | 0.00 | 0.00 | 0.00 | 1,074.13 | 89,404.00 | 18,520.69 | 19,594.82 |
| CHARLES MIX | * | 0.00 | 0.00 | 0.00 | 0.00 | 286.70 | 4,098.15 | 1,142,147.00 | 7,381.30 | 11,765.15 |
| CLAY | * | 0.00 | 0.00 | 0.00 | 0.00 | 0.00 | 40.00 | 4,000.00 | 59.50 | 99.50 |
| DAVISON | * | 0.00 | 0.00 | 0.00 | 0.00 | 0.00 | 229.92 | 34,540.00 | 354.10 | 584.02 |
| DOUGLAS | * | 0.00 | 0.00 | 0.00 | 0.00 | 449.73 | 3,852.05 | 647,697.00 | 3,450.61 | 7,752.39 |
| HANSON | * | 0.00 | 0.00 | 0.00 | 0.00 | 0.00 | 1,073.60 | 281,853.00 | 2,815.28 | 5,888.88 |
| HUTCHINSON | * | 0.00 | 0.00 | 0.00 | 0.00 | 0.00 | 789.51 | 227,846.26 | 1,185.50 | 1,975.01 |
| LINCOLN | | 0.00 | 0.00 | 0.00 | 0.00 | 0.00 | 177.22 | 59,925.00 | 300.50 | 477.72 |
| TRIPP FSA | ** * | 0.00 | 0.00 | 0.00 | 0.00 | 0.00 | 0.00 | 0.00 | 5.90 | 5.90 |
| TURNER | * | 0.00 | 0.00 | 0.00 | 0.00 | 0.00 | 850.09 | 530,066.90 | 479.90 | 1,329.99 |
| UNION | | 0.00 | 0.00 | 0.00 | 0.00 | 0.00 | 96.02 | 22,331.00 | 0.00 | 96.02 |
| YANKTON | | 0.00 | 0.00 | 0.00 | 0.00 | 0.00 | 794.63 | 178,562.00 | 546.90 | 641.53 |
| WMD TOTAL | 13 | 0.00 | 0.00 | 0.00 | 0.00 | 735.43 | 18,467.57 | 4,988,086.06 | 68,894.03 | 87,597.03 |

TABLE 4 - WATERFOWL PRODUCTION AREA COUNTIES

| STATE AND UNIT | RESERVED FROM PUBLIC DOMAIN | | ACQUIRED BY OTHER FEDERAL AGENCY | | DEVISE OR GIFT | PURCHASED | | AGREEMENT EASEMENT OR LEASE | TOTAL ACRES |
|---|---|---|---|---|---|---|---|---|---|
| | SOLE OR PRIMARY | SECONDARY | SOLE OR PRIMARY | SECONDARY | | ACRES | COST ($) | | |
| SOUTH DAKOTA | | | | | | | | | |
| MADISON WMD | | | | | | | | | |
| BROOKINGS * | 0.00 | 0.00 | 0.00 | 0.00 | 158.25 | 6,079.50 | 1,430,278.70 | 8,179.78 | 14,415.63 |
| DEUEL * | 0.00 | 0.00 | 0.00 | 0.00 | 0.00 | 3,186.37 | 459,099.00 | 23,929.03 | 27,115.40 |
| HAMLIN * | 0.00 | 0.00 | 0.00 | 0.00 | 0.00 | 3,400.89 | 954,563.00 | 6,519.14 | 9,720.03 |
| KINGSBURY * | 0.00 | 0.00 | 0.00 | 0.00 | 0.00 | 6,924.04 | 1,455,469.80 | 23,806.78 | 30,730.82 |
| LAKE * | 0.00 | 0.00 | 0.00 | 0.00 | 359.34 | 5,742.09 | 1,304,607.75 | 6,907.72 | 13,008.65 |
| MCCOOK * | 0.00 | 0.00 | 0.00 | 0.00 | 0.00 | 3,362.96 | 640,845.60 | 7,151.87 | 10,514.83 |
| MINER * | 40.00 | 0.00 | 0.00 | 0.00 | 0.00 | 1,537.04 | 151,040.00 | 19,583.92 | 21,130.96 |
| MINNEHAHA * | 0.00 | 0.00 | 0.00 | 0.00 | 0.00 | 4,499.63 | 1,100,286.00 | 1,650.96 | 6,150.59 |
| MOODY * | 0.00 | 0.00 | 0.00 | 0.00 | 277.22 | 2,903.78 | 927,478.85 | 2,387.69 | 5,568.69 |
| WMD TOTAL 9 | 40.00 | 0.00 | 0.00 | 0.00 | 794.81 | 37,642.80 | 8,846,929.70 | 99,866.99 | 138,333.80 |
| SAND LAKE WMD | | | | | | | | | |
| BROWN | 0.00 | 0.00 | 0.00 | 0.00 | 452.62 | 4,094.93 | 819,223.80 | 48,885.67 | 53,463.23 |
| CAMPBELL | 340.00 | 0.00 | 0.00 | 0.00 | 0.00 | 1,919.71 | 185,341.00 | 22,352.15 | 24,611.86 |
| CORSON FSA ** * | 0.00 | 0.00 | 0.00 | 0.00 | 0.00 | 0.00 | 0.00 | 1,105.90 | 1,105.90 |
| DEWEY FSA ** * | 0.00 | 0.00 | 0.00 | 0.00 | 0.00 | 0.00 | 0.00 | 956.80 | 956.80 |
| EDMUNDS * | 0.00 | 0.00 | 0.00 | 0.00 | 160.00 | 8,965.76 | 1,717,201.00 | 115,743.72 | 134,869.48 |
| FAULK * | 0.00 | 0.00 | 0.00 | 0.00 | 0.00 | 2,566.68 | 480,995.00 | 127,741.59 | 130,508.27 |
| MCPHERSON * | 160.45 | 0.00 | 0.00 | 0.00 | 1,381.23 | 19,414.42 | 5,599,600.80 | 139,205.86 | 160,161.96 |
| POTTER * | 0.00 | 0.00 | 0.00 | 0.00 | 0.00 | 952.63 | 71,179.00 | 23,673.83 | 24,526.46 |
| SPINK * | 520.00 | 0.00 | 0.00 | 0.00 | 200.00 | 2,226.43 | 588,680.00 | 75,752.00 | 78,698.43 |
| WALWORTH * | 335.71 | 0.00 | 0.00 | 0.00 | 0.00 | 1,524.54 | 191,600.00 | 17,948.71 | 19,808.96 |
| WMD TOTAL 8 | 1,256.16 | 0.00 | 0.00 | 0.00 | 2,229.85 | 41,665.50 | 7,294,220.60 | 573,366.03 | 568,211.34 |
| WAUBAY WMD | | | | | | | | | |
| CLARK * | 95.73 | 0.00 | 0.00 | 0.00 | 0.00 | 6,053.11 | 845,303.90 | 45,032.53 | 51,181.37 |
| CODINGTON * | 31.23 | 0.00 | 0.00 | 0.00 | 1,188.47 | 5,089.31 | 982,837.70 | 10,230.03 | 16,538.99 |
| DAY | 208.75 | 0.00 | 0.00 | 0.00 | 0.00 | 6,411.50 | 466,964.00 | 44,836.51 | 51,456.76 |
| GRANT | 0.00 | 0.00 | 0.00 | 0.00 | 0.00 | 5,362.99 | 1,005,000.00 | 15,921.94 | 21,284.93 |
| MARSHALL * | 16.89 | 0.00 | 0.00 | 0.00 | 204.95 | 10,484.77 | 1,351,929.00 | 56,097.91 | 66,804.56 |
| ROBERTS * | 0.00 | 0.00 | 0.00 | 0.00 | 0.00 | 5,052.73 | 625,710.80 | 50,803.48 | 55,856.21 |
| WMD TOTAL 6 | 352.60 | 0.00 | 0.00 | 0.00 | 1,393.37 | 38,414.44 | 5,775,747.40 | 222,942.40 | 263,102.80 |
| STATE TOTAL 44 | 1,768.76 | 0.00 | 340.00 | 0.00 | 8,154.58 | 149,053.53 | 28,411,419.79 | 1,094,956.76 | 1,254,153.60 |
| WISCONSIN | | | | | | | | | |
| LEOPOLD WMD | | | | | | | | | |
| ADAMS | 0.00 | 0.00 | 0.00 | 0.00 | 0.00 | 544.00 | 172,500.00 | 0.00 | 544.00 |
| COLUMBIA | 0.00 | 0.00 | 0.00 | 0.00 | 0.00 | 2,974.64 | 2,495,066.45 | 0.00 | 2,974.64 |
| DANE | 0.00 | 0.00 | 0.00 | 0.00 | 0.00 | 1,591.08 | 2,109,875.65 | 0.00 | 1,591.08 |
| DODGE | 0.00 | 0.00 | 0.00 | 0.00 | 0.00 | 689.01 | 880,652.33 | .43 | 689.44 |
| FOND DU LAC | 0.00 | 0.00 | 0.00 | 0.00 | 0.00 | 949.56 | 1,166,452.00 | 0.00 | 949.56 |
| JEFFERSON | 0.00 | 0.00 | 0.00 | 0.00 | 0.00 | 249.79 | 241,239.00 | 0.00 | 249.79 |
| MANITOWOC | 0.00 | 0.00 | 0.00 | 0.00 | 0.00 | 120.00 | 88,000.00 | 0.00 | 120.00 |
| MARQUETTE | 0.00 | 0.00 | 0.00 | 0.00 | 0.00 | 259.97 | 119,450.00 | 0.00 | 259.97 |
| OZAUKEE | 0.00 | 0.00 | 0.00 | 0.00 | 0.00 | 736.30 | 679,413.40 | 0.00 | 736.30 |
| ROCK | 0.00 | 0.00 | 0.00 | 0.00 | 0.00 | 349.32 | 302,358.71 | 0.00 | 349.32 |
| SHEBOYGAN | 0.00 | 0.00 | 0.00 | 0.00 | 0.00 | 729.91 | 1,658,658.94 | 0.00 | 729.91 |
| WAUSHARA | 0.00 | 0.00 | 0.00 | 0.00 | 0.00 | 232.30 | 343,000.00 | 0.00 | 232.30 |
| WINNEBAGO | 0.00 | 0.00 | 0.00 | 0.00 | 0.00 | 1,778.27 | 1,151,300.00 | 0.00 | 1,778.27 |
| WMD TOTAL 13 | 0.00 | 0.00 | 0.00 | 0.00 | 0.00 | 10,923.95 | 11,418,976.48 | .43 | 10,924.38 |
| ST. CROIX WMD | | | | | | | | | |
| DUNN | 0.00 | 0.00 | 0.00 | 0.00 | 0.00 | 471.96 | 698,200.00 | 0.00 | 471.96 |
| POLK | 0.00 | 0.00 | 0.00 | 0.00 | 0.00 | 1,045.07 | 509,094.00 | 0.00 | 1,045.07 |

TABLE 4 - WATERFOWL PRODUCTION AREA COUNTIES

| STATE AND UNIT | | RESERVED FROM PUBLIC DOMAIN | | ACQUIRED BY OTHER FEDERAL AGENCY | | DEVISE OR GIFT | PURCHASED | | AGREEMENT EASEMENT OR LEASE | TOTAL ACRES |
|---|---|---|---|---|---|---|---|---|---|---|
| | | SOLE OR PRIMARY | SECONDARY | SOLE OR PRIMARY | SECONDARY | | ACRES | COST ($) | | |
| WISCONSIN | | | | | | | | | | |
| ST CROIX WMD ST. CROIX | | 0.00 | 0.00 | 0.00 | 0.00 | 0.00 | 5,091.90 | 5,356,004.56 | 1.64 | 5,093.54 |
| WMD TOTAL | 5 | 0.00 | 0.00 | 0.00 | 0.00 | 0.00 | 6,758.95 | 6,561,296.56 | 1.64 | 6,760.59 |
| STATE TOTAL | 16 | 0.00 | 0.00 | 0.00 | 0.00 | 0.00 | 17,682.90 | 17,982,275.04 | 2.07 | 17,684.97 |
| GRAND TOTAL | 208 | 15,897.64 | 0.00 | 26,756.41 | 0.00 | 14,240.96 | 686,580.71 | 197,197,975.74 | 2,293,670.90 | 2,995,098.22 |

\* — COUNTY WHERE WPA PROGRAM CURRENTLY EXISTS AND NEW FSA INTERESTS ARE ACQUIRED.

\*\* — SUMMARY BY COUNTY OF ALL OTHER ACRES, BOTH FEE AND LESS THAN FEE, ACQUIRED FROM THE FSA, NOT REPORTED WITHIN AN EXISTING PROJECT. SUMMARY MAY CONTAIN ONE OR MORE OWNERSHIPS. FSA COUNTY SUMMARY ACRES ARE INCLUDED IN THE TOTAL ACRES FOR EACH STATE BUT ARE NOT SEPARATE UNITS IN THE WATERFOWL PRODUCTION AREA STATE TOTALS.

WMD — WETLANDS MANAGEMENT DISTRICT

FSA — FARM SERVICE AGENCY (FORMERLY FARMERS HOME ADMINISTRATION, DEPARTMENT OF AGRICULTURE)

TABLE 9 — COORDINATION AREAS

| STATE AND UNIT | RESERVED FROM PUBLIC DOMAIN | | ACQUIRED BY OTHER FEDERAL AGENCY | | DEVISE OR GIFT | PURCHASES | | AGREEMEN EASEMENT OR LEASE | TOTAL ACRES |
|---|---|---|---|---|---|---|---|---|---|
| | SOLE OR PRIMARY | SECONDARY | SOLE OR PRIMARY | SECONDARY | | ACRES | COST ($) | | |
| **ARIZONA** | | | | | | | | | |
| GILA RIVER | 6,896.14 | 0.00 | 0.00 | 0.00 | 0.00 | 0.00 | 0.00 | 0.00 | 6,896.14 |
| STATE TOTAL  1 | 6,896.14 | 0.00 | 0.00 | 0.00 | 0.00 | 0.00 | 0.00 | 0.00 | 6,896.14 |
| **CALIFORNIA** | | | | | | | | | |
| HONEY LAKE | 1,050.29 | 0.00 | 0.00 | 0.00 | 0.00 | 0.00 | 0.00 | 0.00 | 1,050.29 |
| TOPAZ LAKE | 200.00 | 0.00 | 0.00 | 0.00 | 0.00 | 0.00 | 0.00 | 0.00 | 200.00 |
| STATE TOTAL  2 | 1,250.29 | 0.00 | 0.00 | 0.00 | 0.00 | 0.00 | 0.00 | 0.00 | 1,250.29 |
| **COLORADO** | | | | | | | | | |
| HOT SULPHUR | 1,115.00 | 0.00 | 0.00 | 0.00 | 0.00 | 0.00 | 0.00 | 0.00 | 1,115.00 |
| MACK MESA | 37.53 | 0.00 | 0.00 | 0.00 | 0.00 | 0.00 | 0.00 | 0.00 | 37.53 |
| STATE TOTAL  2 | 1,152.53 | 0.00 | 0.00 | 0.00 | 0.00 | 0.00 | 0.00 | 0.00 | 1,152.53 |
| **IDAHO** | | | | | | | | | |
| C. J. STRIKE | 1,544.90 | 0.00 | 0.00 | 0.00 | 0.00 | 0.00 | 0.00 | 0.00 | 1,544.90 |
| CAREY LAKE | 520.00 | 0.00 | 0.00 | 0.00 | 0.00 | 0.00 | 0.00 | 0.00 | 520.00 |
| HAGERMAN | 0.00 | 0.00 | 0.00 | 0.00 | 0.00 | 219.78 | 13,070.00 | 0.00 | 219.78 |
| NORTH LAKE | 2,705.32 | 0.00 | 0.00 | 0.00 | 0.00 | 0.00 | 0.00 | 0.00 | 2,705.32 |
| SAND CREEK | 1,000.00 | 0.00 | 0.00 | 0.00 | 0.00 | 0.00 | 0.00 | 0.00 | 1,000.00 |
| STATE TOTAL  5 | 5,570.22 | 0.00 | 0.00 | 0.00 | 0.00 | 219.78 | 13,070.00 | 0.00 | 5,790.00 |
| **ILLINOIS** | | | | | | | | | |
| MISSISSIPPI RIVER | 0.00 | 0.00 | 0.00 | E 26,626.00 | 0.00 | 0.00 | 0.00 | 0.00 | 26,626.00 |
| STATE TOTAL  1 | 0.00 | 0.00 | 0.00 | 26,626.00 | 0.00 | 0.00 | 0.00 | 0.00 | 26,626.00 |
| **IOWA** | | | | | | | | | |
| GREEN ISLAND | 0.00 | 0.00 | 0.00 | E 2,571.00 | 0.00 | 82.00 | 410.00 | 0.00 | 2,653.00 |
| LAKE ODESSA | 0.00 | 0.00 | 0.00 | F 3,154.00 | 0.00 | 0.00 | 0.00 | 0.00 | 3,154.00 |
| PRINCETON | 0.00 | 0.00 | 0.00 | E 794.00 | 0.00 | 0.00 | 0.00 | 0.00 | 794.00 |
| STATE TOTAL  3 | 0.00 | 0.00 | 0.00 | 6,499.00 | 0.00 | 82.00 | 410.00 | 0.00 | 6,581.00 |
| **MINNESOTA** | | | | | | | | | |
| BELTRAMI | 0.00 | 0.00 | 51,651.58 | 0.00 | 0.00 | 0.00 | 0.00 | 0.00 | 51,651.58 |
| PIPESTONE | 0.00 | 0.00 | 117.72 | 0.00 | 0.00 | 0.00 | 0.00 | 0.00 | 117.72 |
| STATE TOTAL  2 | 0.00 | 0.00 | 51,769.10 | 0.00 | 0.00 | 0.00 | 0.00 | 0.00 | 51,769.10 |
| **MISSOURI** | | | | | | | | | |
| CLARKSVILLE | 0.00 | 0.00 | 0.00 | E 282.00 | 0.00 | 0.00 | 0.00 | 0.00 | 282.00 |
| ELSBERRY | 0.00 | 0.00 | 0.00 | E 1,486.00 | 0.00 | 0.00 | 0.00 | 0.00 | 1,486.00 |
| MISSISSIPPI RIVER | 0.00 | 0.00 | 0.00 | E 10,265.00 | 0.00 | 0.00 | 0.00 | 0.00 | 10,265.00 |
| WEST QUINCY | 0.00 | 0.00 | 0.00 | E 242.00 | 0.00 | 0.00 | 0.00 | 0.00 | 242.00 |
| STATE TOTAL  4 | 0.00 | 0.00 | 0.00 | 12,075.00 | 0.00 | 0.00 | 0.00 | 0.00 | 12,075.00 |
| **MONTANA** | | | | | | | | | |
| BULL MOUNTAIN | 1,599.52 | 0.00 | 0.00 | 0.00 | 0.00 | 0.00 | 0.00 | 0.00 | 1,599.52 |
| DODSON | 120.00 | 0.00 | 0.00 | 0.00 | 0.00 | 0.00 | 0.00 | 0.00 | 120.00 |
| FOX LAKE | 160.00 | 0.00 | 0.00 | 0.00 | 0.00 | 0.00 | 0.00 | 0.00 | 160.00 |
| FREEZEOUT LAKE | 434.80 | 0.00 | 0.00 | 0.00 | 0.00 | 0.00 | 0.00 | 0.00 | 434.80 |
| JUDITH RIVER | 234.49 | 0.00 | 0.00 | 0.00 | 0.00 | 0.00 | 0.00 | 0.00 | 234.49 |
| SUN RIVER | 4,144.63 | 0.00 | 0.00 | 0.00 | 0.00 | 0.00 | 0.00 | 0.00 | 4,144.63 |
| STATE TOTAL  6 | 6,693.44 | 0.00 | 0.00 | 0.00 | 0.00 | 0.00 | 0.00 | 0.00 | 6,693.44 |
| **NEVADA** | | | | | | | | | |
| STILLWATER | 0.00 | 0.00 | 0.00 | 0.00 | 0.00 | 0.00 | 0.00 | 63,544.00 | 63,544.00 |
| STATE TOTAL  1 | 0.00 | 0.00 | 0.00 | 0.00 | 0.00 | 0.00 | 0.00 | 63,544.00 | 63,544.00 |

TABLE 9 - COORDINATION AREAS

| STATE AND UNIT | RESERVED FROM PUBLIC DOMAIN | | ACQUIRED BY OTHER FEDERAL AGENCY | | DEVISE OR GIFT | PURCHASED | | AGREEMENT EASEMENT OR LEASE | TOTAL ACRES |
| --- | --- | --- | --- | --- | --- | --- | --- | --- | --- |
| | SOLE OR PRIMARY | SECONDARY | SOLE OR PRIMARY | SECONDARY | | ACRES | COST ($) | | |
| NEW YORK | | | | | | | | | |
| LIDO BEACH | 0.00 | 0.00 | 22.42 | 0.00 | 0.00 | 0.00 | 0.00 | 0.00 | 22.42 |
| STATE TOTAL 1 | 0.00 | 0.00 | 22.42 | 0.00 | 0.00 | 0.00 | 0.00 | 0.00 | 22.42 |
| NORTH DAKOTA | | | | | | | | | |
| LAKE WASHINGTON | 3.68 | 0.00 | 0.00 | 0.00 | 0.00 | 0.00 | 0.00 | 0.00 | 3.68 |
| STATE TOTAL 1 | 3.68 | 0.00 | 0.00 | 0.00 | 0.00 | 0.00 | 0.00 | 0.00 | 3.68 |
| OREGON | | | | | | | | | |
| GOVERNMENT ISLAND | 1.79 | 0.00 | 0.00 | 0.00 | 0.00 | 0.00 | 0.00 | 0.00 | 1.79 |
| OCHOCO RESERVOIR | 40.00 | 0.00 | 0.00 | 0.00 | 0.00 | 0.00 | 0.00 | 0.00 | 40.00 |
| SUMMER LAKE | 7,127.65 | 0.00 | 0.00 | 0.00 | 0.00 | 0.00 | 0.00 | 0.00 | 7,127.65 |
| STATE TOTAL 3 | 7,169.44 | 0.00 | 0.00 | 0.00 | 0.00 | 0.00 | 0.00 | 0.00 | 7,169.44 |
| UTAH | | | | | | | | | |
| DESERT LAKES | 880.00 | 0.00 | 1,741.23 | 0.00 | 0.00 | 0.00 | 0.00 | 0.00 | 2,621.23 |
| ROCK ISLAND | 1.74 | 0.00 | 0.00 | 0.00 | 0.00 | 0.00 | 0.00 | 0.00 | 1.74 |
| TOPAZ LAKE | 3,662.13 | 0.00 | 480.00 | 0.00 | 0.00 | 0.00 | 0.00 | 0.00 | 4,142.13 |
| STATE TOTAL 3 | 4,543.87 | 0.00 | 2,221.23 | 0.00 | 0.00 | 0.00 | 0.00 | 0.00 | 6,765.10 |
| WASHINGTON | | | | | | | | | |
| COLOCKUM | 4,957.23 | 0.00 | 0.00 | 0.00 | 0.00 | 0.00 | 0.00 | 0.00 | 4,957.23 |
| LENORE | 5,787.00 | 0.00 | 0.00 | 0.00 | 0.00 | 0.00 | 0.00 | 0.00 | 5,787.00 |
| NARROWSTONE | 16.25 | 0.00 | 0.00 | 0.00 | 0.00 | 0.00 | 0.00 | 0.00 | 16.25 |
| METHOW | 3,037.97 | 0.00 | 0.00 | 0.00 | 0.00 | 0.00 | 0.00 | 0.00 | 3,037.97 |
| PHALON LAKE | 9.70 | 0.00 | 0.00 | 0.00 | 0.00 | 0.00 | 0.00 | 0.00 | 9.70 |
| SHERMAN CREEK | 560.00 | 0.00 | 0.00 | 0.00 | 0.00 | 0.00 | 0.00 | 0.00 | 560.00 |
| STMLANEKIN | 2,833.83 | 0.00 | 0.00 | 0.00 | 0.00 | 0.00 | 0.00 | 0.00 | 2,833.83 |
| SUNNYSIDE | 320.00 | 0.00 | 0.00 | 0.00 | 0.00 | 0.00 | 0.00 | 0.00 | 320.00 |
| STATE TOTAL 8 | 17,521.98 | 0.00 | 0.00 | 0.00 | 0.00 | 0.00 | 0.00 | 0.00 | 17,521.98 |
| WISCONSIN | | | | | | | | | |
| NECEDAH | 33.18 | 0.00 | 55,260.72 | 0.00 | 0.00 | 579.35 | 0.00 | 0.00 | 55,873.25 |
| STATE TOTAL 1 | 33.18 | 0.00 | 55,260.72 | 0.00 | 0.00 | 579.35 | 0.00 | 0.00 | 55,873.25 |
| WYOMING | | | | | | | | | |
| EAST FORK | 3,432.04 | 0.00 | 0.00 | 0.00 | 0.00 | 0.00 | 0.00 | 0.00 | 3,432.04 |
| GREYS RIVER | 927.31 | 0.00 | 0.00 | 0.00 | 0.00 | 0.00 | 0.00 | 0.00 | 927.31 |
| OCEAN LAKE | 0.00 | 0.00 | 0.00 | R 10,539.14 | 0.00 | 0.00 | 0.00 | 0.00 | 10,539.14 |
| SHERIDAN | 160.00 | 0.00 | 0.00 | 0.00 | 0.00 | 0.00 | 0.00 | 0.00 | 160.00 |
| SYBILLE | 681.44 | 0.00 | 0.00 | 0.00 | 0.00 | 0.00 | 0.00 | 0.00 | 681.44 |
| TONGUE RIVER | 551.05 | 0.00 | 0.00 | 0.00 | 0.00 | 0.00 | 0.00 | 0.00 | 551.05 |
| STATE TOTAL 6 | 5,751.84 | 0.00 | 0.00 | 10,539.14 | 0.00 | 0.00 | 0.00 | 0.00 | 16,290.98 |
| GRAND TOTAL 30 | 56,586.61 | 0.00 | 159,273.47 | 55,739.14 | 0.00 | 681.13 | 13,480.00 | 63,544.00 | 515,624.59 |

C — CORPS OF ENGINEERS — DEPARTMENT OF THE ARMY
R — BUREAU OF RECLAMATION — DEPARTMENT OF THE INTERIOR

TABLE 6 - ADMINISTRATIVE SITES

| STATE AND UNIT | RESERVED FROM PUBLIC DOMAIN | | ACQUIRED BY OTHER FEDERAL AGENCY | | DEVISE OR GIFT | PURCHASED | | AGREEMENT EASEMENT OR LEASE | TOTAL ACRES |
|---|---|---|---|---|---|---|---|---|---|
| | SOLE OR PRIMARY | SECONDARY | SOLE OR PRIMARY | SECONDARY | | ACRES | COST ($) | | |
| **ALASKA** | | | | | | | | | |
| BETHEL | 5.08 | 0.00 | 0.00 | 0.00 | 0.00 | 7.08 | 63,600.00 | 0.00 | 7.16 |
| BETTLES | 0.00 | 0.00 | 0.00 | 0.00 | 0.00 | 0.00 | 0.00 | 1.74 | 1.74 |
| COLD BAY HANGAR | 0.00 | 0.00 | 0.00 | 0.00 | 0.00 | 0.00 | 0.00 | .59 | .59 |
| DILLINGHAM | 0.00 | 0.00 | 0.00 | 0.00 | 0.00 | 13.73 | 499,900.00 | 0.00 | 13.73 |
| FAIRBANK | 0.00 | 0.00 | 0.00 | 0.00 | 0.00 | 0.00 | 0.00 | .17 | .17 |
| FAIRBANKS HANGAR | 0.00 | 0.00 | 0.00 | 0.00 | 0.00 | 0.00 | 0.00 | 2.04 | 2.04 |
| FAIRBANKS OFFICE WILDLIFE | 0.00 | 0.00 | 1.89 | 0.00 | 0.00 | .26 | 7,024.05 | 0.00 | 2.15 |
| FAIRBANKS WAREHOUSE | .64 | 0.00 | 0.00 | 0.00 | 0.00 | 0.00 | 0.00 | 0.00 | .64 |
| FORT YUKON | .52 | 0.00 | 0.00 | 0.00 | 0.00 | 0.00 | 0.00 | .19 | .71 |
| GALENA | .44 | 0.00 | 0.00 | 0.00 | 0.00 | 2.99 | 50,100.00 | 0.00 | 3.43 |
| HOMER | 0.00 | 0.00 | 0.00 | 0.00 | .75 | 57.80 | 1,009,000.00 | 0.00 | 58.55 |
| JUNEAU DOCK | 0.00 | 0.00 | 0.00 | 0.00 | 0.00 | 0.00 | 0.00 | .67 | .67 |
| JUNEAU HANGAR | 0.00 | 0.00 | 0.00 | 0.00 | 0.00 | 0.00 | 0.00 | 1.06 | 1.06 |
| KAKTOVIK | 0.00 | 0.00 | 0.00 | 0.00 | 0.00 | 0.00 | 0.00 | .46 | .46 |
| KENAI HANGAR | 0.00 | 0.00 | 0.00 | 0.00 | 0.00 | 0.00 | 0.00 | .91 | .91 |
| KETCHIKAN | 0.00 | 0.00 | 0.00 | 0.00 | 0.00 | 0.00 | 0.00 | .51 | .51 |
| KING SALMON | 6.29 | 0.00 | 0.00 | 0.00 | 0.00 | 5.42 | 64,000.00 | 0.00 | 11.71 |
| KODIAK | 2.04 | 0.00 | 0.00 | 0.00 | 0.00 | 0.00 | 0.00 | 0.00 | 2.04 |
| KODIAK FLOAT PLANE | 0.00 | 0.00 | 0.00 | 0.00 | 0.00 | 0.00 | 0.00 | .06 | .06 |
| KODIAK OFFICE | 0.00 | 36.00 | 0.00 | 0.00 | 0.00 | 0.00 | 0.00 | 0.00 | 36.00 |
| KOTZEBUE | 0.00 | 0.00 | 0.00 | 0.00 | 0.00 | .50 | 209,500.00 | 0.00 | .50 |
| KUSTATAN RIVER | 0.00 | 0.00 | 0.00 | 0.00 | 0.00 | 0.00 | 0.00 | 7.00 | 7.00 |
| LAKE HOOD SEAPLANE BASE | 14.90 | 0.00 | 0.00 | 0.00 | 0.00 | 0.00 | 0.00 | 2.26 | 17.16 |
| MCGRATH | 0.00 | 0.00 | 0.00 | 0.00 | 0.00 | 2.44 | 51,000.00 | 0.00 | 2.44 |
| MOSES LAKE | 0.00 | 0.00 | 0.00 | 0.00 | 0.00 | 0.00 | 0.00 | .01 | .01 |
| MORTENSENS CREEK | 0.00 | 0.00 | 0.00 | 0.00 | 0.00 | 0.00 | 0.00 | 1.50 | 1.50 |
| PILOT POINT | 1.00 | 0.00 | 0.00 | 0.00 | 0.00 | 0.00 | 0.00 | 0.00 | 1.00 |
| SOLDOTNA AIRPORT | 0.00 | 0.00 | 0.00 | 0.00 | 0.00 | 0.00 | 0.00 | 3.92 | 3.92 |
| ST. GEORGE | 0.00 | 0.00 | 0.00 | 0.00 | 0.00 | 0.00 | 0.00 | 1.00 | 1.00 |
| ST. PAUL | 0.00 | 0.00 | 0.00 | 0.00 | 0.00 | 0.00 | 0.00 | 1.11 | 1.11 |
| TOK | 0.00 | 0.00 | 0.00 | 0.00 | 0.00 | 17.86 | 45,000.00 | 0.00 | 17.86 |
| WHITEFISH LAKE | 0.00 | 0.00 | 0.00 | 0.00 | 0.00 | 0.00 | 0.00 | .50 | .50 |
| STATE TOTAL 32 | 30.91 | 36.00 | 1.89 | 0.00 | .75 | 108.10 | 1,994,924.05 | 25.30 | 197.95 |
| **ARIZONA** | | | | | | | | | |
| CABEZA PRIETA | 10.00 | 0.00 | 0.00 | 0.00 | 0.00 | .44 | 25,500.00 | 0.00 | 10.44 |
| KOFA | 0.00 | 0.00 | 0.00 | 0.00 | 0.00 | 1.00 | 0.00 | 0.00 | 1.00 |
| STATE TOTAL 2 | 10.00 | 0.00 | 0.00 | 0.00 | 0.00 | 1.44 | 25,500.00 | 0.00 | 11.44 |
| **COLORADO** | | | | | | | | | |
| NAT'L BLACK-FOOTED FERRET | 0.00 | 0.00 | 0.00 | 0.00 | 0.00 | 40.05 | 17,000.00 | 0.00 | 40.05 |
| STATE TOTAL 1 | 0.00 | 0.00 | 0.00 | 0.00 | 0.00 | 40.05 | 17,000.00 | 0.00 | 40.05 |
| **HAWAII** | | | | | | | | | |
| HAWAII | 0.00 | 0.00 | .23 | 0.00 | 0.00 | 0.00 | 0.00 | 0.00 | .23 |
| MAKENA BEACH | 0.00 | 0.00 | 0.00 | 0.00 | 0.00 | 0.00 | 0.00 | .50 | .50 |
| OLINDA | 0.00 | 0.00 | 4.20 | 0.00 | 0.00 | 0.00 | 0.00 | 0.00 | 4.20 |
| STATE TOTAL 3 | 0.00 | 0.00 | 4.43 | 0.00 | 0.00 | 0.00 | 0.00 | .50 | 4.93 |
| **IOWA** | | | | | | | | | |
| MCGREGOR | 0.00 | 0.00 | 0.00 | 0.00 | 0.00 | 4.33 | 155,000.00 | 0.00 | 4.33 |
| STATE TOTAL 1 | 0.00 | 0.00 | 0.00 | 0.00 | 0.00 | 4.33 | 155,000.00 | 0.00 | 4.33 |
| **KANSAS** | | | | | | | | | |
| GREAT PLAINS NATURE CTR | 0.00 | 0.00 | 0.00 | 0.00 | 0.00 | 8.33 | 450,000.00 | 6.22 | 14.55 |

TABLE 6 - ADMINISTRATIVE SITES

| STATE AND UNIT | RESERVED FROM PUBLIC DOMAIN | | ACQUIRED BY OTHER FEDERAL AGENCY | | DEVISE OR GIFT | PURCHASED | | AGREEMENT EASEMENT OR LEASE | TOTAL ACRES |
|---|---|---|---|---|---|---|---|---|---|
| | SOLE OR PRIMARY | SECONDARY | SOLE OR PRIMARY | SECONDARY | | ACRES | COST ($) | | |
| KANSAS | | | | | | | | | |
| STATE TOTAL 1 | 0.00 | 0.00 | 0.00 | 0.00 | 0.00 | 8.33 | 400,000.00 | 6.22 | 14.55 |
| MICHIGAN LAMPREY EEL | 0.00 | 0.00 | 0.00 | 0.00 | 0.00 | 0.00 | 0.00 | 1.00 | 1.00 |
| STATE TOTAL 1 | 0.00 | 0.00 | 0.00 | 0.00 | 0.00 | 0.00 | 0.00 | 1.00 | 1.00 |
| NEW MEXICO SAN ANDRES | 0.00 | 0.00 | 0.00 | 0.00 | 0.00 | 2.16 | 14,000.00 | 0.00 | 2.16 |
| STATE TOTAL 1 | 0.00 | 0.00 | 0.00 | 0.00 | 0.00 | 2.16 | 14,000.00 | 0.00 | 2.16 |
| OREGON CLARK R. BAVIN (A) | 0.00 | 0.00 | 0.00 | 0.00 | 0.00 | 0.00 | 0.00 | 4.02 | 4.02 |
| KLAMATH | 10.04 | 0.00 | 0.00 | 0.00 | 0.00 | 0.00 | 0.00 | 0.00 | 10.04 |
| LAKEVIEW | 0.00 | 0.00 | .25 | 0.00 | 0.00 | 0.00 | 0.00 | 0.00 | .25 |
| STATE TOTAL 3 | 10.04 | 0.00 | .25 | 0.00 | 0.00 | 0.00 | 0.00 | 4.02 | 14.31 |
| WASHINGTON MOSES LAKE | 0.00 | 0.00 | .88 | 0.00 | 0.00 | 0.00 | 0.00 | 0.00 | .88 |
| STATE TOTAL 1 | 0.00 | 0.00 | .88 | 0.00 | 0.00 | 0.00 | 0.00 | 0.00 | .88 |
| WEST VIRGINIA NCTC/TRAINING CENTER | 0.00 | 0.00 | 0.00 | 0.00 | 0.00 | 865.74 | 7,949,045.00 | 0.00 | 865.74 |
| STATE TOTAL 1 | 0.00 | 0.00 | 0.00 | 0.00 | 0.00 | 865.74 | 7,949,045.00 | 0.00 | 865.74 |
| GRAND TOTAL 47 | 50.95 | 36.00 | 7.40 | 0.00 | .75 | 1,025.15 | 10,570,269.05 | 57.04 | 1,157.29 |

(A) - FISH AND WILDLIFE FORENSICS LAB

CG - COAST GUARD, DEPARTMENT OF HOMELAND SECURITY

* - NOT COUNTED

TABLE 7 — NATIONAL FISH HATCHERIES

| STATE AND UNIT | RESERVED FROM PUBLIC DOMAIN | | ACQUIRED BY OTHER FEDERAL AGENCY | | DEVISE OR GIFT | PURCHASED | | AGREEMENT EASEMENT OR LEASE | TOTAL ACRES |
|---|---|---|---|---|---|---|---|---|---|
| | SOLE OR PRIMARY | SECONDARY | SOLE OR PRIMARY | SECONDARY | | ACRES | COST ($) | | |
| ARIZONA | | | | | | | | | |
| ALCHESAY | 0.00 | 0.00 | 0.00 | 0.00 | 0.00 | 0.00 | 0.00 | 20.88 | 20.83 |
| WILLIAMS CREEK | 0.00 | 0.00 | 0.00 | 0.00 | 0.00 | 0.00 | 0.00 | 91.89 | 91.89 |
| WILLOW BEACH | 0.00 | R 47.81 | 0.00 | 0.00 | 0.00 | 0.00 | 0.00 | 0.00 | 47.81 |
| STATE TOTAL 3 | 0.00 | 47.81 | 0.00 | 0.00 | 0.00 | 0.00 | 0.00 | 112.72 | 160.53 |
| ARKANSAS | | | | | | | | | |
| GREERS FERRY | 0.00 | 0.00 | 0.00 | E 31.97 | 0.00 | 0.00 | 0.00 | 0.00 | 31.97 |
| MAMMOTH SPRING | 0.00 | 0.00 | 0.00 | 0.00 | 0.00 | 36.84 | 55,925.00 | 0.00 | 36.84 |
| NORFORK | 0.00 | 0.00 | 0.00 | E 46.00 | 0.00 | 0.00 | 0.00 | 0.00 | 46.00 |
| STATE TOTAL 3 | 0.00 | 0.00 | 0.00 | 77.97 | 0.00 | 36.84 | 55,925.00 | 0.00 | 114.81 |
| CALIFORNIA | | | | | | | | | |
| COLEMAN | 0.00 | 0.00 | 55.28 | 0.00 | 0.00 | 22.52 | 153,221.00 | 62.97 | 140.77 |
| LIVINGSTON STONE | 0.00 | 0.00 | 0.00 | 0.00 | 0.00 | 0.00 | 0.00 | .04 | .04 |
| TEHAMA-COLUSA (2) * | 0.00 | 0.00 | 0.00 | R 350.00 | 0.00 | 0.00 | 0.00 | 0.00 | 350.00 |
| STATE TOTAL 2 | 0.00 | 0.00 | 55.28 | 350.00 | 0.00 | 22.52 | 153,221.00 | 65.01 | 490.81 |
| COLORADO | | | | | | | | | |
| HOTCHKISS | 10.00 | 0.00 | 129.17 | 0.00 | 0.00 | 0.00 | 0.00 | 2.54 | 141.71 |
| LEADVILLE | 2,966.54 | 0.00 | 0.00 | 0.00 | 0.00 | 98.79 | 14,400.00 | .75 | 3,065.88 |
| STATE TOTAL 2 | 2,976.54 | 0.00 | 129.17 | 0.00 | 0.00 | 98.79 | 14,400.00 | 3.29 | 3,307.59 |
| FLORIDA | | | | | | | | | |
| WELAKA | 0.00 | 0.00 | 385.04 | 0.00 | 0.00 | 0.00 | 0.00 | 0.00 | 385.04 |
| STATE TOTAL 1 | 0.00 | 0.00 | 385.04 | 0.00 | 0.00 | 0.00 | 0.00 | 0.00 | 385.04 |
| GEORGIA | | | | | | | | | |
| BO GINN (A) * | 0.00 | 0.00 | 0.00 | 0.00 | 106.89 | 20.12 | 10.00 | 0.00 | 127.01 |
| CHATTAHOOCHEE FOREST | 0.00 | 0.00 | 0.00 | F 44.80 | 0.00 | 0.00 | 0.00 | 0.00 | 44.80 |
| WARM SPRINGS (B) | 0.00 | 0.00 | 0.00 | 0.00 | 18.97 | 57.24 | 24,916.00 | 0.00 | 56.21 |
| STATE TOTAL 3 | 0.00 | 0.00 | 0.00 | 44.80 | 125.86 | 77.36 | 24,926.00 | 0.00 | 228.02 |
| IDAHO | | | | | | | | | |
| CLEARWATER (A) * | 0.00 | 0.00 | 17.62 | 0.00 | 0.00 | 0.00 | 0.00 | 1.33 | 18.95 |
| DWORSHAK | 0.00 | 0.00 | 0.00 | 0.00 | 0.00 | 0.00 | 0.00 | 25.54 | 25.54 |
| EAGLE FISH (B) * | 0.00 | 0.00 | 1.21 | 0.00 | 0.00 | 0.00 | 0.00 | .18 | 1.39 |
| HAGERMAN | 0.00 | 0.00 | 0.00 | 0.00 | 0.00 | 78.79 | 4,566.22 | 0.00 | 78.79 |
| KOOSKIA | 125.20 | 0.00 | 0.00 | 0.00 | 0.00 | 3.25 | 1.00 | 8.99 | 137.44 |
| MAGIC VALLEY (A) * | 0.00 | 0.00 | 25.46 | 0.00 | 0.00 | 0.00 | 0.00 | 16.98 | 42.44 |
| MCCALL (A) * | 0.00 | 0.00 | 10.91 | 0.00 | 0.00 | 0.00 | 0.00 | 19.05 | 29.96 |
| SAWTOOTH (A) * | 0.00 | 0.00 | 71.66 | 0.00 | 0.00 | 0.00 | 0.00 | 11.68 | 83.29 |
| STATE TOTAL 5 | 125.20 | 0.00 | 126.86 | 0.00 | 0.00 | 82.04 | 4,567.22 | 83.70 | 415.80 |
| KENTUCKY | | | | | | | | | |
| WOLF CREEK | 0.00 | 0.00 | 0.00 | E 20.47 | 0.00 | 0.00 | 0.00 | 0.00 | 20.47 |
| STATE TOTAL 1 | 0.00 | 0.00 | 0.00 | 20.47 | 0.00 | 0.00 | 0.00 | 0.00 | 20.47 |
| LOUISIANA | | | | | | | | | |
| NATCHITOCHES | 0.00 | 0.00 | 0.00 | 0.00 | 0.00 | 96.99 | 3,954.95 | 0.00 | 96.99 |
| STATE TOTAL 1 | 0.00 | 0.00 | 0.00 | 0.00 | 0.00 | 96.99 | 3,954.95 | 0.00 | 96.99 |

TABLE 7 - NATIONAL FISH HATCHERIES

| STATE AND UNIT | RESERVED FROM PUBLIC DOMAIN | | ACQUIRED BY OTHER FEDERAL AGENCY | | DEVISE OR GIFT | PURCHASED | | AGREEMENT EASEMENT OR LEASE | TOTAL ACRES |
|---|---|---|---|---|---|---|---|---|---|
| | SOLE OR PRIMARY | SECONDARY | SOLE OR PRIMARY | SECONDARY | | ACRES | COST ($) | | |
| **MAINE** | | | | | | | | | |
| CRAIG BROOK | 0.00 | 0.00 | 0.00 | 0.00 | 0.00 | 134.65 | 7,000.00 | 0.00 | 134.65 |
| GREEN LAKE | 0.00 | 0.00 | 0.00 | 0.00 | 0.00 | 129.86 | 32,000.00 | 1.00 | 129.86 |
| STATE TOTAL 2 | 0.00 | 0.00 | 0.00 | 0.00 | 0.00 | 264.51 | 54,000.00 | 1.00 | 264.51 |
| **MASSACHUSETTS** | | | | | | | | | |
| BERKSHIRE (A) * | 0.00 | 0.00 | 0.00 | 0.00 | 136.90 | 0.00 | 7,500.00 | 0.00 | 136.90 |
| NORTH ATTLEBORO | 0.00 | 0.00 | 0.00 | 0.00 | 228.48 | .06 | 1,500.00 | 0.00 | 228.54 |
| RICHARD CRONIN | 0.00 | 0.00 | 0.00 | 0.00 | 59.69 | 0.00 | 0.00 | 0.00 | 59.69 |
| STATE TOTAL 3 | 0.00 | 0.00 | 0.00 | 0.00 | 425.07 | .06 | 4,000.00 | 0.00 | 425.13 |
| **MICHIGAN** | | | | | | | | | |
| OTTAWHA FOREST | 0.00 | 0.00 | 0.00 | 6.67 | 0.00 | 0.00 | 0.00 | 0.00 | 6.67 |
| JORDAN RIVER | 0.00 | 0.00 | 0.00 | 0.00 | 116.84 | 0.00 | 0.00 | 0.00 | 116.84 |
| PENDILLS CREEK | 0.00 | 0.00 | 0.00 | 1,648.65 | 0.00 | 84.83 | 4,000.00 | 0.00 | 1,731.46 |
| STATE TOTAL 3 | 0.00 | 0.00 | 0.00 | 1,653.32 | 116.84 | 84.83 | 4,000.00 | 0.00 | 1,854.97 |
| **MISSISSIPPI** | | | | | | | | | |
| MERIDIAN (A) * | 0.00 | 0.00 | 0.00 | 0.00 | 105.86 | 0.00 | 0.00 | 0.00 | 105.86 |
| PRIVATE JOHN ALLEN | 0.00 | 0.00 | 0.00 | 0.00 | 0.00 | 28.40 | 1,990.00 | 0.00 | 28.40 |
| STATE TOTAL 1 | 0.00 | 0.00 | 0.00 | 0.00 | 105.86 | 28.40 | 1,990.00 | 0.00 | 134.26 |
| **MISSOURI** | | | | | | | | | |
| NEOSHO | 0.00 | 0.00 | 0.00 | 0.00 | 0.00 | 261.33 | 46,027.97 | 11.50 | 272.83 |
| STATE TOTAL 1 | 0.00 | 0.00 | 0.00 | 0.00 | 0.00 | 261.33 | 46,027.97 | 11.50 | 272.83 |
| **MONTANA** | | | | | | | | | |
| BOZEMAN (F) * | 0.00 | 0.00 | 0.00 | 0.00 | 42.79 | 130.30 | 4,565.00 | .28 | 173.37 |
| CRESTON | 0.00 | 0.00 | 73.56 | 0.00 | 0.00 | 0.00 | 0.00 | 0.00 | 73.56 |
| ENNIS | 0.00 | 0.00 | 0.00 | 0.00 | 0.00 | 160.00 | 4,000.00 | 9.32 | 169.32 |
| STATE TOTAL 4 | 0.00 | 0.00 | 73.56 | 0.00 | 42.79 | 290.50 | 8,565.00 | 9.60 | 416.25 |
| **NEVADA** | | | | | | | | | |
| AMARGOSA PUPFISH (T) * | 0.00 | 159.28 | 0.00 | 0.00 | 0.00 | 0.00 | 0.00 | 0.00 | 159.28 |
| LAHONTAN | 0.00 | 0.00 | 0.00 | 0.00 | 0.00 | 24.84 | 12,200.00 | 11.06 | 35.90 |
| MARBLE BLUFF (O) * | 0.00 | 0.00 | 0.00 | 623.20 | 0.00 | 0.00 | 0.00 | 0.00 | 623.20 |
| STATE TOTAL 3 | 0.00 | 159.28 | 0.00 | 623.20 | 0.00 | 24.84 | 12,200.00 | 11.06 | 818.38 |
| **NEW HAMPSHIRE** | | | | | | | | | |
| MERRIMACK RIVER (O) * | 0.00 | 0.00 | 0.00 | 0.00 | 0.00 | 8.00 | 24,000.00 | 0.00 | 8.00 |
| NASHUA | 0.00 | 0.00 | 0.00 | 0.00 | 0.00 | 39.40 | 4,000.00 | 0.00 | 39.40 |
| STATE TOTAL 1 | 0.00 | 0.00 | 0.00 | 0.00 | 0.00 | 47.40 | 28,000.00 | 0.00 | 47.40 |
| **NEW MEXICO** | | | | | | | | | |
| DEXTER (G) | 0.00 | 0.00 | 0.00 | 0.00 | 0.00 | 640.93 | 3,266.90 | 0.00 | 640.93 |
| MORA (G) | 0.00 | 0.00 | 0.00 | 0.00 | 0.00 | 116.79 | 241,000.00 | 2.00 | 118.79 |
| STATE TOTAL 2 | 0.00 | 0.00 | 0.00 | 0.00 | 0.00 | 757.72 | 244,266.90 | 2.00 | 759.72 |
| **NORTH CAROLINA** | | | | | | | | | |
| EDENTON | 0.00 | 0.00 | 0.00 | 0.00 | 0.00 | 63.59 | 30,000.00 | 0.00 | 63.59 |
| MCKINNEY LAKE (A) * | 0.00 | 0.00 | 408.07 | 0.00 | 0.00 | 14.21 | 72,000.00 | 0.00 | 422.27 |
| STATE TOTAL 2 | 0.00 | 0.00 | 408.07 | 0.00 | 0.00 | 77.79 | 102,000.00 | 0.00 | 485.86 |

TABLE 7 - NATIONAL FISH HATCHERIES

| STATE AND UNIT | RESERVED FROM PUBLIC DOMAIN | | ACQUIRED BY OTHER FEDERAL AGENCY | | DEVISE OR GIFT | PURCHASED | | AGREEMENT EASEMENT OR LEASE | TOTAL ACRES |
|---|---|---|---|---|---|---|---|---|---|
| | SOLE OR PRIMARY | SECONDARY | SOLE OR PRIMARY | SECONDARY | | ACRES | COST ($) | | |
| **NORTH DAKOTA** | | | | | | | | | |
| BALDHILL DAM (D) * | 0.00 | 0.00 | 0.00 E | 57.10 | 0.00 | 0.00 | 0.00 | 0.00 | 57.10 |
| GARRISON DAM | 0.00 | 0.00 | 0.00 E | 186.40 | 0.00 | 0.00 | 0.00 | 0.00 | 186.40 |
| VALLEY CITY | 0.00 | 0.00 | 0.00 | 0.00 | 71.49 | 0.00 | 0.00 | .95 | 72.52 |
| STATE TOTAL 2 | 0.00 | 0.00 | 0.00 | 233.50 | 71.49 | 0.00 | 0.00 | .95 | 295.92 |
| **OKLAHOMA** | | | | | | | | | |
| TISHOMINGO | 0.00 | 0.00 | 0.00 | 0.00 | 0.00 | 230.95 | 99,137.00 | 3,428.55 | 3,659.50 |
| STATE TOTAL 1 | 0.00 | 0.00 | 0.00 | 0.00 | 0.00 | 230.95 | 99,137.00 | 3,428.55 | 3,659.50 |
| **OREGON** | | | | | | | | | |
| EAGLE CREEK | 40.00 | 560.00 | 0.00 | 0.00 | 0.00 | 176.37 | 17,000.00 | 1.03 | 727.40 |
| UMATILLA SATELLITES (A) * | 0.00 | 0.00 | 15.14 | 0.00 | 0.00 | 0.00 | 0.00 | 1.27 | 16.41 |
| LOOKINGGLASS (A) * | 0.00 | 0.00 | 13.49 | 0.00 | 0.00 | 0.00 | 0.00 | 0.00 | 13.49 |
| WARM SPRINGS | 0.00 | 0.00 | 0.00 | 0.00 | 0.00 | 0.00 | 0.00 | 84.79 | 84.79 |
| STATE TOTAL 2 | 40.00 | 560.00 | 31.63 | 0.00 | 0.00 | 176.37 | 17,000.00 | 87.09 | 845.09 |
| **PENNSYLVANIA** | | | | | | | | | |
| ALLEGHENY | 0.00 | 0.00 | 0.00 E | 45.04 | 0.00 | 0.00 | 0.00 | 0.00 | 45.04 |
| LAMAR (H) | 0.00 | 0.00 | 0.00 | 0.00 | 0.00 | 177.21 | 30,557.31 | 0.00 | 177.21 |
| STATE TOTAL 2 | 0.00 | 0.00 | 0.00 | 45.04 | 0.00 | 177.21 | 30,557.31 | 0.00 | 222.25 |
| **SOUTH CAROLINA** | | | | | | | | | |
| BEARS BLUFF | 0.00 | 0.00 | 50.40 | 0.00 | 0.00 | 0.00 | 0.00 | 0.00 | 50.40 |
| ORANGEBURG | 0.00 | 0.00 | 0.00 | 0.00 | 0.00 | 50.65 | 6,578.40 | 0.00 | 50.65 |
| ORANGEBURG COUNTY (O) * | 0.00 | 0.00 | 0.00 | 0.00 | 134.01 | 46.65 | 7,500.00 | 0.00 | 180.66 |
| STATE TOTAL 2 | 0.00 | 0.00 | 50.40 | 0.00 | 134.01 | 97.30 | 14,078.40 | 0.00 | 261.71 |
| **SOUTH DAKOTA** | | | | | | | | | |
| D. C. BOOTH (T) * | 0.00 | 0.00 | 0.00 | 0.00 | 0.00 | 10.67 | 4,100.00 | .12 | 10.79 |
| GAVINS POINT | 0.00 | 0.00 | 0.00 E | 581.00 | 0.00 | 0.00 | 0.00 | 0.00 | 581.00 |
| STATE TOTAL 1 | 0.00 | 0.00 | 0.00 | 581.00 | 0.00 | 10.67 | 4,100.00 | .12 | 591.79 |
| **TENNESSEE** | | | | | | | | | |
| DALE HOLLOW | 0.00 | 0.00 | 0.00 E | 58.51 | 0.00 | 0.00 | 0.00 | 0.00 | 58.51 |
| ERWIN | 0.00 | 0.00 | 0.00 | 0.00 | 0.00 | 52.25 | 2,698.34 | 0.00 | 52.25 |
| STATE TOTAL 2 | 0.00 | 0.00 | 0.00 | 58.51 | 0.00 | 52.25 | 2,698.34 | 0.00 | 70.76 |
| **TEXAS** | | | | | | | | | |
| TAWS DAM | 0.00 | 0.00 | 0.00 | 0.00 | 84.70 | 0.00 | 0.00 | 89.20 | 173.90 |
| SAN MARCOS (G) | 0.00 | 0.00 | 0.00 | 0.00 | 115.78 | 0.00 | 0.00 | 2.79 | 118.57 |
| UVALDE | 0.00 | 0.00 | 0.00 | 0.00 | 100.00 | 0.00 | 0.00 | 1.06 | 101.06 |
| STATE TOTAL 3 | 0.00 | 0.00 | 0.00 | 0.00 | 300.48 | 0.00 | 0.00 | 93.05 | 393.53 |
| **UTAH** | | | | | | | | | |
| JONES HOLE | 465.55 | 0.00 | 0.00 | 0.00 | 0.00 | 0.00 | 0.00 | 66.30 | 531.85 |
| OURAY (B) | 0.00 | 0.00 | 0.00 | 0.00 | 0.00 | 0.00 | 0.00 | 0.00 | 0.00 |
| STATE TOTAL 2 | 465.55 | 0.00 | 0.00 | 0.00 | 0.00 | 0.00 | 0.00 | 66.30 | 531.85 |
| **VERMONT** | | | | | | | | | |
| PITTSFORD | 0.00 | 0.00 | 0.00 | 0.00 | 0.00 | 35.09 | 13,010.00 | 0.00 | 35.09 |
| WHITE RIVER | 0.00 | 0.00 | 0.00 | 0.00 | 0.00 | 53.50 | 155,500.00 | 15.00 | 68.50 |

TABLE 7 - NATIONAL FISH HATCHERIES

| STATE AND UNIT | RESERVED FROM PUBLIC DOMAIN | | ACQUIRED BY OTHER FEDERAL AGENCY | | DEVISE OR GIFT | PURCHASED | | AGREEMENT EASEMENT OR LEASE | TOTAL ACRES |
|---|---|---|---|---|---|---|---|---|---|
| | SOLE OR PRIMARY | SECONDARY | SOLE OR PRIMARY | SECONDARY | | ACRES | COST ($) | | |
| **VERMONT** | | | | | | | | | |
| STATE TOTAL 2 | 0.00 | 0.00 | 0.00 | 0.00 | 0.00 | 88.79 | 146,530.00 | 15.00 | 103.59 |
| **VIRGINIA** | | | | | | | | | |
| HARRISON LAKE | 0.00 | 0.00 | 0.00 | 0.00 | 0.00 | 444.73 | 116,368.50 | 0.00 | 444.73 |
| PAINT BANK (A) * | 0.00 | 0.00 | 0.00 | 0.00 | 0.00 | 0.00 | 31,500.00 | 0.00 | 0.00 |
| WYTHEVILLE (A) * | 0.00 | 0.00 | 0.00 | 0.00 | 0.00 | .00 | 97,000.00 | 0.00 | .00 |
| STATE TOTAL 1 | 0.00 | 0.00 | 0.00 | 0.00 | 0.00 | 444.73 | 219,868.50 | 0.00 | 444.73 |
| **WASHINGTON** | | | | | | | | | |
| ABERNATHY (C) * | 0.00 | 0.00 | 0.00 | 0.00 | 0.00 | 98.52 | 10,789.00 | 3.10 | 101.62 |
| CARSON | 0.00 | F 220.00 | 0.00 | 0.00 | 0.00 | 0.00 | 0.00 | 0.00 | 220.00 |
| ENTIAT | 0.00 | 0.00 | 34.27 | 0.00 | 0.00 | 0.00 | 0.00 | .08 | 34.35 |
| LEAVENWORTH | 0.00 | 0.00 | 861.15 | 0.00 | 11.40 | 4.07 | 84,000.00 | .43 | 877.05 |
| LITTLE WHITE SALMON | 0.00 | 0.00 | 211.39 | 0.00 | 1.34 | 202.44 | 476,518.00 | 17.42 | 432.59 |
| LYONS FERRY (A) * | 0.00 | 0.00 | 110.28 | 0.00 | 0.00 | 0.00 | 0.00 | 28.61 | 138.89 |
| MAKAH | 0.00 | 0.00 | 0.00 | 0.00 | 0.00 | 0.00 | 0.00 | 81.85 | 81.85 |
| NISQUALLY (B) * | 0.00 | 0.00 | 0.00 | 0.00 | 0.00 | 0.00 | 0.00 | 155.81 | 155.81 |
| QUILCENE | 0.00 | 0.00 | 0.00 | 0.00 | 3.38 | 51.50 | 454,590.00 | 12.52 | 67.40 |
| QUINAULT | 0.00 | 0.00 | 81.37 | 0.00 | 0.00 | 0.00 | 6,510.00 | 15.06 | 96.43 |
| SPRING CREEK | 0.00 | 0.00 | 0.00 E | 34.20 | 0.00 | 75.70 | 177,473.00 | 9.67 | 109.57 |
| TUCANNON (A) * | 0.00 | 0.00 | 16.62 | 0.00 | 0.00 | 0.00 | 0.00 | 32.10 | 48.92 |
| WILLARD | 0.00 | 0.00 | 0.00 | 0.00 | 0.00 | 80.10 | 6,750.00 | 3.70 | 83.80 |
| WINTHROP | 0.00 | 0.00 | 41.56 | 0.00 | 0.00 | 0.00 | 0.00 | 12.37 | 53.93 |
| STATE TOTAL 10 | 0.00 | 220.00 | 1,356.84 | 34.20 | 16.12 | 492.33 | 1,216,577.00 | 372.72 | 2,652.21 |
| **WEST VIRGINIA** | | | | | | | | | |
| WHITE SULPHUR SPRINGS | 0.00 | 0.00 | 0.00 | 0.00 | 0.00 | 25.24 | 2,500.00 | 0.00 | 25.24 |
| STATE TOTAL 1 | 0.00 | 0.00 | 0.00 | 0.00 | 0.00 | 25.24 | 2,500.00 | 0.00 | 25.24 |
| **WISCONSIN** | | | | | | | | | |
| GENOA (C) | 0.00 | 0.00 | 0.00 | 0.00 | 0.00 | 0.00 | 0.00 | 0.00 | 0.00 |
| IRON RIVER | 0.00 | 0.00 | 0.00 | 0.00 | 0.00 | 1,200.84 | 525,480.00 | 0.00 | 1,200.84 |
| STATE TOTAL 2 | 0.00 | 0.00 | 0.00 | 0.00 | 0.00 | 1,200.84 | 525,480.00 | 0.00 | 1,200.84 |
| **WYOMING** | | | | | | | | | |
| JACKSON (2) | 0.00 | 0.00 | 0.00 | 0.00 | 0.00 | 0.00 | 0.00 | 0.00 | 0.00 |
| SARATOGA | 0.00 | 0.00 | 0.00 | 0.00 | 0.00 | 118.73 | 174,800.00 | 1.21 | 119.94 |
| STATE TOTAL 2 | 0.00 | 0.00 | 0.00 | 0.00 | 0.00 | 118.73 | 174,800.00 | 1.21 | 119.94 |
| **GRAND TOTAL 69** | 3,607.09 | 907.09 | 2,596.85 | 3,682.01 | 1,338.52 | 5,273.90 | 3,196,960.99 | 4,360.85 | 21,846.31 |

(A) - HATCHERY MANAGED/OPERATED BY STATE
(B) - HATCHERY MANAGED/OPERATED BY TRIBE
(C) - FISH TECHNOLOGY CENTER
(D) - OTHER NON-NATIONAL FISH HATCHERY OR FISHERIES FACILITY
(E) - HISTORIC NATIONAL FISH HATCHERY
(F) - FISH TECHNOLOGY CENTER AND FISH HEALTH CENTER
(G) - NATIONAL FISH HATCHERY AND FISH TECHNOLOGY CENTER
(H) - NATIONAL FISH HATCHERY, FISH TECHNOLOGY CENTER AND FISH HEALTH CENTER
(I) - FISH HEALTH LAB MANAGED/OPERATED BY STATE

(1) - LOCATED ON THE UPPER MISSISSIPPI REFUGE
(2) - LOCATED ON THE NATIONAL ELK REFUGE
(3) - LOCATED ON THE OURAY NATIONAL WILDLIFE REFUGE

E - CORPS OF ENGINEERS, DEPARTMENT OF THE ARMY
F - FOREST SERVICE, DEPARTMENT OF AGRICULTURE
LM - BUREAU OF LAND MANAGEMENT, DEPARTMENT OF THE INTERIOR
R - BUREAU OF RECLAMATION, DEPARTMENT OF THE INTERIOR

* - NOT COUNTED AS A NATIONAL FISH HATCHERY

TABLE 6 — WILDERNESS AREAS IN NATIONAL WILDLIFE REFUGES

UNITS ALSO INCLUDED IN TABLE 5

| STATE AND UNIT | WILDERNESS NAME | WILDERNESS ACRES | REFUGE ACRES | PUBLIC LAW | |
|---|---|---|---|---|---|
| | | | | NUMBER | DATE |
| **ALASKA** | | | | | |
| ALASKA MARITIME | ALEUTIAN ISLANDS | 1,300,000.00 | 3,465,048.79 | 96-487 | 12-02-80 |
| ALASKA MARITIME | BERING SEA | 81,340.00 | 0.00 | 91-504 | 10-23-70 |
| ALASKA MARITIME | BOGOSLOF | 175.00 | 0.00 | 91-504 | 10-23-70 |
| ALASKA MARITIME | CHAMISSO | 455.00 | 0.00 | 94-662 | 01-03-75 |
| ALASKA MARITIME | FORRESTER ISLAND | 2,832.00 | 0.00 | 91-504 | 10-23-70 |
| ALASKA MARITIME | HAZY ISLAND | 32.00 | 0.00 | 91-504 | 10-23-70 |
| ALASKA MARITIME | SEMIDI | 250,000.00 | 0.00 | 96-487 | 12-02-80 |
| ALASKA MARITIME | SIMIONOF | 25,855.00 | 0.00 | 94-557 | 10-19-76 |
| ALASKA MARITIME | ST. LAZARIA | 65.00 | 0.00 | 91-504 | 10-23-70 |
| ALASKA MARITIME | TUXEDNI | 5,566.00 | 0.00 | 91-504 | 10-23-70 |
| ALASKA MARITIME | UNIMAK | 910,000.00 | 0.00 | 96-487 | 12-02-80 |
| ARCTIC | MOLLIE BEATTIE | 8,000,000.00 | 19,286,082.39 | 96-487 | 12-02-80 |
| BECHAROF | BECHAROF | 400,000.00 | 1,200,020.53 | 96-487 | 12-02-80 |
| INNOKO | INNOKO | 1,240,000.00 | 3,850,321.02 | 96-487 | 12-02-80 |
| IZEMBEK | IZEMBEK | 307,981.76 | 311,075.75 | 96-487 | 12-02-80 |
| KENAI | KENAI | 1,354,247.00 | 1,912,425.40 | 96-487 | 12-02-80 |
| KOYUKUK | KOYUKUK | 400,000.00 | 3,550,000.53 | 96-487 | 12-02-80 |
| SELAWIK | SELAWIK | 240,000.00 | 2,150,002.01 | 96-487 | 12-02-80 |
| TOGIAK | TOGIAK | 2,270,799.79 | 4,099,457.96 | 96-487 | 12-02-80 |
| YUKON DELTA | ANDREAFSKY | 1,300,000.00 | 19,166,894.48 | 96-487 | 12-02-80 |
| | NUNIVAK | 600,000.00 | | 96-487 | 12-02-80 |
| STATE TOTAL | | 18,689,348.55 | 58,990,506.49 | | |
| **ARIZONA** | | | | | |
| CABEZA PRIETA | CABEZA PRIETA | 803,418.00 | 860,041.52 | 101-628 | 11-28-90 |
| HAVASU | HAVASU | 14,606.00 | 93,279.62 | 101-628 | 11-28-90 |
| IMPERIAL | IMPERIAL REFUGE WILDERNESS | 9,220.00 | 17,809.76 | 101-628 | 11-28-90 |
| KOFA | KOFA | 516,200.00 | 666,480.00 | 101-628 | 11-28-90 |
| STATE TOTAL | | 1,343,444.00 | 1,574,610.90 | | |
| **ARKANSAS** | | | | | |
| BIG LAKE | BIG LAKE | 2,143.60 | 11,036.10 | 94-557 | 10-19-76 |
| STATE TOTAL | | 2,143.60 | 11,036.10 | | |
| **CALIFORNIA** | | | | | |
| FARALLON | FARALLON | 141.00 | 211.00 | 93-550 | 12-26-74 |
| HAVASU | HAVASU | 3,195.00 | 7,285.34 | 103-433 | 10-31-94 |
| IMPERIAL | IMPERIAL | 5,836.00 | 7,908.19 | 103-433 | 10-31-94 |
| STATE TOTAL | | 9,172.00 | 15,404.53 | | |
| **COLORADO** | | | | | |
| LEADVILLE * | MOUNT MASSIVE | 2,560.00 | 3,065.88 | 96-560 | 12-22-80 |
| STATE TOTAL | | 2,560.00 | 3,065.88 | | |
| **FLORIDA** | | | | | |
| CEDAR KEYS | CEDAR KEYS | 379.00 | 891.15 | 93-564 | 09-07-73 |
| CHASSAHOWITZKA | CHASSAHOWITZKA | 23,579.95 | 30,842.91 | 94-557 | 10-19-76 |
| GREAT WHITE HERON | FLORIDA KEYS | 1,900.00 | 192,787.43 | 93-632 | 01-03-75 |
| ISLAND BAY | ISLAND BAY | 20.24 | 20.24 | 91-504 | 10-23-70 |
| J. N. "DING" DARLING | J.N. "DING" DARLING | 2,619.15 | 6,390.68 | 94-557 | 10-19-76 |
| KEY WEST | FLORIDA KEYS | 2,019.00 | 208,308.17 | 93-632 | 01-03-75 |
| LAKE WOODRUFF | LAKE WOODRUFF | 1,066.00 | 21,559.02 | 94-557 | 10-19-76 |
| NATIONAL KEY DEER | FLORIDA KEYS(1) | 2,278.00 | 8,982.94 | 93-632 | 01-03-75 |
| PASSAGE KEY | PASSAGE KEY | 36.37 | 63.87 | 91-504 | 10-23-70 |
| PELICAN ISLAND | PELICAN ISLAND | 5.50 | 3,375.93 | 91-504 | 10-23-70 |
| ST. MARKS | ST. MARKS | 17,350.00 | 67,491.01 | 93-632 | 01-03-75 |

| STATE AND UNIT | WILDERNESS NAME | WILDERNESS ACRES | REFUGE ACRES | PUBLIC LAW | |
|---|---|---|---|---|---|
| | | | | NUMBER | DATE |
| FLORIDA | | | | | |
| STATE TOTAL | | 51,252.17 | 542,913.55 | | |
| GEORGIA | | | | | |
| BLACKBEARD ISLAND | BLACKBEARD ISLAND | 5,000.00 | 5,617.64 | 95-652 | 10-23-70 |
| OKEFENOKEE | OKEFENOKEE | 353,981.00 | 391,401.99 | 93-429 | 10-01-74 |
| WOLF ISLAND | WOLF ISLAND | 5,125.82 | 5,125.82 | 95-652 | 01-03-75 |
| STATE TOTAL | | 362,106.82 | 402,145.45 | | |
| ILLINOIS | | | | | |
| CRAB ORCHARD | CRAB ORCHARD | 4,050.00 | 43,888.52 | 94-557 | 10-19-76 |
| STATE TOTAL | | 4,050.00 | 43,888.52 | | |
| LOUISIANA | | | | | |
| BRETON | BRETON | 5,000.00 | 9,047.00 | 93-632 | 01-01-75 |
| LACASSINE | LACASSINE | 3,345.60 | 34,378.77 | 94-557 | 10-19-76 |
| STATE TOTAL | | 8,345.60 | 43,425.77 | | |
| MAINE | | | | | |
| MOOSEHORN | BARING UNIT | 4,680.00 | 27,704.76 | 95-652 | 01-03-75 |
| | BIRCH ISLANDS UNIT | 6.00 | | 91-504 | 10-23-70 |
| | EDMUNDS UNIT | 2,706.00 | | 91-504 | 10-23-70 |
| STATE TOTAL | | 7,392.00 | 27,704.76 | | |
| MASSACHUSETTS | | | | | |
| MONOMOY | MONOMOY | 2,420.00 | 2,701.85 | 91-504 | 10-23-70 |
| STATE TOTAL | | 2,420.00 | 2,701.85 | | |
| MICHIGAN | | | | | |
| HURON | HURON ISLANDS | 147.50 | 146.85 | 91-504 | 10-23-70 |
| MICHIGAN ISLANDS | MICHIGAN ISLANDS | 12.00 | 397.39 | 91-504 | 10-23-70 |
| SENEY | SENEY | 25,150.00 | 95,344.81 | 91-504 | 10-23-70 |
| STATE TOTAL | | 25,309.50 | 95,889.05 | | |
| MINNESOTA | | | | | |
| AGASSIZ | AGASSIZ | 4,000.00 | 61,500.93 | 94-557 | 10-19-76 |
| TAMARAC | TAMARAC | 2,180.00 | 35,191.38 | 94-557 | 10-19-76 |
| STATE TOTAL | | 6,180.00 | 96,692.31 | | |
| MISSOURI | | | | | |
| MINGO | MINGO | 7,730.00 | 21,745.86 | 94-557 | 10-19-76 |
| STATE TOTAL | | 7,730.00 | 21,745.86 | | |
| MONTANA | | | | | |
| MEDICINE LAKE | MEDICINE LAKE | 11,366.00 | 31,484.01 | 94-557 | 10-19-76 |
| RED ROCK LAKES | RED ROCK LAKES | 32,350.00 | 53,932.50 | 94-557 | 10-19-76 |
| UL BEND | UL BEND | 20,819.00 | 56,049.56 | 94-557 | 10-19-76 |
| | | | | 98-140 | 10-31-84 |
| STATE TOTAL | | 64,535.00 | 141,466.07 | | |
| NEBRASKA | | | | | |
| FORT NIOBRARA | FORT NIOBRARA | 4,635.00 | 19,132.53 | 94-557 | 10-19-76 |
| STATE TOTAL | | 4,635.00 | 19,132.53 | | |
| NEW JERSEY | | | | | |
| EDWIN B. FORSYTHE | BRIGANTINE | 6,681.00 | 45,743.24 | 93-632 | 01-03-75 |
| GREAT SWAMP | GREAT SWAMP | 3,660.00 | 7,382.36 | 90-532 | 09-28-68 |
| STATE TOTAL | | 10,341.00 | 53,327.60 | | |
| NEW MEXICO | | | | | |
| BITTER LAKE | SALT CREEK | 9,621.00 | 24,608.64 | 91-504 | 10-23-70 |
| BOSQUE DEL APACHE | CHUPADERA WILDERNESS AREA | 5,289.00 | 57,191.10 | 93-632 | 01-03-75 |
| | INDIAN WELL WILDERNESS AREA | 5,159.00 | | 93-632 | 01-03-75 |

| STATE AND UNIT | WILDERNESS NAME | WILDERNESS ACRES | REFUGE ACRES | PUBLIC LAW | |
|---|---|---|---|---|---|
| | | | | NUMBER | DATE |
| NEW MEXICO | | | | | |
| | LITTLE SAN PASCUAL WILDERNESS | 19,859.00 | | 93-632 | 01-03-75 |
| STATE TOTAL | | 57,908.00 | 81,799.74 | | |
| NORTH CAROLINA | | | | | |
| SWANQUARTER | SWANQUARTER | 8,784.95 | 16,411.09 | 94-557 | 10-19-76 |
| STATE TOTAL | | 8,784.95 | 16,411.09 | | |
| NORTH DAKOTA | | | | | |
| CHASE LAKE | CHASE LAKE | 4,155.00 | 4,449.47 | 93-632 | 01-03-75 |
| LOSTWOOD | LOSTWOOD | 5,577.00 | 26,903.99 | 94-632 | 01-03-75 |
| STATE TOTAL | | 9,732.00 | 31,353.46 | | |
| OHIO | | | | | |
| WEST SISTER ISLAND | WEST SISTER ISLAND | 77.00 | 80.15 | 93-632 | 01-04-75 |
| STATE TOTAL | | 77.00 | 80.15 | | |
| OKLAHOMA | | | | | |
| WICHITA MOUNTAINS | CHARONS GARDEN UNIT | 5,725.00 | 59,019.60 | 91-504 | 10-23-70 |
| | NORTH MOUNTAIN UNIT | 2,847.00 | | 91-504 | 10-23-70 |
| STATE TOTAL | | 8,570.00 | 59,019.60 | | |
| OREGON | | | | | |
| OREGON ISLANDS | OREGON ISLANDS | 925.06 | 1,079.61 | 91-504 | 10-23-70 |
| | | | | 95-450 | 10-11-78 |
| | | | | 104-333 | 11-12-96 |
| THREE ARCH ROCKS | THREE ARCH ROCKS | 15.00 | 15.00 | 91-504 | 10-23-70 |
| STATE TOTAL | | 940.06 | 1,096.61 | | |
| SOUTH CAROLINA | | | | | |
| CAPE ROMAIN | CAPE ROMAIN | 29,000.00 | 65,268.66 | 93-632 | 01-03-75 |
| STATE TOTAL | | 29,000.00 | 65,268.66 | | |
| WASHINGTON | | | | | |
| COPALIS | WASHINGTON ISLANDS | 60.80 | 60.80 | 91-504 | 10-23-70 |
| FLATTERY ROCKS | WASHINGTON ISLANDS | 125.00 | 125.00 | 91-504 | 10-23-70 |
| QUILLAYUTE NEEDLES | WASHINGTON ISLANDS | 300.20 | 300.20 | 91-504 | 10-23-70 |
| SAN JUAN ISLANDS | SAN JUAN ISLANDS | 353.00 | 448.93 | 94-557 | 10-19-76 |
| STATE TOTAL | | 849.00 | 934.56 | | |
| WISCONSIN | | | | | |
| GRAVEL ISLAND | WISCONSIN ISLANDS | 27.00 | 27.00 | 91-504 | 10-23-70 |
| GREEN BAY | WISCONSIN ISLANDS | 2.00 | 2.00 | 91-504 | 10-23-70 |
| STATE TOTAL | | 29.00 | 29.00 | | |
| GRAND TOTAL | | 70,698,845.45 | 62,541,748.24 | | |

* Located on the Leadville National Fish Hatchery

46

| STATE AND UNIT | ACRES UNDER PRIMARY CONTROL OF | | | | TOTAL ACRES |
|---|---|---|---|---|---|
| | CORPS OF ENGINEERS | BUREAU OF RECLAMATION | TENNESSEE VALLEY AUTHORITY | FISH AND WILDLIFE SERVICE | |
| ALABAMA | | | | | |
| CHOCTAW | 4,218.00 | 0.00 | 0.00 | 0.00 | 4,218.00 |
| EUFAULA | 7,929.00 | 0.00 | 0.00 | 24.19 | 7,953.19 |
| WHEELER | 0.00 | 0.00 | 25,674.62 | 8,756.04 | 34,430.66 |
| STATE TOTAL | 12,147.00 | 0.00 | 25,674.62 | 8,780.23 | 46,601.85 |
| ARIZONA | | | | | |
| BILL WILLIAMS | 0.00 | 1,699.07 | 0.00 | 4,355.69 | 6,054.76 |
| CIBOLA | 0.00 | 623.38 | 0.00 | 7,982.66 | 8,606.04 |
| HAVASU | 0.00 | 20,235.28 | 0.00 | 10,044.54 | 30,279.82 |
| IMPERIAL | 0.00 | 17,166.14 | 0.00 | 643.62 | 17,809.76 |
| STATE TOTAL | 0.00 | 39,723.87 | 0.00 | 23,026.51 | 62,750.38 |
| ARKANSAS | | | | | |
| WHITE RIVER | 45.80 | 0.00 | 0.00 | 158,368.92 | 158,414.72 |
| STATE TOTAL | 45.80 | 0.00 | 0.00 | 158,368.92 | 158,414.72 |
| CALIFORNIA | | | | | |
| CLEAR LAKE | 0.00 | 11,103.43 | 0.00 | 13,020.07 | 24,123.50 |
| HAVASU | 0.00 | 7,225.54 | 0.00 | 10.00 | 7,235.54 |
| IMPERIAL | 0.00 | 7,958.19 | 0.00 | 0.00 | 7,958.19 |
| SONNY BONO SALTON SEA | 0.00 | 23,424.58 | 0.00 | 14,234.29 | 37,658.87 |
| STATE TOTAL | 0.00 | 49,711.54 | 0.00 | 27,264.36 | 76,975.90 |
| GEORGIA | | | | | |
| EUFAULA | 3,231.00 | 0.00 | 0.00 | 0.00 | 3,231.00 |
| STATE TOTAL | 3,231.00 | 0.00 | 0.00 | 0.00 | 3,231.00 |
| IDAHO | | | | | |
| DEER FLAT | 0.00 | 9,993.28 | 0.00 | 554.29 | 10,547.57 |
| MINIDOKA | 0.00 | 17,835.19 | 0.00 | 2,866.42 | 20,701.61 |
| STATE TOTAL | 0.00 | 27,828.47 | 0.00 | 3,420.71 | 31,249.18 |
| ILLINOIS | | | | | |
| GREAT RIVER | 5,490.81 | 0.00 | 0.00 | 1,619.82 | 7,110.63 |
| PORT LOUISA | 1,466.00 | 0.00 | 0.00 | 4.89 | 1,470.89 |
| TWO RIVERS | 7,017.00 | 0.00 | 0.00 | 1,016.20 | 8,033.20 |
| UPPER MISSISSIPPI RIVER | 26,502.00 | 0.00 | 0.00 | 6,334.70 | 32,836.70 |
| STATE TOTAL | 40,475.81 | 0.00 | 0.00 | 8,975.61 | 49,451.42 |
| IOWA | | | | | |
| PORT LOUISA | 10,425.94 | 0.00 | 0.00 | 12,199.44 | 22,625.38 |
| UPPER MISSISSIPPI RIVER | 30,315.00 | 0.00 | 0.00 | 20,724.21 | 51,039.21 |
| STATE TOTAL | 40,738.94 | 0.00 | 0.00 | 32,923.65 | 73,662.59 |
| KANSAS | | | | | |
| FLINT HILLS | 18,463.21 | 0.00 | 0.00 | .15 | 18,463.36 |
| KIRWIN | 0.00 | 10,778.00 | 0.00 | 0.00 | 10,778.00 |
| STATE TOTAL | 18,463.21 | 10,778.00 | 0.00 | .15 | 29,241.36 |
| MINNESOTA | | | | | |
| BIG STONE | 254.20 | 0.00 | 0.00 | 11,265.93 | 11,520.13 |
| UPPER MISSISSIPPI RIVER | 15,420.77 | 0.00 | 0.00 | 18,259.99 | 33,680.76 |
| STATE TOTAL | 15,674.97 | 0.00 | 0.00 | 29,525.92 | 45,200.89 |
| MISSISSIPPI | | | | | |
| PANTHER SWAMP | 7,070.45 | 0.00 | 0.00 | 28,201.40 | 35,271.85 |
| STATE TOTAL | 7,070.45 | 0.00 | 0.00 | 28,201.40 | 35,271.85 |
| MISSOURI | | | | | |
| TWO RIVERS | 232.00 | 0.00 | 0.00 | 0.00 | 232.00 |
| STATE TOTAL | 232.00 | 0.00 | 0.00 | 0.00 | 232.00 |
| MONTANA | | | | | |
| CHARLES M. RUSSELL | 328,300.14 | 0.00 | 0.00 | 584,048.18 | 912,348.32 |

| STATE AND UNIT | ACRES UNDER PRIMARY CONTROL OF | | | | TOTAL ACRES |
| --- | --- | --- | --- | --- | --- |
| | CORPS OF ENGINEERS | BUREAU OF RECLAMATION | TENNESSEE VALLEY AUTHORITY | FISH AND WILDLIFE SERVICE | |
| MONTANA | | | | | |
| UL BEND | 14,823.36 | 0.00 | 0.00 | 41,226.20 | 56,049.56 |
| STATE TOTAL | 549,125.50 | 0.00 | 0.00 | 479,274.58 | 968,597.88 |
| NEBRASKA | | | | | |
| NORTH PLATTE | 0.00 | 2,684.81 | 0.00 | 788.42 | 3,473.23 |
| STATE TOTAL | 0.00 | 2,684.81 | 0.00 | 788.42 | 3,473.23 |
| NEVADA | | | | | |
| FALLON | 0.00 | 17,901.94 | 0.00 | 0.00 | 17,901.94 |
| STATE TOTAL | 0.00 | 17,901.94 | 0.00 | 0.00 | 17,901.94 |
| NEW MEXICO | | | | | |
| MAXWELL | 0.00 | 438.52 | 0.00 | 3,260.07 | 3,698.59 |
| STATE TOTAL | 0.00 | 438.52 | 0.00 | 3,260.07 | 3,698.59 |
| NORTH DAKOTA | | | | | |
| AUDUBON | 14,739.19 | 0.00 | 0.00 | 0.00 | 14,739.19 |
| STATE TOTAL | 14,739.19 | 0.00 | 0.00 | 0.00 | 14,739.19 |
| OKLAHOMA | | | | | |
| OPTIMA | 4,552.81 | 0.00 | 0.00 | 0.00 | 4,552.81 |
| SALT PLAINS | 11,565.28 | 0.00 | 0.00 | 20,491.84 | 32,057.12 |
| SEQUOYAH | 20,800.00 | 0.00 | 0.00 | 0.00 | 20,800.00 |
| TISHOMINGO | 16,464.18 | 0.00 | 0.00 | 0.00 | 16,464.18 |
| WASHITA | 0.00 | 8,061.61 | 0.00 | 13.56 | 8,075.37 |
| STATE TOTAL | 53,162.27 | 8,061.61 | 0.00 | 20,505.40 | 81,729.48 |
| OREGON | | | | | |
| COLD SPRINGS | 0.00 | 7,679.95 | 0.00 | 436.88 | 3,116.83 |
| MCKAY CREEK | 0.00 | 1,813.00 | 0.00 | 23.50 | 1,836.50 |
| UMATILLA | 7,430.37 | 0.00 | 0.00 | 1,477.00 | 8,907.37 |
| STATE TOTAL | 7,430.37 | 4,492.95 | 0.00 | 1,937.38 | 13,860.70 |
| SOUTH CAROLINA | | | | | |
| TYBEE | 100.00 | 0.00 | 0.00 | 0.00 | 100.00 |
| STATE TOTAL | 100.00 | 0.00 | 0.00 | 0.00 | 100.00 |
| TENNESSEE | | | | | |
| CROSS CREEKS | 2,442.00 | 0.00 | 0.00 | 6,419.49 | 8,861.49 |
| TENNESSEE | 0.00 | 0.00 | 50,830.30 | 529.16 | 51,359.46 |
| STATE TOTAL | 7,442.00 | 0.00 | 50,830.30 | 6,948.65 | 60,220.95 |
| TEXAS | | | | | |
| HAGERMAN | 11,319.84 | 0.00 | 0.00 | 0.00 | 11,319.84 |
| STATE TOTAL | 11,319.84 | 0.00 | 0.00 | 0.00 | 11,319.84 |
| WASHINGTON | | | | | |
| COLUMBIA | 0.00 | 2,662.00 | 0.00 | 26,934.27 | 29,596.27 |
| MCNARY | 11,895.00 | 0.00 | 0.00 | 3,564.46 | 15,459.46 |
| UMATILLA | 13,209.50 | 0.00 | 0.00 | 1,666.33 | 14,875.83 |
| STATE TOTAL | 25,104.50 | 2,662.00 | 0.00 | 44,165.06 | 59,931.56 |
| WISCONSIN | | | | | |
| UPPER MISSISSIPPI | 40,341.00 | 0.00 | 0.00 | 49,126.64 | 89,467.64 |
| STATE TOTAL | 40,341.00 | 0.00 | 0.00 | 49,126.64 | 89,467.64 |
| WYOMING | | | | | |
| PATHFINDER | 0.00 | 14,512.06 | 0.00 | 2,294.84 | 16,806.90 |
| STATE TOTAL | 0.00 | 14,512.06 | 0.00 | 2,294.84 | 16,806.90 |
| GRAND TOTAL | 845,841.85 | 178,795.97 | 76,504.92 | 854,586.75 | 1,955,931.04 |

# Notes

In addition to the changes noted in the accomplishments on page 7 and those noted below, the figures in our tables may show some changes from previous annual reports. For example, decreases in acreage figures may reflect expired leases, real property disposals made in land exchanges, or property transfers. An increase or decrease may be noted after new property surveys are completed or when additional information is entered into the database after the data has been transmitted from the regions for publication. Other changes result from corrections that are made when errors are found in the historical data previously entered into the database systems or when information was not previously entered into the database (e.g., see Table 3, Clear Lake NWR in California where a duplicate entry was removed and Cabo Rojo NWR in Puerto Rico where the total acreage is corrected due to a survey).

**Table 2A**: Negative acreage will appear in Table 2A when we dispose of or transfer more acres than we acquire during the fiscal year. For example, acreage totaling 188 acres was exchanged on McNary NWR, Washington, for other land within the acquisition boundary.

**Table 3**: Two additional refuges were established: Baca NWR in Colorado and Mountain Longleaf NWR in Alabama (see Accomplishments section of this report). Also, a Memorandum of Understanding was signed with the Office of Insular Affairs, and the Service is now managing the surrounding submerged lands and waters of the Midway Atoll NWR out to 12 nautical miles. This presents a significant acreage adjustment at Midway.

**Tables 3 and 4**: The report summarizes Farm Service Agency (formerly Farmers Home Administration), Department of Agriculture, units in Table 3 by state and in Table 4 by state and county. These entries, identified as "FSA Interest" consist of lands or interests in lands acquired from the Farm Service Agency that are not located within existing project boundaries. We include FSA units in state and county acreage totals, but do not count them as separate units.

**Table 4**: The Waterfowl Production Areas are units of the National Wildlife Refuge System established under the Migratory Bird Hunting and Conservation Stamp Act. For purposes of this report, the acreage of the WPAs are rolled up by county in each state and the total number of NWRS Waterfowl Production Area units are shown as the total number of approved counties with WPA acres.

**Table 6**: San Simeon, California was removed because the permit expired and Lewis River, Alaska was also removed. We no longer have a property interest in either site.

**Table 7**: The Ouray hatchery in Utah is counted as a National Fish Hatchery but it is located on the Ouray National Wildlife Refuge and the acreage is included in Table 3 rather than Table 7. The Hagerman National Fish Hatchery in Idaho is managed by the Service, but the remainder of the land is managed by the State and appears in Table 5 as the Hagerman Coordination Area.

www.ingramcontent.com/pod-product-compliance
Lightning Source LLC
Chambersburg PA
CBHW052015280526
45793CB00005B/988

*9 781505 439403*